Reaching
Learners
Through
Telecommunications

Becky S. Duning
Marvin J. Van Kekerix
Leon M. Zaborowski

Reaching Learners Through Telecommunications

Management
and Leadership
Strategies for
Higher Education

Jossey-Bass Publishers • San Francisco

Substantial discounts on bulk quantities of Jossey-Bass books are available to corporations, professional associations, and other organizations. For details and discount information, contact the special sales department at Jossey-Bass Inc., Publishers. (415) 433-1740; Fax (415) 433-0499.

For sales outside the United States, contact Maxwell Macmillan International Publishing Group, 866 Third Avenue, New York, New York 10022.

Manufactured in the United States of America

The paper used in this book is acid-free and meets the State of California requirements for recycled paper (50 percent recycled waste, including 10 percent postconsumer waste), which are the strictest guidelines for recycled paper currently in use in the United States.

10% POST CONSUMER WASTE

The ink in this book is either soy- or vegetable-based and during the printing process emits fewer than half the volatile organic compounds (VOCs) emitted by petroleum-based ink.

Library of Congress Cataloging-in-Publication Data

Duning, Becky S., date.
  Reaching learners through telecommunications : management and leadership strategies for higher education / Becky S. Duning, Marvin J. Van Kekerix, Leon M. Zaborowski. — 1st ed.
      p.   cm. — (Jossey-Bass higher and adult education series)
  Includes bibliographical references (p.   ) and index.
  ISBN 1-55542-501-1
  1. Telecommunication in education.   2. Distance education.
3. Education, Higher.   I. Van Kekerix, Marvin J., date.
II. Zaborowski, Leon M., date.   III. Title.   IV. Series.
LB1044.84.D86   1993
371.3'35—dc20   92-30051
                                                 CIP

FIRST EDITION
HB Printing   10 9 8 7 6 5 4 3 2 1   *Code 9305*

●●●●●●●●●●●●●

The
Jossey-Bass
Higher and Adult Education
Series

Consulting Editor
Adult and Continuing Education

Alan B. Knox
University of Wisconsin, Madison

Contents

Preface

The advent of new telecommunications technologies and a growing recognition of their potential for meeting educational needs has raised many questions about how to integrate telecommunications with existing educational programs. Telecommunications technology is increasingly regarded as the key to access to education for many learners who have been bypassed in the past, but for professionals in education who do not know how to manage and lead successful efforts in this area, the obstacles can appear to be insurmountable. Even those with experience find that rapid changes in technology can turn a specialist into a novice overnight.

The task of integrating telecommunications with existing programs can appear to be confusing and frustrating in the absence of examples and guidance drawn from others' experience. Moreover, the seemingly limitless potential of the technology itself can distort rather than further a vision of how educational telecommunications systems can enhance an institution's ability to achieve its purpose. At the same time, those who focus only on the complexities and costs often fail to see how this potential can be achieved.

Genesis of the Book

This book evolved from the coauthors' shared belief that individuals who are engaged in the management and leadership of educational telecommunications systems could benefit from others' experience. Those seeking to integrate telecommunications with existing educational activities frequently say that they are overwhelmed by the immensity of their task and the absence of guidance. Too often it seems that the wrong questions are asked or that questions are asked in the wrong context. Much of the available literature in the field of telecommunications-based education is geared toward considerations of equipment or instructional design rather than management and administration. Furthermore, the existing managerial literature in distance learning and continuing education is primarily descriptive rather than conceptual or analytical and is spread among many sources.

In our view what was needed was a book that would provide a context for decision making under a variety of conditions. Newcomers as well as the experienced require a frame of reference that goes beyond technical considerations and incorporates considerations of many other areas — personal and organizational strategy; organizational values as well as structure; budget and staffing; marketing and quality guidelines that take issues of equity seriously; and institutional policy development — that support programmatic goals and organizational vision.

We gave much consideration to the question of when and where electronic technologies should be defined in the book. We concluded that most definitions would be placed solely in the Glossary. Our premise is that the manager's chief concern is to conceptualize how emerging needs among educators and learners relate to nontraditional approaches to teaching and learning, and to the mission of the parent organization. Too often a nontechnical manager is led to believe that knowledge about equipment will explain what needs to be done. In fact, just the opposite is true. It is only after a manager has developed a rationale for responding to needs or setting new goals that electronic technologies can be explained meaningfully. Only at that point will comparative descriptions of technical capabilities, installation costs, and long-term technical considerations be understandable for purposes of decision making.

Purpose and Audience

This book is written for managers and leaders in postsecondary education as well as those in business and industry, health, the military, government, and other settings who have a responsibility for ensuring that telecommunications-based education and training achieves its potential — and more. The educational point of view in this book may introduce important considerations that are not immediately apparent to nontechnical professionals in other environments. There is no reason to lose one's way in the complex array of options that unfold daily. Indeed, this evolving set of conditions offers nearly unlimited choice to discerning managers. At the heart of this book is an attempt to help such managers clarify the set of choices that will work best for learners of great diversity, and make those choices work. Each chapter contributes to the development of an organizing framework within which choices, recommendations, and decisions can become more meaningful in relationship to each other. Figures and tables are provided to help make the framework illuminating and inspiring.

A number of themes are presented and developed throughout the text. Chapters One, Two, Five, and Twelve discuss how the demands of telecommunications and its myriad possibilities influence perceptions of who we are, who we deal with, and how we carry out our work. Even where it is evident that new partnerships are necessary and that telecommunications adds urgency to these transitions, one may learn from fields and experiences outside one's own to provide perspective and continuing guidance.

A second theme is that the learner's needs, aspirations, and requirements are a primary consideration in the success of any educational telecommunications system. This theme appears throughout the book and is particularly addressed in Chapters Seven and Eleven. The primacy of the learner promises to be the inspiration for much that managers of educational telecommunications systems can achieve. It also gives new meaning to an organizational mission that sets implicit or explicit goals for telecommunications-based education in two areas: access and equity.

The disparities in levels of participation among those who need educational opportunities are well documented. The inequities that have surfaced over time are viewed in this book less as problems to be overcome than as inspiration for bringing different lenses to all our efforts, in particular our ways of evaluating how we are doing. These "access lenses" not only indicate the distance we have to go but also can focus and direct our attention. In a field in which everything seems possible, continual and systematic reflection on how and why we work in the ways we do yields new perspectives. This can, in turn, add clarity and purpose to future efforts.

Chapters Three, Four, Six, Eight, and Nine address a third theme: how we look at ourselves as educational leaders, managers, and staff working within structures and procedures that require constant revision and change. At one level, this theme—organizational change—is familiar. At another level, however, it leads to a consideration of values such as individual and organizational integrity. A discussion of integrity is appropriate here because telecommunications forces individuals and organizations to address issues of quality and equity. Organizational values of inclusiveness meet head-on with the reality that unequal participation currently exists in continuing and alternative forms of education and training. Our ability to deliver education any time to any place inevitably raises questions about how and why we choose to do what we do with this powerful tool; therefore, a reexamination of personal and organizational values in the presence of such opportunities is both desirable and necessary.

Yet there is little to suggest that such a reexamination will yield satisfactory results. There is a silent undertow in many organizations. Too many people no longer find it possible to take ownership and to be accountable for their work. They are present, yet they act like dropouts. The resulting undertow has subtle and little-examined effects on the new, more enterprising relationships that telecommunications demands. Among the numerous suggestions in this book, the vocabulary of telecommunications-based education management is questioned for its continuing relevance in a multicultural society; we suggest that it may, in fact, have the unintended effect of leading us to serve the same relatively narrow audience, which is less and less reflective of the makeup of our wider society.

Little in telecommunications-based education can be done single-handedly. New personal interrelationships severely test organizational and personal ways of doing things, as well as how we think about what we do. These concerns are considered throughout the book and are brought together in Chapter Ten, where useful resources are presented.

This book itself is a combined effort. We have reconsidered and reconnected information and experience to support and encourage newcomers and to bring a different perspective to their efforts. For organizational leaders and others who may be somewhat removed from daily telecommunications activities, the themes introduced may also suggest how and where to place resources, time, and attention — and why. We have sought above all to develop a text with information that will carry over time, place, and circumstance. Most importantly, the book is written to be used variously by those whose needs, conditions, and purposes have only their diversity in common.

Organization

This book is written by practitioners for advocates of integrating telecommunications-based education into existing educational programming. It is not intended to be a technical primer, nor is it written for the person seeking technical proficiency. Instead, it is geared toward management and leadership issues. The primary audiences are those leaders and managers who are attempting to put educational resources within reach of a diverse public.

This book has been arranged in the sequence of a strategic planning model; thus, the progression of chapters offers readers the opportunity to scan the major phases in strategic planning. Readers who can place themselves at a particular phase of the process may want to use the chapter that covers that phase as their point of departure. Readers who are new to telecommunications-based education can read each chapter in sequence and experience how strategic planning is applied, phase by phase. Chapter Four summarizes key steps in strategic planning. A complete review of the entire strategic planning process in continuing education is presented in Simerly and Associates (1987).

Chapter One points out that successful managers approach telecommunications systems as networks of human relationships rather than as networks of electronic linkages, and that they seek congruence with wider organizational purposes. The complexity of technical choices is transformed into a continuum of choices that are made possible by the richness of technology. From this perspective the appropriate starting point is nontechnical and involves choices concerning purpose, audience, needs, and content. Successful advocates of integrating telecommunications and education look for a lasting "fit" with the larger, longer-term aspirations and values of their organization. Throughout the discussion the need to adopt a balanced perspective is emphasized.

Chapter Two delineates eight guiding assumptions that provide new lenses for viewing the opportunities and benefits of telecommunications technology. Attention is directed to five groups that directly affect the success of telecommunications systems: student support services, technical support services, faculty, the learner, and the organizational leadership. The assumptions that form the basis for successful systems are identified. Among the most important assumptions are the primacy of the learner, the movement of telecommunications from the periphery of institutional effort to the mainstream, the emergence of partnership relationships with learners, the movement toward more individualized learning, and the need for leaders to be increasingly aware of their own biases regarding the purpose of the organization. Each theme is elaborated and discussed in terms of its implications for telecommunications managers, and a new, more comprehensive vision for telecommunications-based education and training is introduced.

Chapter Three provides a conceptual framework to guide integration of telecommunications with existing educational activities. The effort at integration can be undertaken as either framebreaking, which is abrupt and traumatic, or incremental change. Selection of a change strategy depends on an analysis of conditions in the environment as well as on the position of the change agent. In either case a comprehensive change strategy will include cultural-ideological, political, and technical components. Throughout the discussion there is an emphasis on assessing the fit between the strategy and the environment in which the change will take place. Finally, the chapter points to the importance of defining success before it can be achieved.

Chapter Four shifts the discussion to a consideration of how to assess the telecommunications choices available in terms of the purpose or vision for the system. The strategic planning process is integrated with elements of instructional design to help guide the decision maker toward the design of a system congruent with the particular environment in which it will function. Seven characteristics are discussed: type of program, learning situation, service area, number of receive sites, learner dispersion, system utilization level, and unit cost; a set of tables matches the technological preferences of each of the most common technologies for these seven characteristics. A case study shows how to use the tables to fashion a distance-learning system that will meet the unique requirements of the parent organization.

Chapter Five addresses the need to adapt management concerns to the dynamic qualities of organizational life. Too often, leaders of change efforts strive to put into place a single structure and staffing pattern that they assume will guarantee success. A conceptual framework built upon organizational life cycle literature is used to analyze the evolution of management strategy that is required to integrate telecommunications and educational efforts. Inherent in this approach is the recognition that management strategies that were found to be successful at one point in the history of an organization may be so inappropriate at another time as to present problems.

Chapter Six addresses the issues surrounding budgeting for educational telecommunications systems. Financial assumptions about these systems are reviewed and the impact of organizational objectives and structure on the budgeting process is analyzed. In addition, various budget types are defined, and typical expenditures and revenue sources for budgets are presented. The chapter concludes by bringing the various components together in a sample master budget. The discussion is informed by the recognition that although individual circumstances dictate the precise nature of a budget, common elements will emerge.

Chapter Seven offers a framework for conceptualizing telecommunications-based education within the general evolution of marketing strategy. The key element is finding a product that the organization wishes to produce and the learner wishes to have. How telecommunications-based education fits into the current educational marketplace as a value-added product is addressed and special considerations related to finding an appropriate market mix and producing an effective promotional message are described in some detail.

Chapter Eight reviews the recent history and current practices of media and technical support units in postsecondary educational institutions as a backdrop for exploring where forces are directing those units. In most organizational settings, the resources needed to integrate telecommunications and existing educational or training activities are widely dispersed. A strong case is made for incorporating these services within an instructional-design unit that functions as a component of the telecommunications effort. The importance of managing relationships is emphasized as a key element for success.

Chapter Nine addresses the question of what characteristics distinguish quality in telecommunications-based education and training. It is argued that nowhere is there a greater opportunity to provide leadership than in the area of defining and ensuring quality. The need for managers to develop and follow a consistent approach to quality is seen as a high priority. No single model or checklist can apply universally to the varying combinations of equipment; subject matter; staffing; learner needs and expectations; and organizational history, circumstances, mission, and resources. Five values that speak to the issue of quality are described and the chapter advocates value-based outcomes as a means of establishing quality benchmarks.

Chapter Ten elaborates nine areas in which professionals are likely to seek the information they require to keep informed about developments in the field. The chapter focuses on ways to build a personal repertoire of information sources that is selective but comprehensive. Publications, associations, conferences, and agencies that can provide valuable information to both the novice and experienced distance education professional are described, and the links between the sources identified in the chapter and core managerial concerns are discussed.

Chapter Eleven deals with policy issues that must be of concern to managers of educational telecommunications systems. These issues and the types of policy decision makers who are in a position to influence the success of the integration effort are identified and discussed. Among the key issues are access to educational opportunity by underserved audiences, the state's interest in regulating telecommunications-based education, and institutional policy. The discussion emphasizes the need to develop a shared and informed view of the wider social potential for telecommunications-based education in the areas of access and equity.

Chapter Twelve argues that telecommunications-supported programming will move from the periphery to the mainstream of academic endeavors with the emergence of a new learner who is neither "traditional" nor "nontraditional." The focus on teaching and training skills inherent in this development will also revitalize teaching and training in traditional environments. Three types of postsecondary institutions are described: the elite higher education institution, the mass higher education institution, and the universal-access higher education institution. Development of telecommunications-based education is placed within the context of institutional evolution from one type to another. The chapter includes a vision of how the new learner might use telecommunications.

Acknowledgments

Becky wishes to express gratitude to her professional colleagues for their generosity, patience, and understanding during the course of preparing this work. Marvin would like to acknowledge his wife, Becci, and his family for their support. He also wishes to thank Robert G. Simerly, dean of the division of continuing studies at the University of Nebraska, Lincoln, as well as the staff of the department of academic telecommunications and professional development for their contributions to this project. Leon thanks his wife, Jeanne Bortz, for her advice and encouragement. He also acknowledges his colleagues at the University of Northern Colorado and numerous members of the National University Continuing Education Association for their insights on educational telecommunications.

December 1992   Becky S. Duning
                                             Greeley, Colorado

                                             Marvin J. Van Kekerix
                                             Lincoln, Nebraska

                                             Leon M. Zaborowski
                                             Greeley, Colorado

●●●●●●●●●●●●●●

The Authors

Becky S. Duning is manager for sponsored programs in the College of Continuing Education at the University of Northern Colorado. She received her B.A. degree (1957) from the University of Iowa in history and her M.A. degree (1962) from the University of California, Berkeley in history. Before coming to the University of Northern Colorado, she worked with distance education and telecommunications in continuing education at the University of Colorado, Boulder; the University of Maryland, University College; Auburn University; the University of North Carolina, Chapel Hill; and Murdoch University in Australia.

Duning received the Leadership Award of the National University Teleconference Network in 1988. She has chaired the Independent Study Division and the Division of Educational Telecommunications of the National University Continuing Education Association. Currently, she is on the board of the National University Teleconference Network and the editorial board of the *American Journal of Distance Education*.

Duning's writing activities have focused on issues in distance education and telecommunications applications to education. Her article "Independent Study in Higher Education: A Captive of Legendary Resilience" (1987) received the Charles A. Wedemeyer Award and was included in an edited collection (1989) on principles of distance education. Among her most recent works are an article, "The Coming of the New Distance Educators in the United States" (1990), published in *Distance Education,* Australia's major distance education research journal, and a chapter (1990) in a book on issues in distance education.

Marvin J. Van Kekerix is director of the Department of Academic Telecommunications and Professional Development in the Division of Continuing Studies at the University of Nebraska, Lincoln. In this capacity he provides the administrative leadership for a department that offers a variety of credit and noncredit professional development programs across the state of Nebraska and across the nation. A major delivery system for the department is Nebraska CorpNet, an on-site training network for business and industry that distributes "live" broadcast television to network members. The department serves approximately ten thousand people annually.

Van Kekerix received his B.A. degree (1966) from the University of South Dakota in mathematics, his M.A. degree (1968) from the University of South Dakota in history, and his Ph.D. degree (1986) from the University of Nebraska, Lincoln, in community and human resources. His dissertation, a study of the life cycle of the State University of Nebraska or SUN Project, won the Charles A. Wedemeyer Award for Distinguished Scholarship and Publication from the Independent Study Division of the National University Continuing Education Association in 1987. He is coauthor, with James P. Andrews, of a chapter entitled "Electronic Media and Independent Study" in *Foundations of American Distance Education: A Century of Collegiate Correspondence Study* (1992). In addition, he has presented numerous workshops on various aspects of distance education.

Before assuming the position of director of academic telecommunications and professional development, Van Kekerix was director of extended campus programs at the University of Nebraska, Lincoln. Prior to that he held a number of curricular and administrative positions within the Department of Independent Study at the University of Nebraska, Lincoln, and taught at the secondary and postsecondary levels.

Van Kekerix has been active in adult and continuing education associations on the state, regional, and national levels. He has served as president of the Adult and Continuing Education Association of Nebraska and chair of the Division of Educational Telecommunications for the National University Continuing Education Association, has been a member of the Administrative Committee of the Independent Study Division of the National University Continuing Education Association, and has served on the editorial board of the Independent Study Division Commemorative Anthology and the board of directors of the Missouri Valley Adult Education Association.

Leon M. Zaborowski is dean of the College of Continuing Education at the University of Northern Colorado. He received his B.S. degree (1966) from the University of Wisconsin, River Falls, in secondary education (chemistry) and his Ph.D. degree (1970) from the University of Idaho in chemistry.

Before assuming his current position in 1988, Zaborowski served as the director of continuing education programs at the University of Wisconsin, River Falls; University of Massachusetts, Boston; and Winona State University, Rochester Center. He has been involved in the development of a number of educational telecommunications systems and programs, including public service programming on cable television, live-via-satellite teleconference origination and reception, large-scale audioconferencing programs, and two-way interactive video systems using either fiber-optic or compressed-video transport systems.

Zaborowski has presented numerous papers on a variety of adult and continuing education topics. He has been a member of the National University Continuing Education Association since 1978.

Reaching
Learners
Through
Telecommunications

● ● ● ● ● ● ● ● ● ● *Chapter* 1

Mapping the Transition to Telecommunications-Based Education

Myth: Success in telecommunications-based education is a matter of identifying the single best model and applying it.

Reality: Telecommunications-based education is an enterprise that synthesizes components of many educational telecommunications systems and tailors a response to particular circumstances.

The advent of telecommunications-based education and training turned many experienced educators and administrators into novices overnight. First, the rapid pace and unfamiliar vocabulary of the field produced confusion about when, why, and how to adopt new electronic technologies. Second, the basis from which to make decisions about introducing a new system was unclear. Was the decision primarily technical, managerial, or educational? A third source of frustration centered on the thorny

1

questions inevitably raised concerning the relationship of the telecommunications system to the fundamental purposes of the parent organization. Most organizations confront such questions irregularly and seldom have a good strategy for doing so.

Managers in business, health care, and governmental agencies who come to telecommunications-based education with widely differing backgrounds will be able to transfer many of the authors' perspectives to their environments. The educational point of view in this book may introduce important considerations that are not immediately apparent to those working in other circumstances.

One consideration is to determine which issues deserve most of a manager's attention. Successful managers approach telecommunications systems as networks of human relationships. Defining new relationships before seeking the "fit" between specific electronic technologies and redefined roles, priorities, and objectives is a central preoccupation in managing and sustaining these systems.

For our purposes, *educational telecommunications system* refers to a collection of four components:

1. Hardware
2. Software that provides directions for operating and manipulating hardware
3. Transport, referring to electronic methods for receiving and sending programming among locations with educators and learners
4. Professionals who lead, manage, support, and use the system, and who respond to instructors' and learners' needs

Telecommunications-based education refers to any educational offering, whether at a distance or not, that depends on some or all of these components. Electronic technologies are integral to teaching and learning in telecommunications-based education.

This chapter looks at the importance of telecommunications-based education and what it can do, particularly in meeting the educational needs of adults. The issues encountered as this technology is integrated into the parent organization are explained and an approach to typical questions and concerns is offered.

The chapter begins with a case study that explores the origins and development of an educational telecommunications system in a postsecondary educational institution. The unfolding process of decision making is described in terms of the internal and external forces that influenced planning over a number of years and the kinds of issues that were encountered. We move next to the major expectations of telecommunications-based education and the qualities that successful managers bring to the planning process. Approaches to anticipating and minimizing the complexities of applying technologies to education, and the resistance it can inspire, are presented. We close the chapter with an overview of the themes developed throughout the book, which are identified as six lessons from experience.

Following are some of the most common concerns of managers who are unfamiliar with telecommunications-based education:

- What questions need to be asked and where are the best answers found?
- How should information be organized for decision making?
- What decisions need to be made first?
- How can the uncertainty and risk associated with electronic technologies be reduced?
- How are costs and revenues determined and projected?
- What are the pitfalls and how are they avoided?
- What factors are critical to success?
- How can experience with educational telecommunications systems in one environment be transferred to different circumstances?
- What kinds of organizational changes should be anticipated with telecommunications-based education?

The need to keep technical and human considerations in balance is embedded in all of these concerns and is introduced in this chapter as a central theme of the book.

The case study that follows illustrates how these kinds of issues can be addressed by describing the internal and external considerations that accompanied the introduction of an educational telecommunications system. The forces that came into play are discussed in terms of their influence on the reasoning that went into decision making. Many features of the case study foreshadow the approaches to planning and management developed throughout the book. There are examples of ideological elements such as accessibility to education, political elements represented by the role of a state education commission, and technical elements such as learner-support activities. The turning points described in the case study are noteworthy for their role in planning. All of these elements illustrate important aspects of the planning process presented in the book.

Case Study

During the 1980s the legislature of a Rocky Mountain state assigned one of the state's universities, an institution with a long history of leadership in teacher education, the primary responsibility for delivering complete graduate degree programs statewide to public school teachers and educational administrators. This mandate was consistent with the mission of the institution, and its specificity and exclusiveness was a key factor in subsequent decisions to introduce an educational telecommunications system.

Continuing education was given the responsibility for introducing and managing the program. It was decided in the early years of the program that the off-campus effort would be integrated into the academic fabric of the university. As a result, instruction was accomplished by increasing the regular faculty in the colleges affected and using a broad cross section of professors, with each normally teaching no more than two courses off campus during the school year. This resulted in a program that applied uniform standards of quality comparable to on-campus degree programs.

The university was expected to deliver this program across one of the largest states in the nation, which included a majority of the highest mountains in the country. Data from the state's Department of Education during the 1980s showed that there were approximately 33,000 public school teachers spread throughout the 176 school districts covering the state. Roughly 50 percent of these teachers did not have a master's degree. About 82 percent of the teachers resided in a concentrated area within eight of the state's sixty-three counties. These demographics were important in determining how to proceed and what impediments had to be taken into account.

By the fall of 1986 the university was able to start offering master's degree programs in three locations. Since then the program has had significant annual growth. For 1992, over thirty degree programs were planned for delivery at eleven different sites across the state. Each master's program runs for two to two and one-half years, covering six or seven consecutive semesters including summer. Fifteen to twenty-five practicing teachers or administrators enroll at the beginning of the typical program to form a cohort that takes an average of two courses per term for the duration of the degree.

Environmental scanning began at the inception of the program by means of a statewide needs assessment. This assessment, combined with demographic data about each school district, provided a substantial data base that was useful in indicating the types of programs needed as well as the communities in which to offer the programs. Data from the state's higher education commission provided information on programs being offered by other institutions. With these data and preexisting coordination between public colleges and universities, it was possible to avoid unnecessary interinstitutional duplication and unwarranted competition.

With the encouragement of the higher education commission, sites were restricted primarily to the campuses of other postsecondary institutions, most often community colleges or state colleges without graduate programs. This strategy improved the possibilities for obtaining suitable classrooms, instructional support equipment, and library facilities. Library resources were supplemented with materials from the university library or were enhanced by connection to an existing statewide computer-based data resource that provided the capability for on-line bibliographic search, faxing of articles, and a two-day interlibrary loan service. The statewide on-line bibliographic library resource had come into existence a few years before the start of the off-campus degree program.

Not long after the university received the statewide teacher education mandate, discussions began on the need for some type of educational telecommunications system to support the off-campus degree program. In 1987, a consultant completed an analysis and provided a set of recommendations for the creation of such a system. After two years, the off-campus program had demonstrated that it was viable. Yet the hardships of travel to distant instructional sites began to mount. By 1988, an extensive support base had developed that favored a distance-learning educational telecommunications system. An Educational Telecommunications Steering Committee was formed in 1989 to develop a proposal for a statewide telecommunications system to support the off-campus program effort. The committee had representation from the faculty, continuing education, media services, and the administration. Two faculty members with instructional-design expertise provided leadership. The continuing education unit was also asked by the administration to put up seed funds to cover the first phase of the system.

A substantial amount of strategic planning information had been gathered by 1989 that provided information on six strategic issues:

1. Potential student market
2. Possible programs
3. Service area
4. Potential competition
5. Most appropriate electronic technology
6. Costs

The *potential student market* was well defined at the school district level. Identifying *possible programs* was not a problem. The 1986 needs assessment combined with individual targeted regional assessments conducted on a program-by-program basis was providing a high level of reliability. Only about one in fifteen degree programs had to be canceled. The legislature had defined the *service area*—the state. The coordinating function of the state's higher education commission coupled with the unique statewide mandate positioned the university well with regard to *potential competition.* Settling on the most appropriate *electronic technology* and determining *costs,* however, proved more challenging.

The university's mission and mandate required the university to serve a *large service area* with an overall *low density of learners.* While the total number of teachers was substantial, about half already had a master's degree. Second, because of the large number of graduate degrees in demand, a dozen different programs were commonly requested. The net result was typically one or two teachers per building having interest in the same program. The one major metropolitan area was an exception, however, and a number of universities were accessible to serve students. The most vocal expressions of need came from the rural areas that comprise the bulk of the area in the state. The higher education commission, in fact, had set funding priorities that favored the offering of rural programs.

Experience had shown that rural educators were willing to travel an hour or more for the opportunity to participate in the university's degree programs. The desirability of using other postsecondary campuses for program sites established the requirement to have the *learners in a group;* therefore, a *multiple-site approach,* with twelve to thirteen strategically placed locations across the state, was selected as appropriate for both instructional and telecommunications sites. This strategy also increased the density of learners by requiring the students to converge at a central location. All residents would be a reasonable commute from any one site. The large number of programs being offered also suggested the need for a *dedicated educational telecommunications system.* In addition, graduate programs typically require considerable interaction between students and faculty or advisers; this also supported the notion of a dedicated system. Finally, the high level of interaction, with two-way video as a desirable characteristic, suggested that the telecommunications system would yield a *high cost per learner per program.*

With this information, the Educational Telecommunications Steering Committee evaluated various technical delivery systems. The large service area with its multiple-site, high-density combination of characteristics suggested that satellite delivery might be appropriate; however, the total number of students available to the system was still relatively low. The significant number of degree programs that would need to be transmitted simultaneously also worked against satellite delivery. The mountainous terrain precluded the distribution of significant amounts of optical fiber, a form of transport laid in the ground, and the mountains and large service area made microwave distribution difficult.

Instructional designers in the university's telecommunications planning group reasoned that the system should blend a number of electronic technologies, thereby allowing use of the most appropriate technology for the learning objective. It was agreed to support this approach and to introduce a set of technologies that would permit interactive instruction. It was also decided to select a backbone or base electronic technology that would serve as the primary conduit for the rest of the electronic technologies used. Terrestrial telephone transport was selected. A review of the technology preference tables in Chapter Four confirms how this decision was made. Telephone technology fit within the physical and operational parameters of the project and also provided an opportunity to develop the blended-technology concept supported by the instructional designers.

Early in 1990, some four years after the need for a distance-learning support system was expressed, the university initiated the first phase of a five-year plan for its educational telecommunications system. The electronic technology of choice for interactive instruction, advising, and a number of administrative functions was compressed video augmented by a number of other technologies.

Organizational change and the necessity of having an infrastructure to support and implement the system have been the most challenging aspects of the project. Three elements are critical to success: (1) faculty development and faculty commitment, (2) a feeling of familiarity and comfort with a new way of doing things throughout the organizational unit and the parent organization, and (3) an infrastructure that implements the educational telecommunications system.

The distance-learning project resurrected the idea of an instructional-design organizational unit at the university. The idea had been discussed off and on for a number of years and numerous reports and recommendations had encouraged the creation of such a unit. In the spring of 1991, a small task force was appointed; it developed the concept into a proposal that combined the existing media services unit, which was a part of the university libraries; the new educational telecommunications unit from continuing education; and the academic computer labs across campus. Instructional-design faculty from the college of education were made available on a project-by-project basis. The director of the new organizational unit was asked to serve on the task force, and a coordinating agent was designated during the start-up phase.

In this example, we see the kinds of considerations, forces, choices, decisions, and turning points that can play a part in planning and introducing an educational telecommunications system. We move next to an examination of the most powerful rationales for the introduction of telecommunications-based education, each of which was alluded to in the case study.

What Telecommunications-Based Education Can Do

Telecommunications-based education responds to opportunities that either depend on or are more powerfully realized with electronic delivery. These opportunities are often centered on sustaining or extending the parent organization's mission, improving instruction, or responding to learners' needs.

Extending the Mission

Telecommunications-based education needs to be conceptualized and perceived as an extension of the parent organization's mission. Opportunities to apply electronic technologies to education invariably give rise to a reassessment of purposes and a rethinking of priorities. Their introduction can lead to new and stimulating collaborative endeavors with local, national, or international scope that may significantly alter the image of both the organizational unit responsible for telecommunications-based education and the parent organization. Teaching is reconceptualized and a new perspective is brought to the content and delivery of education, the needs of individual learners and underserved constituencies, and the parent organization's mission and competitive position.

Individualizing Instruction

Responding to adults' requirements ranging from basic to advanced skills requires the individualization of instruction and flexibility of scheduling and location that telecommunications-based education can potentially offer. Such education can be responsive to learning differences through the use of electronic technologies with their potential for powerfully individualized instructional formats. The importance of electronic delivery of education to learners at a distance was initially most evident in the education of professionals in such fields as health care and engineering. These career-oriented professionals look for flexible instruction that is adapted to the practical urgencies of the workplace and to their own academic preparation, career progression, and scheduling constraints. The equally important promise of telecommunications-based education for less privileged, more culturally diverse and underserved learners who need individualized instruction is still unfolding.

Meeting the Needs of Adults

A key decision in the introduction of telecommunications-based education is the determination of who is to be served — in other words, accessibility. This type of education can alter and extend instruction within and beyond the parent organization. The unmet educational and training needs of adults in an increasingly multicultural population are acknowledged by business, government, and educators. The frame of reference proposed in this chapter and in Chapter Two reflects the growing importance of cultural diversity and adult learners' needs. If these are the primary reasons for introducing telecommunications-based education, what do managers do first to initiate the process? The next section describes the qualities that successful managers bring to the consideration of electronic technologies and educational telecommunications systems.

Characteristics of the Successful Manager

The nontechnical manager is often in a better position than one who is technically experienced to ensure that considerations such as user services, program goals, and the purposes of the organizational unit and the parent organization stay in balance with technical issues during decision making. Yet professionals in telecommunications-based education who are not technical specialists often find it difficult to know where to start when the pros and cons of introducing new systems are being explored. It is important to keep in mind that over the long run it will not be the electronic technology that is the measure of a program's success. Instead, its success will be determined by the extent to which the program's purposes, identified at the outset, are shown to be congruent with larger organizational purposes over time.

Managers typically express the following concerns about their lack of knowledge from which to judge the implications of telecommunications-based education for their own operations and those of the parent organization:

- Given my lack of technical expertise, how can I know what my organizational unit will face over the short run and in the future?
- Does my organizational unit have what it takes to successfully start this type of project?
- What aspects of my parent organization's circumstances matter most when considering the introduction of an educational telecommunications system?
- Where are the most reliable sources of information and how do I go about applying what I learn to my own circumstances?

Perceiving Choices, Not Confusion

Successful managers view the many options generated by new electronic technologies as a source of freedom rather than a distracting maze. Where others see confusion, the successful manager sees a continuum of choices. This reconceptualization of the situation is a form of reframing that is treated thoroughly by Bolman and Deal (1991). It is well to keep in mind that such choices were not being weighed by anyone until relatively recently. There is no extensive history of successful reconceptualization to serve as a baseline for telecommunications-based education. At the center of an approach that can bring clarity to confusion is the recognition, expressed in the statement that introduced this chapter, that managers are not searching for one best answer.

Successful managers of telecommunications-based education develop a focus on a cluster of nontechnical issues, which will be considered later in this chapter. Technological considerations are placed in the larger context of these nontechnical decisions, an orientation that enables managers to assess conflicting information and to explain their priorities. This focus is the most vital skill managers bring to the earliest phases of consideration of telecommunications-based education for two reasons: (1) it enables managers to resist pressures to achieve unnecessary levels of technical proficiency and (2) it prevents technical considerations from being introduced too early in the decision-making process.

Distinguishing Problem Setting from Problem Solving

Managers who successfully introduce telecommunications-based education make distinctions between problem setting and problem solving. Problem solving is concerned with means to an end. The appropriate choice of electronic technologies is a problem-solving task. Problem setting deals with ends, that is, the goals and purposes to which the electronic technologies will be applied. Questions of means are technical and managerial, while questions of ends require both management and leadership skills. Managers skilled at problem setting use this ability to marshal opinion around the possibilities of educational telecommunications systems.

Extracting Meaning from Others' Experiences

A crucial skill in the application of electronic technologies to education is the ability to extract meaning from others' experience. Ad hoc telecommunications-based education as well as entire systems often develop idiosyncratically. Such systems require collaboration between people who may not have worked closely together before. Managers frequently have difficulty making sense of the variations in the process, particularly those regarding the myriad possible applications of electronic technologies. If they have no technical background, managers usually do not feel confident or competent to understand what technologies can do or to assess their cost implications over time. Yet there are ways to consider technical equipment that can cut through the complexity. Becoming familiar with the language used to describe educational telecommunications systems is useful; however, it is not illuminating as a first step. A better first step is to explore what electronic technologies can accomplish in general. Integrating technologies, networking people, and combining locations are examples of capabilities that introduce useful distinctions in a range of choices.

Minimizing the Complexities of Equipment

Integrating Technologies

Video, audio, and other components have roles, functions, and characteristics that can alter as they are combined. Nearly limitless combinations of traditional distance-learning methods based on correspondence study and interactive teaching and learning can then be joined with electronic technologies and integrated into educational telecommunications systems. These integrating capabilities only become meaningful, however, in light of the needs they are intended to serve in a particular environment.

After a manager becomes familiar with the language of electronic technology, it will be apparent that when these technologies are introduced the primary concerns are not technical. Instead, the major issues relate to the needs and expectations of learners and educators and the relationships between providers of telecommunications-based education and their partners.

Networking People

A primary capability of many electronic technologies is the electronic linking of people for "real-time" interaction. The new vocabulary of this capability can make familiar technology appear unnecessarily complex. For example, a telephone has functions in a telecommunications system that alter its usual role. Even the language used to describe this familiar instrument changes when hardware is combined in an educational telecommunications system. "Bridging" into a conference call rather than "phoning" indicates that the call, while technically no more than a telephone call, is accomplishing a different objective.

The term *bridging* refers to phoning an electronic device known as an audioconference bridge where the caller encounters a person or a message that serves the function of a telephone operator. The caller who bridges is linked to a larger set of electronic technologies that provides more powerful phone operations. Now, with a single phone call, the caller can talk instantaneously with any number of other callers, who are all networked simultaneously simply by phoning the bridging mechanism.

There is almost no technical limit to the number of callers who can be bridged. The number is limited by the same considerations that limit any meeting or instructional session: the nature of the subject and the amount of individual exchange desired. From a technician's viewpoint this kind of networking is a technical feat, but from a manager's perspective it is a meeting or a class, not a technical achievement. Like most meetings, electronic ones become an experience in human interactions that are initiated, sustained, deepened, or expanded.

Combining Locations

Electronic technologies are often described not only in terms of how they present information — by picture, audio, and so on — or by their implications for networking people, but also as linking mechanisms housed at origination and reception sites. Unlike video screens, telephones, and other tools, these linking mechanisms are often invisible to educators and learners who use electronic telecommunications systems. Linking mechanisms such as fiber optics, microwave and Instructional Television Fixed Service (ITFS) networks, satellites, cable, and audio bridges, as well as all of the electronic technologies referred to in this book, are defined in the Glossary.

Linking can refer merely to ad hoc audio communication between two or more separated locations. In other cases, it may involve converting video from still pictures, called *freeze frame,* to partial- or full-motion video. The video may or may not be accompanied by live, talkback arrangements. The capacities to integrate hardware, network people, or combine dispersed locations may all sound desirable at first, but these strengths must be weighed against other considerations and requirements within a particular context as described in Chapter Four.

Major Descriptors of Telecommunications

As noted earlier, a full description of an educational telecommunications system refers to hardware, software, transport, instructors and learners, and professional staff. The term *electronic technology* by itself is often used to describe entire systems. For example, educational telecommunications systems may be referred to as microwave or satellite systems. Complex systems might be described as an integration of microwave and satellite technologies, audio and video, computers, fax machines, telephones, and other electronic tools. Systems are usually described, however, by some dimension that comes to have overriding importance in a particular set of circumstances.

Origination and Reception

How learners access telecommunications-based education depends in part on how the management of the telecommunications system is structured. One common structural descriptor distinguishes systems by the physical location of the educator who is teaching, called the *origination site,* and the location of the learners, called *reception sites.* Multiple reception sites may all be located within the same building or on the same property. Sites may also be dispersed throughout a geographical area that includes cities, states, regions, the nation, or the world.

Distinctions between origination and reception sites can blur over time. When both faculty and learners are located at all sites, rather than faculty being solely at an origination site, the interactive technical capability that has networked the locations can also be used to initiate instruction from all the sites. Under these circumstances the notion of a primary, or origination, site becomes less meaningful as a managerial construct.

Whether the origination of instruction should be centralized, decentralized, or a hybrid is initially a managerial rather than a technical issue. The determination of the most desirable arrangement is based on considerations regarding the wider purposes of the educational telecommunications system for the organizational unit, the parent organization, and the educators and learners.

Potential for Integration

A second broad characteristic of educational telecommunications systems from the manager's perspective is the extent to which they are capable of integrating current and emerging technologies. This might initially appear to be largely a technical matter, because the capacity to integrate technologies might seem to be a desirable feature under all conditions. Yet managerial, financial, service, maintenance, and learner-support implications are associated with this capacity. The relative importance of these factors has a bearing on how desirable it is to maximize technical integration in a particular context.

Content

A third descriptor has to do with the nature and purposes of the material conveyed by the system. The type of content that might be carried is frequently reduced to just three words: voice, data, or video. *Data* allow some economies in the use of an educational telecommunications system because some types of data can be transmitted electronically at less cost during times of lowest system demand. *Voice* refers to two-way audio, for example, used in a conference call using the telephone. *Video* can refer to one-way or two-way video between an origination site and receiving locations, in combination with one-way or two-way audio. Few educational telecommunications systems, however, are dedicated solely to a single type of content, since multiple use is one of the strengths of this technology.

Users

A fourth descriptor is related to the audience for whom a system is designed. Educational telecommunications systems are sometimes described in terms of narrowly defined groups of learners with highly focused requirements, for example, a group of systems engineers seeking postgraduate academic coursework. Targeting a system to a mix of learners influences how the system's purpose is conceptualized. Descriptors can provide general professional development with or without academic credit, as well as entire academic degrees or specialized professional certification. Audiences also include general users who are less concerned with academic credit than with broad professional updating, skills enhancement, or public issues.

Early attempts at introducing telecommunications-based education typically identified a relatively narrow clientele with specific needs. Academic or professional certification offerings were often viewed as the safest starting point. Yet in many environments, this may not be the best initial use of telecommunications-based education. Depending on the circumstances, a response to educational needs where learners are not seeking academic credit may be the best place to start.

It is not until the immediate purposes, audiences, and overarching goals of telecommunications-based education have been articulated and have received wide agreement within the parent organization that descriptors become meaningful and electronic technologies can be compared. Diagramming a possible system can be helpful. The diagram can be configured into various combinations of descriptors; for example, just three of the descriptors alluded to earlier can be combined into a number of choices:

1. Centralized or decentralized origination
2. A broad versus a narrow set of learners
3. Education carrying academic credit versus a noncredit emphasis

A manager can make fundamental conceptual decisions by seeing how the distinctions among these choices fit some circumstances but not others.

Extending or diversifying access to education is a major capability of electronic technologies. At the same time, much of the resistance to telecommunications-based education is concerned with the issue of accessibility.

Overcoming Resistance to Electronic Technologies

This book is not intended as a technical primer nor is it written for the person seeking technical proficiency. We believe that nontechnical managers, faculty, and leaders of the parent organization most often lead in achieving greater access to resources and meeting other goals through telecommunications-based education.

The decision to move forward in the application of new electronic technologies depends on the availability of resources to one or more organizational units and often to the parent organization, the relationship of telecommunications-based education to the parent organization's mission, and its ability to alter or confirm a vision of the future.

The idea that access to education can be extended or diversified is a common reason for considering the introduction of telecommunications-based education. Yet the meanings attached to such accessibility are in part a product of assumptions, values, and goals that may be unexamined or in conflict. Varying perceptions of the effects of electronic technologies on education offer clues to underlying assumptions within the organizational unit and the parent organization that require managerial attention.

Chief among environmental considerations in educational change is the resistance of many educators to electronic technologies. Their skepticism about nontraditional instruction in general, particularly when learners and faculty are at a distance from each other, has long been acknowledged. The ambivalence among faculty in postsecondary education with regard to applying new methodologies to teaching is also well known. Lack of know-how, loss of control, and loss of privacy are grounds for educators' reluctance to embrace educational telecommunications systems that are seldom explored in the literature. These sources of resistance are not insurmountable barriers to the introduction of telecommunications activity; they do, however, require greater attention to feelings than is commonly acknowledged.

Threat or Enhancement to Teaching?

The introduction of educational telecommunications systems connotes for some educators a degradation of the teaching process. The skeptical anticipate educational disruption, not linkages, and view electronic technology as an imposition that diminishes human interaction in instruction and learning. The alteration in the traditional contact between the educator and the learner is seen as undermining an essential element in the quality of the educational experience, causing scholars to resist their seeming transformation into mere facilitators of information or operators of equipment. The team approach to instructional technology arouses understandable concern. The emphasis on planning, equipment, and methodologies is out of keeping with instructors' experiences of creativity, inspiration, and the serendipitous learning moment that cannot be scripted in advance.

By contrast, academicians, trainers, and administrators who embrace technological innovation are willing to place themselves in the position of neophytes in order to explore how teaching methods might benefit from electronic technologies. Such faculty are frequently found in professions with a history of providing continuing professional education, such as law, engineering, and health care. A practical incentive may also exist in these fields through rewards for nontraditional instruction in the form of compensation, reduced workload, or credits toward academic tenure.

There are a number of other sources of educators' resistance to electronic technologies that are understandable and can be overcome. Studies throughout this century have documented that learners working at a distance from faculty do as well as those in conventional educational settings no matter what mode of instruction is used. Yet educators' concepts of teaching and learning are tied to intense feelings about their academic field that cannot be expected to yield readily to such evidence.

As Bok (1986, p. 62) observes, "Most faculty members believe passionately in knowledge for its own sake. This belief may strike some as effete. But it accounts for much of the enthusiasm professors feel toward their disciplines." He goes on to note that a new educational proposal that runs counter to the basis of this enthusiasm "can easily come into conflict with the deepest feelings professors have toward their subjects" (p. 62). He sees a "pattern of avoidance" tied to certain academic preoccupations, most notably the curriculum, and states: "But curriculum debates only involve the arrangement and rearrangement of individual courses and do not touch upon the ways in which professors organize their material, teach their classes, and examine their students. Hence, the fascination with curriculum, so typical of American undergraduate education, protects traditional faculty prerogatives at the cost of diverting attention away from the kinds of inquiry and discussion that are most likely to improve the process of learning" (p. 71). These feelings help to explain why movement into educational telecommunications systems is comparatively cautious and underscore the need to approach such education primarily as a network of relationships.

Lack of Know-How

Educators and others often resist new undertakings because they don't know how to do what is being asked of them (Bok, 1986). Bok offers as an example the teaching of new subject matter that is so complex that no one understands it well enough to teach it. The same can be said of understanding how to recast subject matter to make use of new electronic technologies. A complex matrix of working relationships that is wholly at odds with traditional teaching practices is introduced as a result of the teamwork demanded by technical support.

Loss of Control

The loss of privacy and personal control of teaching is a third seldom-acknowledged but understandable reason for educators' reluctance to adopt telecommunications-based education. Telecommunications transforms the privileged status of an educator alone in a classroom without close observation from peers into an effort that may involve educational technologists, technicians, and administrative managers. Even the instructor's place at the center of the team cannot negate the fact that personal latitude has been diminished.

Successful managers resist seeking one "best" answer to these dilemmas. What would raise barriers in one situation can lower them in another. For example, equipping a room with some form of technical capability that is operable without undue assistance can be a useful step in some contexts. In others, minimizing the level of technical interactivity between educators and learners may open the door to electronic technology in unpromising circumstances. Telecommunications-based education requires a rethinking of instructional roles that takes such contextual factors into account. In every context, however, some personal goals must usually give way to shared objectives. For most environments this constitutes a shift in climate, a subject that is treated in Chapter Three.

Loss of Privacy

Academic freedom is exemplified in the tradition of classroom privacy. It transcends faculty concerns regarding control of one's work because it is central to the conception of what it means to be a scholar. The introduction of telecommunications-based education usually eliminates privacy in the classroom. Privacy provides protection from the ebb and flow of fads and political fashions that might otherwise infringe on academic freedom. Moreover, the privacy of the classroom has often shielded educators from peer review. Evaluation is left largely to learners, whose views are routinely disregarded. This traditional prerogative of educators at all educational levels constitutes one of the most emotional and least discussed areas of resistance to telecommunications-based education. Alone with a group of learners, an educator experiences intellectually exciting and personally rewarding moments in teaching. These inspirational peaks are associated with privacy, which is a hallmark of the traditional classroom.

Telecommunications-based education alters these traditional prerogatives profoundly and permanently. Once it has been delivered electronically, instruction is potentially open to review by anyone. An educator's work that has been electronically stored can be examined years later. What this might mean in terms of an educator's reputation and professional rights presents as yet unexplored possibilities. Managers need to acknowledge such value-laden and untested implications of educational telecommunications systems through agreements with educators that address these sources of resistance.

Distrust of Electronic Technology's Claims

Another source of reluctance to use telecommunications-based education is more openly debated: the distrust of electronic technology and its claims. Although rigorous assessment of teaching methodologies is rare in postsecondary education, it is not surprising that educators want evidence that a technical innovation will work as well as or better than present instruction before making the effort required for a transition. These requests for evidence need to be taken seriously. Specific models of telecommunications-based education cannot, however, be expected to be universally applicable.

New systems must invariably be customized and tailored to circumstances and to a specific period in organizational history. New electronic technologies may be viewed as successful in one context because they reach more racial minorities. In other environments success may be measured by opening up new areas of research, satisfying a professional group, improving educational quality, increasing productivity, or reducing turnover among valued staff.

Lessons from Experience

In the chapters that follow, we will explain the issues surrounding the integration of educational telecommunications systems with education from a number of perspectives. Several themes emerge in these discussions, which we mention at this point so that readers can weigh their importance in terms of their personal circumstances. We identify these themes as six lessons from experience.

Lesson No. 1: Involvement from the Top

Successful telecommunications-based education and training programs involve leaders at the highest levels of the parent organization, and success in introducing such systems is more likely with visible support from these levels. Those who paved the way for what is now known as Nebraska CorpNet at the University of Nebraska at Lincoln included the chancellor, the vice chancellor for academic affairs, and the dean of engineering. Nebraska CorpNet is an on-site training network for business and industry using live broadcast television. For the introduction of a multipurpose educational telecommunications system at Portland Community College, leadership came from the president, the vice president for instruction, and the director of what became known as instructional support and industrial television, which served campus and business sites.

This support sometimes, but not always, includes financial resources, although financial resources are seldom supplied indefinitely. Because it is difficult to meet the costs of these systems solely from fees paid by learners, telecommunications-based education is frequently lodged in organizational units that are charged with generating income to underwrite the programs.

Lesson No. 2: Problem Setting

The process of successfully introducing telecommunications-based education concentrates on clusters of problems that can be expected to accompany its introduction. *Hidden concerns of academicians* that need to be directly and indirectly acknowledged constitute one cluster. *Competing goals* among constituent groups within and beyond the parent organization make up a second cluster. These need to be recast as shared goals. *Altered relationships, roles, and fundamental purposes* with respect to telecommunications-based education that must be framed as an extension of the mission of the parent organization are a third problem cluster.

Lesson No. 3: Choices Offer Freedom

Electronic technologies for telecommunications-based education range so widely in cost, complexity, capability, and magnitude that these variations are often misperceived as a barrier. Yet it is this diversity that offers managers freedom of choice and an opportunity for leadership. Managers can approach and assess the uses of electronic technology apart from considerations of individual pieces of equipment and technical mastery. Determining and introducing a balanced combination of electronic technologies and support services is less a technical than a conceptual task. Each combination of options has unique implications for services, staffing, initial and future costs, support systems, and ongoing managerial operations. Focus is achieved through a process of putting problem setting ahead of problem solving and clarifying ends before examining means.

A critical task during the earliest consideration of telecommunications-based education is to ensure that exploration of electronic technologies does not take precedence over analysis of the purposes and uses of the potential system. In short, managers must ask themselves what is to be done, why it is being done, and who will benefit.

The inclination to look first at electronic technologies rather than at purposes and relationships is understandable. An examination of purposes raises questions about the values reflected by the people served by a system, the balance of competing interests for limited resources, and the parent organization's values. Equipment, by contrast, offers an area of exploration that seems more objective. Yet such inquiry nevertheless leads back to the more sensitive area of the parent organization's view of the future. The attributes being sought contribute to a conceptual framework that goes beyond a collection of tactics and offers a set of principles to guide choices.

Lesson No. 4: Collaboration Is Required

Most successful programs confirm that the introduction of telecommunications-based education is necessarily a collaborative effort. In nearly all cases the parties are unaccustomed to working closely with one another. A successful process creates a team that is weighted toward professionals who can best consider the nontechnical questions that are raised.

At the University of Nebraska at Lincoln, a partnership between businesses, University Television, and the university's Division of Continuing Studies has been evolving since 1985. The most memorable problems encountered have been nontechnical. At one point, for example, any change of schedule required the attention of twenty-three people. Among the cooperating businesses, one changed its name four times in the first four years of system operation, and turnover in corporate personnel important to the partnership has been high. The joint administration consisting of University Television (handling technical matters) and the Division of Continuing Studies (responsible for programming and marketing) has been strained by different organizational structures and cultures. One unit is centralized and the other decentralized, leading to divergent approaches to management.

Lesson No. 5: Seeing Opportunities

The introduction of telecommunications systems in higher education can require unusual managerial resourcefulness. The initial effort at one institution was made possible through the use of $120,000 in savings from unrelated operations. This "neutral" money was not a resource vulnerable to debate about its use. The neutral money was called upon more than once as the educational telecommunications system was established.

At another postsecondary institution, resourceful administrators drew on a handful of faculty enthusiasts, along with other factors, to make better use of electronic technology that was already in place throughout the state. At a community college, a fleeting opportunity in the early 1980s to apply for a cable channel dedicated to education was seized upon during a franchise process. Once the channel was established, the need to use it became a driving force in the development of a successful educational telecommunications system.

Lesson No. 6: Readiness for the Unexpected

Unexpected occurrences recounted by seasoned managers show that surprises are common to such activities. Corporate part-

ners experience industrial turmoil, and multimillion-dollar en-
terprises can be reluctant to spend sums as modest as $1,500
to join systems they helped create. Industry training units can
appear to outsiders to be unfamiliar with their own company's
training needs; they may regard options offered by educational
telecommunications systems as a potential threat to the industry's educational programming.

The low levels of technical quality accepted by some educators and learners can make managers of telecommunications-
based education feel compromised. Ongoing operational support in financial and other arrangements is cited by some managers as surprisingly unpredictable. Yet in some instances, the
level of resources allocated to educational telecommunications
systems has exceeded the managers' most optimistic predictions.

Educational telecommunications systems also have borne
out managers' expectations. While telecommunications-based
education in a noncredit format is even more popular than
predicted, degree credit courses were expected to be popular
and have proven to be. Similarly, it was accurately predicted
that professionals who were already looking to an institution
for traditional coursework would accept telecommunications-
based education.

Managers of telecommunications-based education say
that, in retrospect, they would do some things differently. They
would give more attention to:

- Ensuring congruence with the parent organization's mission
  and its rewards to faculty when the new system is introduced
- Gaining faculty cooperation
- Clarifying the primary users of telecommunications-based
  education and their needs, expectations, and locations
- Identifying all stakeholders in the educational telecommu-
  nications system and determining how best to keep them
  informed of developments
- Determining the specific responsibilities of each partner in
  the new system's management
- Probing the expectations of industry partners more thoroughly
- Developing learner-support services, in particular the on-

site coordination of program support in the form of materials, counseling, and logistics
- Specifying sources of expense and income and predicting how they are likely to change over time

Summary

A frame of reference for nontechnical managers engaged in the introduction of telecommunications-based education is proposed that can be summarized in a number of principles. First, it must be presented and perceived as an extension of the mission and fundamental values of the parent organization. The chief officers of the parent organization need to be visibly involved in the conceptualization and planning of the system from the outset.

Second, development of new working relationships within and outside the parent organization is critical. These working relationships need to be identified and formed prior to consideration of specific electronic technologies. Telecommunications-based education must be perceived as consisting of linkages centered on people and their needs, not on equipment. Problem setting that leads to understandings and commitments to specific outcomes should precede technical considerations.

Third, the confusing and sometimes mutually exclusive technical options presented to managers can be clarified with a frame of reference that keeps nontechnical considerations at the forefront of planning and decision making. Nontechnical managers who bring this orientation to the introduction of telecommunications-based education can more readily derive meaning from others' experience, are better able to make sense of conflicting claims, and have a better grasp of the conceptual balance needed in the development process.

Each component of this frame of reference is elaborated as other chapters examine the implications of educational telecommunications systems for planning, partnering, costing, integrating, and staffing the system, and for reaching learners. The next step is to consider a set of guiding assumptions that can inform decision making in all of these areas. These assumptions are the subject of Chapter Two.

●●●●●●●●●● **Chapter 2**

Guiding Assumptions of Educational Telecommunications

Myth: Telecommunications-based education is accomplished by a single responsible organizational unit managing integrated technologies.

Reality: Introducing and sustaining telecommunications-based education centers more on developing networks of relationships than on equipment.

The introduction of telecommunications-based education requires managers to come to terms with conflicting perceptions of the task. Is the task primarily the management of a delivery system or of an educational system? Is the central concern the marketing of self-supporting programming or is it technical, involving the acquisition and application of equipment? Is the managerial task largely financial or should it focus on the use of an educational telecommunications system as a catalyst for widespread organizational change?

Telecommunications-based education is frequently approached as an equipment-driven activity. The task is perceived as technical management with the responsibility resting in organizational units concerned with electronic technologies. On the other hand, when it is perceived primarily as a marketing endeavor, the task is likely to be housed in the organizational unit most accustomed to "selling" educational opportunities to nontraditional learners. And when it is viewed as fundamental to a change of organizational image, it is almost invariably championed by the chief officer of the parent organization. Under these circumstances the organizational leader is personally and publicly associated with telecommunications developments and guides activities through upper-level administrators in an ad hoc fashion.

These three perspectives may not be explicitly stated, yet one or more of them will be the basis of competing opinions within the parent organization. Managers need to be sensitive to this underlying reasoning and recognize the prevailing view even though it may be obscured by ongoing debate. Insight into the basis of contending perspectives can help to clarify deliberations during the confusing early stages of integrating telecommunications-based education into the existing educational system.

The eight guiding assumptions presented in this chapter and elaborated throughout the book can unify the conceptual and operational decisions required by telecommunications-based activities. The assumptions deal with learners' increasing control of learning, the shift in the position of organizational units concerned with telecommunications-based education toward the center of the parent organization, ethics, costs, the mission of the parent organization, the vocabulary of marketing, the individualization of learning, and self-awareness in guiding change.

These assumptions offer a means of assessing managerial and organizational readiness to move into telecommunications, or to carry it beyond present levels. First, the assumptions comprise a rationale for introducing and guiding the program that can resolve conflicting perceptions of the task. Second, examining the conditions and aspirations of the organizational unit in light of these assumptions can bring clarity and flexibility to decision making.

Third, acknowledging these assumptions can contribute to planning that is consistent with the fundamental values of the parent organization and the organizational unit. For example, the parent organization may place a priority on broadening diversity among learners. Managers of telecommunications-based education can begin to operationalize that goal by making multiculturalism an explicit measure of programmatic quality and success and by gathering information about organizational and personal barriers to diversity.

Personal circumstances, geographical setting, time schedules, and financial considerations are often cited as barriers to taking advantage of educational opportunities. Yet telecommunications-based education may make it possible to reduce such seemingly intractable barriers through its power to network individuals, organizations, and resources.

The assumptions presented in this chapter are developed as themes throughout the book. Chapter Three suggests that planning can be organized by grouping issues into interrelated strands that are identified as cultural-ideological, political, and technical. Each of the assumptions discussed in this chapter can be placed in a strand and contribute to the planning strategy. We present the assumptions in a sequence that begins with the most overriding ones: the centrality of the learner and the ultimate centrality of the educational telecommunications system within the parent organization. The most personal of the assumptions — sensitivity to one's own biases — closes the discussion.

Guiding Assumptions

Eight assumptions can assist the introduction and maintenance of telecommunications-based education:

1. The future lies with the learner.
2. Organizational centrality reduces latitude.
3. Ethical considerations will increase.
4. Costs can be managed differently.
5. Congruence with the parent organization's mission is essential.

6. A marketing vocabulary is insufficient.
7. Individualization accompanies telecommunications.
8. Managerial biases influence change.

Learner-Centered

The emerging centrality of the learner is the most powerful of the eight assumptions. Whether the individual is a student, client, constituent, consumer, or learner, his or her expectations will be a paramount consideration for the successful manager.

    Managers who begin with the learner are able to resolve many of the conflicting options offered by electronic technologies. Gauging the extent to which potential change leads toward learners' control over learning offers a useful perspective for decision making.

Centrality of Learners' Needs. Successful telecommunications-based education seeks to place recipients' needs ahead of organizational convenience and at the center of planning and decision making. The "processes" of providing programming become simultaneously more visible to learners and more complex. As learners' choices are widened, their control potentially increases. Thus, the needs of learners as individuals, not merely as students, take on more importance in education that uses electronic technology. Learners' criticism is difficult to ignore because electronic technologies bring greater attention to instructional design and its effects on learning. Their opinions and needs consequently play a more prominent role in decision making than is usual in traditional education.

More Self-Directed Learning. Electronic technologies have characteristics that offer learners the means and the motivation to direct more of their own learning. First, the potential for more varied instructional interactivity than is typical in traditional classrooms is a distinctive attribute of many educational telecommunications systems. Second, interconnectivity of learners to each other enriches the instructional environment and extends the learners' reach geographically from local to national and global resources. Systems with such capabilities thus create a network of learner-based resources beyond those provided by an instructor.

Third, the integration of electronic technologies is shifting educational resources from institutional and organizational centers to dispersed locations that will eventually include the home. Finally, retrievability of educational and related information on one's own terms removes two reasons commonly cited to explain why adult learners ignore educational opportunities: inconvenient time schedules and geographical distance.

Managers who anticipate and prepare to support these forces will foster greater congruence with an organizational mission that responds to learner needs. Such managers will also be among the first professionals in telecommunications-based education to begin operationalizing the shift toward learners who direct more aspects of their own education. Relationships with self-directing learners have implications that require managerial as well as instructional attention.

Management of Relationships. Managers of telecommunications-based education manage relationships, not equipment. Telecommunications encourages and enables students to more actively choose when, where, and how they engage in learning. As their sense of ownership of their own educational progress grows, learners' expectations and perceptions of this technology will change.

Managers can anticipate these changing expectations by planning for the numerous forms of interaction that electronic technologies can so powerfully introduce and support between and among learners, educators, and the organizational unit. As shifts occur in the network of relationships within the telecommunications system, managerial emphasis must also shift to ensure that an orientation toward selling programs is balanced by the establishment of affiliations with learners. Managers must also anticipate a shift in the position of the organizational unit from the margins of the parent organization toward the center of planning.

Gaining Centrality and Losing Latitude

The responsibility for telecommunications-based education frequently resides in organizational units such as continuing and distance education. Such units have traditionally been at the periphery of parent organizations' activities; they will move toward the center of the parent organization as telecommunications-based education grows more important. This transition will erode the latitude that managers of continuing education and other peripheral organizational units frequently gain by virtue of their existence at the organizational margins. The reduction of latitude is not, however, accompanied by a reduction in risk. On the contrary, learners will expect more, not fewer, options in the future.

Managers must understand the effects of being on the organizational margins. The protection from close oversight that this position offers comes at the cost of their ability to make the swift, informed judgments that rapid technological change often requires.

Marginality Delays Action. The ability to take action can be circumscribed by a position on the organizational margins. This was illustrated by an intriguing spectacle that emerged in post-secondary education as the 1980s unfolded. The advent of a powerful, albeit jumbled, collection of new electronic technologies was greeted with outright or implicit dismay by many of the educational entities that were best placed to lead the way in responding to these novel opportunities. Distance educators, who have for decades specialized in providing teaching and support services to learners studying by correspondence, did not readily embrace new and diverse electronic technologies such as more affordable computers and live video available by satellite. What conclusions can be drawn from this response?

There are two primary explanations for this cautious reaction. First, educators had seen promising electronic technologies fade in earlier eras. Enthusiasts at the edges of the organization consequently backed away when chided for what was termed a "gee-whiz" mentality. Second, the skeptics repeatedly asked how these electronic technologies could be made to pay their way through learners' fees.

Other professionals did not step in at once either. Technical specialists, for example, were not well positioned to offer a considered approach to the massive transformation that was so clearly under way. In postsecondary education, they were regarded primarily as issuers of equipment and storers of materials, and they were funded to do little more. Continuing education operations, where postsecondary distance education is typically located, for the most part also took a "wait and see" attitude.

Managers of continuing and distance education in postsecondary education and elsewhere did not, however, stop doing what they do best: their homework. Sessions at national conferences that dealt with advances in applying electronic technology to education were jammed. Pockets of experimentation were visited time and again. Analyses of attempts to apply new electronic technologies were assembled, disassembled, and reexamined in search of the keys to stable educational programming that could cover their costs.

The early and successful activity of some institutions and states, going back in certain instances over decades, generally proved frustrating to onlookers. These early efforts often contained unreplicable elements that made translation to other settings problematic. Early failures, some of them on a large scale, were understandably mined for lessons that served to inhibit rather than spur activity. And most managers lacked a frame of reference within which new information could be made sufficiently meaningful for change of this magnitude to be undertaken confidently.

This scenario can be avoided by creating a frame of reference that allows a confusing barrage of information to be organized. For example, by seeing how opportunities can be presented in terms of the central purposes of the organization, a manager can minimize some of the limitations of a position on the organizational margins.

Marginality Limits Perspective. Managers of telecommunications-based education in postsecondary institutions, and in other educational and business contexts, often possess only incomplete information concerning wider organizational plans. Disparities between organizational units in operations and in their capacity to prepare for change can often be traced to their lack of access to reliable information. Lack of information also narrows managerial perspectives regarding the relationship of the manager's role to the goals of the parent organization.

How will traditional continuing education and distance education managers respond in the coming years to the advice of Votruba (1987) and others that they move from the sidelines and into a leadership position that is closely aligned with the mission of the parent organization? Educational telecommunications systems introduce a number of perceptions that lead their managers toward the organizational center. Electronic technology can be perceived not merely as the acquisition of equipment but as adding value to education through greater accessibility and convenience, or as improving educational quality through effects on teaching and learning that are still to be documented.

Together with marginality, the absence of formulas and the lightning speed of technological developments strain efforts to remain focused on the central objectives of adopting telecommunications-based education. These objectives may include paying more attention to learning differences; advancing teaching effectiveness; widening educational opportunities to include populations who are truly diverse in ethnic background, age, and geographical location; and operationalizing features of the parent organization's mission.

Can areas that are responsible for telecommunications-based education become advocates on behalf of new constituencies and their needs? Moving in from the margins of the parent organization requires more engagement in shaping standards for practices and policies designed for learners. Learners can be as marginalized as the organizational unit. Those who need education and training often gain access based on their ability to circumvent or afford the inconveniences of programming and procedures that the organizational unit takes for granted.

Among the underserved constituencies are those who are less able to adjust to organizational timetables, procedures, and costs that disregard the realities of the adult work life. These constituencies are made up of not only part-time, middle-class, urban adult students but also those with low incomes or lesser skills. Other underserved constituencies include racial minorities, rural residents, and newcomers to the work force such as foreign immigrants and women working for the first time. The most pressing ethical implications of telecommunications-based education in the future will relate to the constituencies it ignores.

Ethics

Ethical considerations are becoming a high priority in the development of telecommunications-based education. Postsecondary education will feel the impact of the perception that only a narrow range of learners has access to education and training. The primarily middle-class, white, urban, and educated character of participants in both traditional and nontraditional educational programs is increasingly viewed as an ethical issue by underrepresented groups. The greater the perceived imbalance, the more insistent the ethical questions will become.

Equitable Access. Successful managers need to prepare themselves to play a major part in addressing issues of equitable access to educational resources; equity in the composition of learners served by programming will be among the most fundamental questions raised about the proper uses of telecommunications in education and training. Managers can begin to prepare for this leadership by asking themselves three questions:

1. What are my current perceptions of the causes of inequities in access to education?
2. What do the causes of such inequities have to do with me as a manager?
3. Which values within current measures of programmatic

success and quality offer greater participation by minorities and other underrepresented constituencies?

The orienting framework presented in Chapter Nine assumes that inequities in access to education for diverse learners will be questioned in the future by those who set policy for educational and training operations. Inequities will not be framed solely as an educational issue. They will increasingly be viewed as exemplifying racism, social control through differential access to resources, and discrepancies between organizational values and organizational behavior.

Aligning Values and Practices. The public nature of telecommunications-based education and its power to reach learners despite time and distance make it inevitable that programs using electronic technologies' far-reaching delivery capabilities will receive increasing public attention. The costs of educational telecommunications systems may mean that less funding is available for other purposes; therefore, any perceived divergence between the espoused values of managers and the outcomes of managerial practices will be on the public agenda in the future. Managers of education and training typically talk about responsiveness to learners' needs, the social objectives of economic progress and well-being for citizens of all ages, and diversity among learners receiving education. Yet practices have not led to outcomes that reflect these values, and measures of outcomes seldom make the values explicit.

Measures of Success. Managers can approach emerging ethical issues by examining the measures of quality and success that are currently applied to the outcomes of telecommunications-based education. Chapter Three presents an example that uses learner access to education as a goal and shows how it might be measured. If in some respects "we are what we assess," our measures of how we are doing can themselves be measured for their consistency with our values, and in light of new imperatives for greater inclusiveness.

Managers can begin to address the ethical dimensions of

management by considering the adoption of one or more measures of programming that influence equity, climate, learner autonomy, and programmatic relationships. *Equity* refers to accessibility to educational resources for underserved constituencies, or other forms of equitableness that lead to a greater diversity of learners. *Climate* is concerned with fostering an inclusive tone in interactions between educators and learners, support staff and learners, and among learners.

Climate also refers to a supportive educational context that is enabling to a diversity of learners and responsive to learning differences. Efforts are required to fashion organizational structures and procedures that give primacy to the comfort and needs of nontraditional learners, rather than merely "accommodating" them. Developing a hospitable environment for minorities, rural dwellers, and others who need but do not now use telecommunications-based education and training must become a priority.

Autonomy acknowledges that in diversifying users, managers will also want to develop practices that anticipate and support the increased autonomy of learners. Autonomy can take the form of learning at places and times, or on schedules, of one's own choosing. It also means permitting learners to approach information in a different sequence or with a different frame of reference or set of learning skills from others studying the same material. Whatever form it takes, the promotion and extension of greater self-direction for learners, as well as the establishment of different kinds of relationships with them, deserve inclusion in a manager's measures of success.

Placing *relationships* within measures of success and quality recognizes that administrative interactions with learners must balance entrepreneurism and marketing of programs with a need for longer-term commitments to learners as individuals. Managers may aspire to be responsive to the "marketplace," yet their programs may meet the needs of only a few sectors of the public.

Relationships can be advanced in ways that transform narrow "markets" into broader "publics." This adds a dimension to measures of program quality and success that is consistent with valuing inclusiveness and reduces the likelihood that such measures will appear to be excessively entrepreneurial.

Guiding Values. An orienting framework made up of values that can guide managerial action and foster greater levels of participation by diverse publics in telecommunications-based education is described in Chapter Nine. Values that speak to relationships include *reciprocity* among learners and between managers, instructors, and learners; *consensus,* the mobilization of opinion on behalf of neglected publics by managers; and *altruism,* managerial advocacy of social justice for neglected constituencies. Other values are *autonomy,* advancing and supporting the self-directing strengths and interests of learners, and *inclusiveness,* which is concerned with the composition of the learners able to take advantage of electronic technologies.

Costs

Costs will be managed differently as electronic technologies are increasingly applied to education. There will be more emphasis on sharing costs through alliances and affiliations with numerous partners rather than relying largely or solely on fees charged to learners. A positive bottom line will no longer be sufficient to justify the existence of telecommunications-based education. It must also respond to urgent educational needs, diverse student requirements, or other institutional commitments to the public.

Safety Nets. Fee-supported activities, such as telecommunications-based continuing education as it is currently funded, are often part of a set of diversified management strategies used by organizational units whose income is derived entirely or largely from program participants. Diversification of activities offers the protection of multiple projects that can back each other up for budgetary protection and operational flexibility. The odds are good that although some programs may do poorly from time to time, others will do well.

These simultaneous projects provide an administrative safety net. Yet the safety net can itself become a priority that drives telecommunications-based education. Carried to extremes, this approach mitigates against the flexibility and responsiveness to change that is vital to this type of system.

Reliance on multiple, loosely connected projects to cushion the ups and downs of a fee-supported budget is reinforced by systems that apply measures of accountability in fragments of time, such as quarters or semesters. This fragmentation is an issue not only for managers of telecommunications-based education but also for the parent organization that values and wishes to encourage strategic planning. Telecommunications-based education requires incentives for long-term calculations and commitments to staff, resources, and a deferred return on investment. This long-term perspective can counterbalance the intermittent and inconclusive information on which determinations regarding the progress of an educational telecommunications system are usually based.

Reliance on student fees also ties activities to short-term considerations that color a manager's view of what constitutes an acceptable risk. Educational programs that are expected to generate revenue must take daily risks, risks linked to the premise that individual fees must cover all direct and indirect program costs. This orientation is insufficient as a fundamental approach to putting telecommunications-based education on a firm financial basis. Thus other alternatives to cushioning risk need to be introduced, including efforts by managers to lead the parent organization toward new thinking about cost recovery for programs that have traditionally been self-supporting.

Cushioning Risk. The initial costs of telecommunications-based education; the long-term unknowns of equipment maintenance, integration, and obsolescence; and the uncertainties of revenue-generating potential require sources of revenue beyond the fees paid by learners. Chapter Six presents a view of budgets that highlights the nature and scale of the financial commitments demanded by electronic technologies and that offers a variety of fiscal options to support educational telecommunications systems. Many options require managers to place themselves in a matrix of relationships within and outside their parent organization that are intended to cushion financial risk.

Alternative programming for nontraditional learners is usually felt to be successful if its revenue covers or exceeds its costs and if attendance projections are met. Yet managers of telecommunications-based education need to anticipate a shifting set of attitudes regarding program viability. With its long-term commitments and powerful delivery mechanisms, this field is particularly vulnerable to questions concerning the rationale behind managerial decision making. A financially successful educational telecommunications system that is only tangentially related to the fundamental goals and image of the parent organization will be more likely to be questioned in the future than has been true in the past.

Congruence with the Larger Mission

Managers who seek ways to achieve new thinking on adult learning and development will be better prepared for the issues that will occupy educational organizations in the future. Thus greater insight into the social as well as the educational and economic implications of the parent organization's mission will strengthen the management of educational telecommunications systems. The ability to respond to the changing needs of learners as individuals was described earlier as a major factor in remaining aligned with the parent organization; managers who school themselves in the tenets, issues, and critical concerns of non-traditional teaching and learning can assist their program in responding to these social imperatives. Merriam and Caffarella (1991, p. 282) refer, for example, to critical pedagogy or critical practice that "directly confronts issues of power and control, conflict and oppression, and mandated action to deal with social inequalities as they are revealed in learning encounters."

Alignment with the parent organization's mission will also be influenced by forces that affect all education. The aging and the racial shading of America are two major forces that are altering public expectations concerning access to education and training. The growing proportion of older people and people of color in the population and the work force is resulting in more explicit calls for just treatment and equal opportunity in education and training services. A work force made up of significant numbers of women and non-Caucasians, many of whom are non-English speakers, will compel educational change. How many managers today know anything about guiding such a diverse work force?

Continuing education often has the appearance of an almost clublike enclave of racial privilege; managers of telecommunications-based education can assist in altering this situation. Information concerning the educational opportunities available to the work force is regularly carried in training periodicals such as the *Training and Development Journal* and indicate a need for change.

In 1990, 86 percent of the work force was Caucasian, yet Caucasians received 92.2 percent of the training. By contrast, 9.5 percent of the work force was African American and 5.5 percent was Hispanic, yet these groups received only 5.1 and 2.7 percent of the training, respectively (Martin and Ross-Gordon, 1990). Becoming knowledgeable about the needs of the ethnic and racial groups who are destined to be the ultimate majority of our population, as well as about other underserved groups of learners such as those living far from sources of education, will be essential to keeping telecommunications-based education aligned with the parent organization's mission. Tentativeness in responding to the concerns of the underserved is not unusual in educational and other organizations; therefore, leadership from managers who have prepared themselves on the issues of ethnicity and access is likely to be needed and welcomed by the parent organization.

As educational, business, and public agencies begin to absorb the effects of an aging and diversified work force, the necessity of education across the life span is a third force affecting public expectations of education and training providers. These expectations are linked to a fourth force, the global economy that is pressuring American business and educational organizations to recast their ways of operating.

This altered environment is felt at local and institutional levels in the form of insistent demands for educational programs that can respond to new national competitive realities. Calls for educational restructuring offer opportunities for new managerial relationships that can network entire educational systems, including those in the workplace. The interconnective power of electronic technologies offers possibilities for interactivity across educational and organizational levels, and between campus, workplace, and home, that have yet to be tapped on a significant scale.

The Vocabulary of Marketing

An entrepreneurial vocabulary permeates postsecondary education. Entrepreneurial values have had a transforming effect on the marketing of both traditional and nontraditional education, producing many benefits. The customer service mentality has transformed learners into "clients." One result of this transformation has been the revitalization of many educational organizations' student services and the introduction of more learner-centered attitudes. Another result has been the perception by businesses that they too are "learning organizations." Customer service relationships between organizational units have become more common, and complaints and seeming injustices are more readily viewed as customer service issues. Personal regard for learners as individual clients of an institution has become a more commonly recognized managerial priority.

Thinking of learners as a market has also brought a customer-oriented tone to many aspects of promoting and managing education in general. The language of marketing and selling has produced more crisp, effective, and attractive catalogues, ads, and direct mail announcements. Marketing educational programs and presenting a forceful image to potential learners now makes up a major industry.

The vocabulary and outlook of entrepreneurism will nevertheless become less useful for telecommunications-based education in the coming years. How effective has a marketing attitude and a seller's vocabulary proved to be as a means of attracting racial minorities, for example? There is a case to be made for greater balance in the language used to attract diverse learners. This also suggests that organizational units must prepare themselves to advance beyond entrepreneurism to the higher level of maturity reflected in the organizational cycle explained in Chapter Five.

A relationship with diverse learners must move beyond the concept of buyers and sellers. A new, more balanced, and more hospitable vocabulary would stress an affiliation with learners and would also more accurately reflect the fundamental values that inspire a commitment to reaching a multicultural set of learners. Such a vocabulary would de-emphasize education as a product and learners as consumers. Instead, more attention would be given to individualized services and the mutual advantages of an affiliative relationship between educational organizations and learners.

Individualization

The introduction of electronic technology drives education toward more, not less, individualization of learners, a development that affects every level of operations. Advancement of the learner's control over learning will be a guiding insight of the most successful systems and a key principle on which to base decision making. Individualization can refer to individually directed pacing, sequencing, and the content of the instruction. It can also mean more individual choice as a result of greater access to existing courses, programs, and academic degrees. In either case the application of electronic technologies can be conceptualized as more than a technical feat. These technologies create a new context in which the quality of interaction receives far more attention from educators and learners than in traditional classrooms.

A central issue is the quality of the human interface that is achieved between learner and teacher. Outstanding managers will move beyond the concept of learners as sets of clients with similar "customer needs"; by advocating learner access to resources, they will help learners individualize their instruction.

Three types of services are integral to excellence in telecommunications-based education: first, services that strengthen the supportiveness of the educational context created by teaching and learning with electronic technologies; second, services that make it easier for individuals to access educational resources for individualized purposes; and third, services that put the educational needs of diverse learners ahead of organizational or administrative convenience. Staff members who previously perceived themselves as functioning relatively autonomously to carry out stable tasks will need to look at themselves differently. They must come to see themselves as providers of many individualized services — a task in telecommunications-based education that is neither predictable nor performed independently of other service providers.

Bias Sensitivity

It is not unusual for nontraditional education to be subject to abrupt change even when the activity is financially sound. Managers of telecommunications-based education can be more responsive to sudden change in the parent organization when they have clarified their own biases regarding the purposes of the organizational unit. Awareness of their biases also influences how they go about building the internal and external partnerships that are fundamental to this type of education.

Sensitivity to multiple and sometimes contradictory goals and values is needed within both the organizational unit and the organization as a whole. Yet important responsibilities are often delegated to newer staff members who are unfamiliar with the parent organization's long-term priorities. One explanation for this common scenario is that telecommunications-based education is regarded as so risky, complex, and time-consuming that accountability for it is shunned.

The view presented in this book is that organizations exist to meet human needs. This assumes that change is more likely to succeed when individual satisfaction and organizational need coincide. A common source of major change in a parent organization is a shift to new leaders who are not impressed by a fiscally responsible management record alone. In addition, they look for a rationale that will explain why telecommunications-based education is being offered on particular topics or in formats that attract particular groups of learners.

Managers who can articulate and act on principles and values as well as maintain fiscal responsibility will be better able to respond to organizational change over time. For example, as a parent organization begins to grasp the implications of the older, more ethnically diverse population of adult learners and workers, a manager's ability to respond to the educational implications of multiculturalism will be a valued attribute. Yet the parent organization will also expect that this response to new realities will temper risk with caution. The eight guiding assumptions convey messages about risk rather than directives for caution.

Balancing Caution and Risk

Managers of the transition to telecommunications-based education have no widely recognized figures to lead the way, and little has been written on leadership in this field. The current managerial literature on educational telecommunications systems is primarily descriptive or technically oriented rather than conceptual or analytical. It is also too fragmented for easy use as a source of working principles or integrated practices.

What the literature documents is that postsecondary education did not lead developments in telecommunications-based education in the handful of states that pioneered the educational applications of electronic technologies. Leadership instead came most often from a governor or from a state telecommunications office in transition from conventional communications systems to information and education networks. This illustrates a failure to read and act on emerging factors in the political arena, a shortcoming of planning that is discussed in Chapter Three.

Cautious Entry Is Common

A 1988 snapshot of technology used by some of the leading universities belonging to the National University Continuing Education Association provides a context for understanding the present status of developments in telecommunications-based education. In 1988 only some five hundred postsecondary institutions, less than 20 percent, were equipped for basic activities such as reception of video signals from satellites. At that time a considerable range of possible telecommunications technologies existed.

The findings of a survey of eighty-three higher education institutions from thirty-eight states and the District of Columbia, reported by Willis and Bridwell (1988), underscore the cautious entry of postsecondary education into applications using electronic technologies. While 68 percent reported having satellite downlinks (the "dishes" that receive signals), there was little in the survey to indicate vigorous use of such technologies. The most prevalent technology used was the videocassette, followed closely by public broadcast television. There were thirteen other technological items; 37 percent or fewer of the institutions indicated using them.

There are a number of explanations for this caution. The nearly unanimous disinterest of the faculty in most developments concerned with electronic technologies in recent decades, in particular developments associated with distance education or continuing education, put a brake on related activities such as telecommunications-based education. Thus, while government officers in a handful of pioneering states acquired knowledge through experimentation, relatively few of their counterparts in postsecondary education around the country were gaining similar know-how. Other sources of obstacles are presented in a publication by Donald R. McNeil issued in 1990 by the Academy for Educational Development, *Wiring the Ivory Tower: A Round Table on Technology in Higher Education*. McNeil categorizes obstacles as attitudinal, technical, and structural. Much experiential evidence points to attitudinal factors as being the most crucial.

Knowns and Unknowns

Many common dilemmas that slow the entry of organizations into telecommunications-based education because of its risks can be anticipated and resolved. One such dilemma is the hesitation that the "unknowns" can inspire. Managers need to reconsider the view that what they already know outweighs what they do not know. Try this brief exercise. Write down everything you know about educational telecommunications systems that could affect outcomes for your current educational programming. Now list the unknowns that could also have important effects. The list of unknowns is usually longer than the list of what is known. The total list of unknowns is even longer since some unknowns are outside the perspective of a novice manager.

It is common in telecommunications-based education to act on the sketchy, anecdotal, and incomplete information in the list of knowns; this can lead to rejection of many opportunities. Managers frequently become anchored to any information they have, even when it is known to be inadequate or questionable. Answers to the complete list of unknowns can also act as a brake on telecommunications-based activities, particularly when the answers run contrary to unexamined assumptions regarding organizational purposes.

Timing

A second brake is insensitivity to the role of chance and the effect of accidents of timing on the success of new projects. The history of the introduction of new commercial products is punctuated by stories of managerial rejection of ideas that are now taken for granted. When the British rejected the concept of the telephone in the 1870s, their reasoning seemed sensible. Why would such a technology be necessary when there would always be messenger boys? Today's seemingly sound reasoning can be similarly flawed by unreflective adherence to past practices, conventional logic, and reluctance to prepare for major change.

Opportunity Costs

A third common brake is the tendency to undertake significant risk only if it appears to be a way to avoid certain loss. This approach to decision making gives undue weight to current or prior circumstances. Risk is viewed from the perspective of expenditures made in the past rather than from an appraisal of future costs and projected benefits. Opportunity costs are ignored or disguised, in part because managers seldom reflect on or document what was lost by actions or projects that were considered but not taken.

Greiner (1972) confirms this dilemma and provides a perspective for managers who are impatient with the caution in applying electronic technologies to teaching and learning. Writing with respect to business organizations, Greiner observes that their problems were "rooted more in past decisions than in present events or outside market dynamics" (p. 38). He takes the position that an organization's future is less a function of the effects of outside forces than of the organization's own history and its current phase of development (p. 38).

Inconsistent Vocabulary

The absence of a common vocabulary for telecommunications activities is a fourth brake on the introduction of even rudimentary telecommunications-based education. The effects of particular electronic technologies and the meaning of technical terms can change from one context to another and from one application to another. In addition, the absence of generally accepted standards of practice together with imprecise language impedes information transfer in this field.

The two dilemmas that are most readily resolved are the problems of inconsistent vocabulary and incomplete information. A necessary first step is to be aware of the role of such obstacles as barriers to planning. Chapter Ten provides a selective list of resources and presents a strategy for linking specific sources of information to particular managerial purposes. These resources are a critical point of departure from which to assemble a working vocabulary and to develop well-informed answers to the kinds of questions that are frequently encountered.

Summary

The assumptions elaborated in this chapter have a number of implications for all managers of telecommunications-based education. First, the time that successful managers spend on issues of technology is far less than might first be assumed. For every hour spent assessing the technical merits of pieces of equipment, a manager will devote perhaps five hours balancing the requirements of relationships that the use of electronic technology demands. All of the guiding assumptions—individualized learning increasingly controlled by the learner, operational shifts from the margins of the parent organization, conceptual alignment of the uses of educational telecommunications systems with the wider mission, ethical considerations that influence the management of costs and revenues, the vocabulary of marketing, and awareness of managerial biases—in one way or another have to do with the centrality of the learner and the new managerial relationships required by telecommunications-based education.

Second, entry into telecommunications is not the same experience for everyone. The guiding assumptions will be experienced differently in different contexts. Management is not unlike the voyage of Columbus as it must have felt to those involved: a thrilling adventure for some, a path to riches for others, a search for a new world and a place in history for still others, and a frightening trip into the unknown for many. To some observers, it was even judged to be a foolish, inconsequential quest promising more trouble than it was worth.

A third implication of the assumptions presented in this chapter concerns the primacy of partnership building in telecommunications-based education. Successful managers develop long-term collaborations within the parent organization as well as collaborations with new kinds of external partners. Important partnerships that require managerial attention are forged with:

- The staff of organizational units, within and outside the parent organization, that provide nontechnical support services to students
- The staff of organizational units that have functions within the technical operations for delivery of telecommunications-based education
- Educators who help develop telecommunications-based education
- Learners who need educational telecommunications systems

- Leaders whose agenda and vision are translated into an organizational image and mission responsive to the larger forces of change

It is important to recognize obstacles and at the same time place them in proper perspective. Critical dilemmas encountered by managers include the problem of assembling complete and accurate information, the pressure to reduce or avoid significant risk, accidents of timing, and the absence of consistent terminology for electronic technologies and their uses.

All of these obstacles can be overcome. Managers who have succeeded in the face of obstacles have, for example, modified some of the vocabulary of selling and marketing that in recent years has had such a galvanizing effect on nontraditional education. Such managers have begun to introduce a vocabulary that cushions risk while speaking to consultation and long-term affiliations with users and providers of telecommunications-based education. Similarly, measures of quality and success can more openly and deliberately incorporate fundamental values and place the opportunities presented by new systems in a different conceptual framework. These alignments make it much more likely that telecommunications-based education will extend and support the larger organizational mission and be responsive to emerging needs. The guiding assumptions proposed in this chapter are a conceptual approach to overcoming barriers to this type of education and reducing uncertainty. Uncertainty is also brought under control by developing an action plan that reduces risk, which is the subject of Chapter Three.

Chapter 3

Developing
an Action Plan
to Minimize Risk

Myth: Planning for the integration of educational telecommunications systems with
existing educational delivery systems is
a rational process, which is driven by
needs assessment, far-sighted systems design, and accurate forecasting.

Reality: Planning for educational telecommunications systems is often driven by
technical capabilities rather than programming needs, by conflicting political
pressures rather than planning, and by
possibilities rather than logic.

The integration of telecommunications systems into an educational enterprise is a formidable task for the manager or leader
to contemplate. Environmental scanning activities often provide ambiguous or highly situation-specific information about
how other organizations are accomplishing this task. Advice
about the general approach or specific actions that should be

taken is likely to vary considerably. The question for the manager is how to analyze this information in a meaningful way and use it to move forward.

In this chapter we address these concerns by describing some ways to conceptualize the change process and by proposing a conceptual framework for thinking about organizations that can be used as a general guide to action. Next, we build upon that framework to suggest the key elements that must be considered when formulating a comprehensive action plan. Finally, we look at the need to identify measures of success for the change effort and suggest some benchmarks for gauging progress toward the goal of establishing a viable system.

Organizational-Change Strategies

Students of organizational change distinguish between two types of change strategies: framebreaking and incremental (Tushman, Newman, and Romanelli, 1986). Framebreaking change is the dramatic stuff of organizational legend. An organization faces a crisis that threatens its continued existence. Its leader boldly articulates a new vision and commands the resources needed to achieve the vision. Within a short, but traumatic, period of time the organization emerges stronger than ever.

Although this scenario is a much-simplified view of framebreaking change, it illustrates several key elements that are usually found where organizations have successfully made dramatic changes. Framebreaking change is more likely to take place when it is proposed in response to a widely recognized crisis situation. Reconsideration of basic organizational goals and movement in a new direction are often central features (London, 1988; Lorsch, 1986; Tushman, Newman, and Romanelli, 1986). Where the strategy is pursued successfully, it usually is led by someone at the very top of the organization who has the authority to secure the resources needed to accomplish the envisioned change.

An incremental-change strategy, on the other hand, is much less dramatic and usually involves the introduction of variations within already existing efforts. The fundamental premise behind incremental change is the idea that it is generally easier to bend one element of an organization's culture than to challenge its core beliefs (Lorsch, 1986). Often the strategy gives the appearance of aimless trial-and-error activity.

Incremental changes may be introduced in a time of crisis, although the crisis is not likely to be one of life-threatening proportions. In addition, the changes are likely to be regarded as elaborations of existing organizational goals, rather than as dramatic new directions. An important characteristic of the strategy is that it can be pursued by people from many different levels of an organization. Thus, an action plan for incremental change must incorporate reflective backtalk from those involved, including considerable discussion, debate, argument, and compromise; it must also leave room for mistakes (Bennis, 1984a). Overall, the incremental-change strategy lends itself well to decentralized organizations where power and authority are diffused (London, 1988).

The selection of an appropriate change strategy becomes an important consideration for the manager or leader who wishes to integrate an educational telecommunications system within an educational institution. This brief discussion of potential change strategies provides a starting point for choosing one and for formulating an action plan that is likely to be successful. A key to making a successful choice is accurate assessment of the change environment itself and the position of the leader or manager within that environment.

Take, for example, the setting of an institution of higher education facing a precipitous decline in on-campus enrollment. To someone searching for additional ways to maintain or even increase enrollment levels, an educational telecommunications system may appear to be a means of extending service to learners who are already associated with the institution. The leader of an institution with a primary mission of teacher preparation may see providing in-service courses to teachers as related to a traditional mission, but still quite distinct from traditional teacher preparation. Under these circumstances, the leader might choose to follow a framebreaking strategy of integrating an educational telecommunications system within the main thrust of activity for the institution. Here the first step is likely to be some reinterpretation or revision of the mission and goals of the institution to incorporate the new service. A second step in the process would undoubtedly be identifying new resources or redirecting existing resources to support the new thrust.

A person in a powerful position might successfully reorient the mission and goals of the parent organization and command the resources needed to make an educational telecommunications system an integral means of achieving the newly defined mission. But even under the most favorable conditions, there is some question whether the impetus for change can be sustained over time if support for it remains the sole property of a single individual. As much as possible, support for the change must be spread across the organization. Otherwise, the change effort may become the victim of political attacks that are designed to discredit the leader, although they have little to do with the merits of the change itself (Van Kekerix, 1986).

Most educational telecommunications managers find that the framebreaking strategy is beyond their resources. They simply do not have enough authority within the parent organization, which is often characterized by diffused authority to begin with. In fact, an important stream of literature in continuing education advocates aligning activities with the mission and goals of the organization and stresses the dangers of straying from them (Votruba, 1987; Simerly and Associates, 1987). Training literature also points to the need to focus efforts on supporting existing goals and missions (London, 1988). Adopting a strategy of framebreaking change, with its emphasis on redefining goals, could put the change advocate in danger of moving outside the mainstream of the organization.

For many managers, the case for pursuing an incremental strategy is strong. Incremental strategies can be used with the existing mission and goals and approach change as a means of enhancing the organization's ability to meet its goals. An incremental approach allows the manager to work within the existing environment in a collaborative way and still assert a leadership role. The beginning stages of the strategy are best envisioned as focused experimentation in contrast to an attempt to design and implement a complete system (Morgan, 1988).

In sum, the choice of an appropriate change strategy depends on the characteristics of the organization, the nature of the change involved, and the position of the change champion. Under the right circumstances either strategy can be successful. Those in the top leadership positions of an organization may choose to pursue a framebreaking strategy as the best available option. Managers at lower levels, on the other hand, lack the resources and the power needed to successfully engage in framebreaking change efforts. They can, however, pursue a strategy of incremental change. In either case, the action plan that evolves from the strategy must be comprehensive enough to embrace the considerable complexities of organizational life.

A Conceptual Framework for Change

Too many action plans are simplistic. Dazzled by the prospects offered by a new electronic technology, a manager or leader of an effort to integrate it into an existing educational delivery mechanism may concentrate on its technical aspects. This tendency is very understandable given the wide range of available choices and their rapid evolution (Long, 1983), but the concentration on technology alone is not sufficient.

An excellent conceptual framework for approaching this problem in a more comprehensive way is provided by Tichy (1980, 1983). Tichy suggests that organizations should be thought of as engaging in ongoing attempts to resolve the problems of cultural-ideological mix, political allocation, and technical design that emerge in cyclical patterns. Furthermore, he argues that the whole of an organization should be thought of as a rope consisting of interdependent cultural-ideological, political, and technical strands. Without three strong strands, the strength of the whole is seriously compromised.

Within this framework, integrating an educational telecommunications system into an organization becomes a matter of deciding how to introduce change into a multifaceted cultural-ideological, political, and technical environment. Tichy's work clearly implies that the manager or leader who wishes to be a change advocate must develop political and ideological skills as well as the technical skills that make the production of desired teaching and learning outcomes possible. Failing to acknowledge the ideological and political aspects of managing change courts disaster. From this perspective the key tasks for the change advocate are to marshal cultural-ideological, political, and technical resources, thereby formulating a comprehensive strategy that incorporates all three strands of the rope.

Formulating a Cultural-Ideological Appeal

The formulation of an effective cultural-ideological appeal should be approached as an exercise in the creation of meaning. In other words, the appeal should set forth the purpose of the change in language that mirrors the values and beliefs of the parent organization and relates them to changes within the external environment.

For the leader following a framebreaking strategy, the appeal must offer a vision of the future that will garner the support of key constituencies. For the manager engaging in an incremental-change strategy, the appeal serves as the basis for collaborative action by defining common interests and providing a sense of common purpose. The primary sources for the appeal are in the history of the organization and the external environment.

Examining the History

The history of an organization sets the historical and cultural context in which the change will take place. Much of the literature on organizational change emphasizes the importance of analyzing history as a means of identifying powerful appeals that can be used to create support for the change effort (Lodahl and Mitchell, 1980). An analysis of organizational history can also show the change advocate how the proposed change may fit within the organization's culture. Even the most innovative organization must acknowledge the need for some degree of compatibility between itself and the environment in which it functions. The closer the fit between the cultural-ideological appeal for the change, the existing culture, and the needs of the environment, the greater the chances for success.

If, for example, the attempt to integrate educational telecommunications is taking place within an institution of higher education with a history of innovative outreach activities, the chances for success are greater than if no such record exists. In such a setting the integration effort can be portrayed as yet another step in the ongoing search for new ways to achieve a well-established organizational mission. In a similar fashion, if an institution has a strong traditional commitment to serving the educational needs of a particular professional group, the new system might be presented as another means of continuing and extending that commitment. Where an institution is the sole source of educational programming in a particular content area, the system can be presented as a means of extending the benefits of that programming to previously unserved or underserved learners.

In any case, the cultural-ideological component of the action plan should be developed with an eye toward attracting support from a variety of internal and external sources. In the same way that aligning any subunit activity with the parent organization's mission legitimizes the subunit's enterprise, the educational telecommunications system becomes more legitimate if it is seen as an integral means of attaining the organization's mission. The appeal needs to incorporate uplifting and idealistic language that focuses on the distinctive aims and methods of the parent organization and on the benefits of the program to society as a whole.

An analysis of the historical context in which the change will take place can also reveal developments that can be of considerable interest to the manager or leader of the change effort. The literature points out that an important element in support of change is a critical shift in events that threatens to disrupt the prevailing state of affairs (Schon, 1971). This crisis creates a demand for new ideas that can be used to explain or remedy the situation. Often the ideas are drawn from areas that were previously considered to be of marginal value to the organization as a whole. When the critical shift takes place, these ideas begin to surface in the mainstream of thought within the organization and are given increasing legitimacy by powerful groups and individuals. For example, if a framebreaking strategy is being pursued, the leader can point to the crisis as a strong argument for making the envisioned changes immediately, thereby using it as an important resource in gaining followers. If, on the other hand, the advocate of change is following an incremental strategy, the change can be presented as an opportunity to solve a crisis that concerns opinion leaders within the organization. To maximize the chances of successfully introducing the change, the advocate must develop an understanding of the concerns of the upper administration and be ready to advance the proposed change at the right moment.

Examining the Environment

A second source of elements that can be combined into a powerful ideological appeal emerge from an examination of the external environment. Much can be learned by scanning the environment and assuming a perspective outside the parent organization (Votruba, 1987). The ability to draw connections between emerging forces in the environment and the characteristics of an envisioned change can be an important factor in improving its chances for success.

For the manager or leader attempting to integrate an educational telecommunications system with existing educational efforts, a primary element in the ideological appeal is likely to be improved access to educational opportunity. This is a widely recognized need within modern society, where the demands for a well-trained and educated work force are great and where the half-life of knowledge continues to shrink dramatically. The proposed system can be advanced as a means of both overcoming geographical barriers and providing access to timely information. Often the system offers a way to serve widely dispersed learners. In rural states, for example, the integration of educational telecommunications with existing educational programming provides opportunities for individuals to achieve educational goals that were previously unattainable.

An ideological appeal based on the benefits of increased access can be particularly effective in cases where an educational program potentially has significant impact, but where the educational resources are scarce and the learner audience is thinly dispersed geographically. Some limitations to the access argument must be acknowledged, however. There is some danger that expectations may be raised beyond what can reasonably be made available. If the gap between expectations and reality is too great, those who are not served will feel betrayed and the credibility of the parent organization and the system's spokespersons will be damaged.

Thus, a cultural-ideological appeal based on the promise of opening higher education to all may be an invitation to disaster if the parent organization is not prepared to offer the courses or the degrees that are required. Similarly, if the parent organization is unprepared to create a supportive climate for the diverse learners who are attracted, the effort is unlikely to achieve much success. A number of highly publicized telecommunications efforts have encountered the problem of inadequately preparing for the changes needed to successfully integrate their systems into existing educational programming. It must also be recognized that although telecommunications systems can lower some barriers to participation, other barriers, such as inadequate financial resources, conflicting schedules, and insufficient learning skills, cannot be overcome by technology alone. Educational telecommunications can be a part of the solution to the problems of access, but not the complete solution.

Formulation of an effective cultural-ideological appeal requires an extensive knowledge of the parent organization and its culture, as well as a keen eye for the opportunities presented by forces in the environment. Becoming an advocate for change means putting oneself in the somewhat precarious position of championing innovation while simultaneously staying within the traditions of the parent organization. Although such a role may be uncomfortable at times, change agents must live with the contradictions between adhering to the mission of the parent organization and developing an external orientation that exploits new opportunities (Offerman, 1987). It is a role often played by continuing education and telecommunications professionals who operate at the margins of the institution. Often the key to this dilemma is building a cultural-ideological appeal that retains the core values and priorities of the organization, but allows for experimentation as well (Rink, 1987).

Devising a Political Strategy

The key to devising a successful political strategy is the ability to manage across organizational lines by generating a shared sense of purpose and identity. The political task is best envisioned as that of mobilizing energies and gaining commitments from people within the operational unit, the parent organization, and the external environment. Even the advocate who is following a framebreaking strategy, and who has the authority and power that strategy demands, cannot simply command a change to take place. Few leaders are successful in pursuing change in the face of fierce internal or external opposition. This is particularly true in higher education settings, where authority and power are diffused. For the manager who is following an incremental strategy, the political task is to become a leader of equals, best envisioned as "a 'framing' and 'bridging' process that can energize and focus the efforts" (Morgan, 1988, pp. 6–7). In both cases, securing the support of key elements within the parent organization is needed in order to achieve success.

A useful framework for assessing the political environment is Mitroff's stakeholder concept (1983). Mitroff suggests analyzing the political problem by identifying those who have an interest in the outcome of the envisioned change. The first step is to categorize stakeholders on the basis of whether they are internal or external to the parent organization. Attempting to assess the change from each stakeholder's perspective provides a second layer of analysis.

Internal Stakeholders

Organizational Leaders

Among the most important stakeholders are those in the upper levels of the organization's leadership. Even if the primary advocate of integrating educational telecommunications is in the top leadership position and is following a framebreaking strategy, there is a need for strong support from the appropriate governing body and the managers of key organizational units. Studies of change in organizations clearly indicate that support from upper-level managers in the parent organization is crucial to success. This is true in part because the beginning phase of a change is often dominated by the need to identify and commit scarce resources. Often only the top leadership is in a position to accomplish this.

For the person who is following an incremental-change strategy, the need to secure the support of top leadership within the parent organization is also crucial. In addition to providing access to resources that would not otherwise be available, top administrative support can establish a climate that is favorable toward creating alliances with other subunits within the parent organization. In addition, the top leadership can often play an important role in securing resources from outside the institution by serving as a link between the organization and important elements in the environment.

Within the context of incremental strategy, a key element in gaining support is acquiring knowledge about the needs and priorities of the parent organization as perceived by the leadership. When there is a match between those perceptions and the attributes of the envisioned change effort, conditions may be very favorable. If, on the other hand, there is no match or the priorities of the institution are directed in other areas, the chances of success are minimal. The more difficult scenario is one in which there is some degree of match, but other contradictory priorities exist as well. In these circumstances, the advocate must try to link the various possibilities together and be ready to advance the change at an opportune moment—a task that will challenge even the most entrepreneurial manager. Often the timing of the proposal is the key to getting the needed support.

Academic Subunits

A second important segment of stakeholders within the parent organization consists of other subunits that may have an interest in the outcome of the effort. In the case of continuing higher education, for example, academic colleges and departments are key stakeholders in any effort to integrate a new telecommunications system with the existing educational program. The support of key deans, department chairs, and faculty is an important factor in determining whether the system will be successful. The ideal is to move forward with the members of those subunits as partners from the beginning, even though there may be indifference or even opposition to the effort (see Chapter Two). Winning support requires the advocate to work closely with the leaders of those subunits, to secure their support from the beginning of the effort, and to provide recognition for their efforts. If overall support is not possible, it may be necessary to work with selected subunits in a pilot project with the goal of using the experience to solidify and expand support. Under these circumstances, the success of the effort may rest on the success of the pilot project.

One very effective tactic in winning needed support for the system is to bring the key decision makers and faculty together with the potential users of the system in face-to-face discussions where the learners can articulate their needs directly. The manager must play an active role in such bridging activities. Direct face-to-face contact often has greater impact than needs-assessment results. It is also helpful to encourage contact between the administrators of academic units and secondary stakeholders such as community representatives of business and industry. For example, a discussion between the chief executive officer of a large manufacturing firm and the dean of a college of engineering can be very effective in winning support for a telecommunications system.

An often-overlooked set of internal stakeholders in educational settings consists of units that provide student and instructional support services. Depending on the nature of the programming envisioned for the educational telecommunications system, such services might include library support for off-campus students, registration and records, financial aid counseling, academic advising, and computer services. Opening a dialogue with these groups at an early stage in the development process provides a way to assess what changes may be necessary in these areas and helps identify barriers that might have to be overcome. In addition, these discussions can provide a wealth of information about the magnitude of the impact that the proposed system may have on the parent organization as a whole.

Technical Units

Other internal stakeholders may include a variety of media and telecommunications units within the parent organization, such as computer services, television and radio broadcast services, and media service units. Depending on the size and purpose of such units, they can be a valuable source of expertise and support. At the same time, the potential for conflict over the control of technology and the funding associated with it may be high if such units interpret the change activity as a threat to their respective domains. The key to success is in knowing where such conflict may develop and focusing attention on the benefits to be gained by both the individual units and the parent institution as a whole. Upper-level administrative support within the institution often plays a key role in mediating these potential conflicts.

External Stakeholders

As learners become more aware of the possibilities, many of them will come to see themselves as stakeholders in decisions related to telecommunications. The existence of an educational telecommunications system can expand the potential audience for any given activity to encompass local, statewide, national, or even international stakeholders. For example, a person who wants to pursue an advanced degree but who is located two hundred miles from the nearest institution of higher education sees the development of a new system as a way to achieve an educational goal and may be motivated to play a role in the decision-making process. In a similar fashion, a person whose work schedule or family obligations make daytime on-campus attendance impossible becomes a stakeholder in the decisions related to telecommunications.

Another factor that tends to widen the circle of stakeholders whenever telecommunications is involved is the cost of
such undertakings. Efforts to integrate educational telecommunications often require funding from local, state, or even national sources, thereby automatically expanding the number of
stakeholders. For example, public funding for a telecommunications system is likely to require the benefits to be spread among
as many taxpayers as possible. Even the reallocation of existing funding within the parent institution to support the change
effort brings new constituencies into the stakeholder realm. Thus,
because questions of access and funding are almost always involved, one of the characteristics of educational telecommunications systems is an expansion of the very definition of who
the pertinent stakeholders are.

Learner and Community Groups

The learners who will benefit from the system are a key group
of external stakeholders. Forging a political alliance with this
group is a high priority. Learners can be extremely effective
advocates on several different levels. They can play an important role in convincing other key stakeholders outside and within
the parent organization to support the system; they also can form
pressure groups and lobby for change within the political arena
external to the parent organization. Such groups have been successful in extending educational delivery systems to learners who
might otherwise have been ignored and thereby denied access.
Effective use of this force requires grass-roots political activity.
Working closely with community leaders and professional groups
becomes a requirement for the telecommunications manager and
goes hand in hand with becoming an articulate spokesperson
for groups of underserved learners.

Another set of external stakeholders consists of the secondary beneficiaries of the system. They include industries and
businesses that benefit because their workers can participate and
thereby become better employees. Communities seeking to upgrade the level of educational opportunities available to their
population also can benefit from the development of these sys-

tems. The motive may be improvement of the overall quality of life within the community, a desire to promote economic development, or both. In any case, the advocate for the system can find support from these groups.

Other Educational Institutions

An often-neglected group of external stakeholders consists of other educational institutions that might be affected. Given the highly public nature and expense of educational telecommunications systems, other educational institutions can play an important role in determining the success or failure of any change effort. Institutions may look on such efforts as a source of direct competition, or as an attempt to reopen issues of turf and service areas that were settled before technology began to complicate matters. Educational telecommunications systems are highly susceptible to this type of concern because they do not respect physical boundaries. Of course, the ideal situation is one in which the envisioned programming or service incorporates elements that are unique to the parent organization and therefore are of little concern to other organizations.

Other institutions can also play a variety of roles within the telecommunications system itself that can be critical to its success. Some are likely to be potential receive sites for the service and may play a direct role in providing expanded educational opportunities to their home community. Other institutions may want to become full partners in the system and share the origination capabilities in a consortium arrangement. Such a partnership approach may be appealing to governing agencies and potential learners who will see an opportunity to gain access to a wider variety of educational programming. Partnerships can also provide a means of sharing system costs across several institutions, which can be appealing to everyone concerned.

State Agencies

Political entities, particularly at the state level, often become stakeholders in the integration process. If the institution is public, the governor and members of the legislature may have a considerable interest in the change effort, since it is likely to involve an educational service paid for by public funds.

Other governmental entities are also potential stakeholders in the change process when telecommunications are involved. Postsecondary coordinating commissions often have a stake in such changes, because telecommunications systems may affect a variety of other educational institutions. Strong alliances with individual learners and communities of learners who would be served by the system can be extremely helpful in dealing with these groups. It should be noted, however, that the political arena is highly volatile. Rapid changes in leadership and political climates can make it difficult to sustain political support on a consistent basis.

Thus, the political dimensions of the action plan must incorporate efforts to identify and secure support from internal and external stakeholders. One means of doing so is to adapt Mitroff's suggestion (1983) of plotting each of the identified stakeholders on a graph that measures their relative importance in the decision-making process on one axis and the degree of certainty about their position on the other. The result is a graphic representation of the political context in which the change effort will take place. Appropriate alliance-building activities are vital to the political success of the action plan. The ability of the manager or leader to foster collaboration through promoting cooperative goals and building trust becomes a key skill in the political arena (Kouzes and Posner, 1987).

Addressing the Technical-Design Dimensions

The final strand of the organizational rope to address in the action plan is the technical design of the telecommunications system. This is not an exploration of the various forms of electronic devices that might be used, but rather an examination of the issues surrounding learning and teaching that uses telecommunications systems. The purpose of this examination is to become knowledgeable about the major issues surrounding the instructional effectiveness of such systems, to study the history of previous attempts to make similar changes within the parent organization, and to identify available resources within the specific environment that can be incorporated.

Addressing the Question of Effectiveness

One element of the technical-design environment that the advocate of change must address is the instructional effectiveness of technology-based education. Many within postsecondary education regard all technology-based instruction as inferior to traditional classroom instruction. Fortunately, a wealth of studies support the basic contention that instruction using a wide variety of educational telecommunications systems is at least as effective as classroom instruction (Clark and Verduin, 1989; Verduin and Clark, 1991; Whittington, 1987).

Perhaps the most important thing for the advocate to understand is the difficulty of convincing skeptics about the effectiveness of educational telecommunications systems through studies alone. Questions about effective instructional methods involve basic beliefs about human nature that are not easily changed. As Hayes (1990) has noted, issues surrounding the question of effectiveness do not lend themselves well to proof based on empirical research. This helps to explain why many educators will insist on clinging to the belief that technology-based instruction is inferior even in the face of overwhelming evidence to the contrary. The question is how to begin to overcome such resistance.

One way of doing so is by shaping the characteristics of the telecommunications system to fit with the core values of the institution. If, for example, the parent organization puts a high value on interaction between teachers and learners, it may be wise to include a technological means of promoting interaction within any envisioned system, even though there may be little support for such interaction in the research on effectiveness. Failure to accommodate core values will make the system vulnerable to criticism that is grounded in the culture of the parent organization.

A second way to overcome resistance is by promoting pilot projects or limited tests of technology as a way for both educators and learners to gain firsthand experience with educational telecommunications systems. Endorsements of the effectiveness of a system by faculty members, based on their personal experience, can be a powerful force in gaining wider acceptance for the change effort. In many cases the learners who are the primary audience are adults whose motivation for learning is very different from that of the traditional student. Highly motivated learners who have an experience base to draw on are likely to be very successful. Thus, the nature of the learner is often more relevant to the effectiveness of the system than the choice of a particular form of technology. Learner endorsements can also be used effectively to win over skeptics.

Separating the Effort from Past Failures

The advocate must recognize that some people in the parent organization or even within the operational unit itself may have doubts about the viability of telecommunications systems that go beyond the question of instructional effectiveness. An examination of the technical history will indicate failures of some systems. There are, of course, well-publicized examples of sizable investments in such systems that have failed to meet expectations in terms of both the size of the audience served and cost-effectiveness (Van Kekerix, 1986). There may even have been an unsuccessful earlier effort at integration within the parent organization.

It is crucial for the advocate of integration to draw distinctions between the new effort and those that failed and to offer an interpretation of the meaning of any previous efforts in light of the current effort. The distinctions may include differences in intended audiences, the program's content, the technology itself, or some combination of these factors. Here knowledge about what other institutions are doing can be more helpful than research findings in countering concerns about the viability of the envisioned effort. An extensive network of fellow telecommunications professionals can provide valuable information about potential technical models that can be effectively distinguished from previous models. Outside consultants can also assist in drawing the needed comparisons.

Assessing Local Technical Resources

The advocate of telecommunications must also make a careful assessment of the technical resources that are available within the parent organization. Of particular interest are developments that hold the promise of expanding delivery capabilities. Such technical resources run the gamut from equipment and delivery capabilities to already existing models for curricular development that might be evolving in other parts of the parent organization.

A careful examination of the technical environment may also uncover sources of expertise in the technology of distance education. In many cases, a comprehensive technical assessment will reveal more resources than were originally thought to be available. An increasing number of faculty in postsecondary institutions have taught classes that use telecommunications as a delivery component. Similarly, the number of students who have participated in learning activities that involve telecommunications is rapidly increasing. Such people can be extremely valuable resources for the manager.

The primary purpose of the technical assessment is to become familiar with the existing and developing telecommunications capabilities within the environment and beyond the parent institution. For example, close attention should be paid to the activities of state commissions on telecommunications, regulatory commissions for telecommunications networks, and telecommunications companies. Careful monitoring of such developments can uncover significant opportunities to reach learners by using existing equipment. The goal in this arena is to become knowledgeable enough to recognize an opportunity within the maze of possibilities.

Thus, by treating the effort to integrate an educational telecommunications system as a series of interactions rather than simply as a technical concern, the change advocate can formulate a plan that attempts to deal with the cultural and political aspects of change as well. One must, however, resist the temptation to simply copy a model used successfully in another organizational setting. Too often an innovation that has achieved apparent success in one setting fails in another. The degree of fit between the model and the specific organizational setting must be examined carefully. Other successful programs should still be studied and freely adapted, but a comprehensive environmental analysis, including a cultural-ideological, political, and technical assessment, must be undertaken in order to properly evaluate the model. Putting together an action plan that systematically incorporates these strands of organizational life can dramatically improve the chances for success.

The Need to Define Success

A comprehensive action plan must also incorporate an attempt to set forth the criteria by which the success or failure of the envisioned telecommunications system can be judged. An organization that is unable to define the terms of its success or to measure its movement toward success increases its chances for failure. All too often little thought is given to what constitutes success, how it might be measured, or what its components might be. As a consequence, success becomes a moving target that is impossible to achieve.

A useful framework for assessing success or failure in educational telecommunications systems is suggested by Gooler's criteria (1977) for evaluating nontraditional postsecondary education programs. According to Gooler, such programs may be assessed in terms of the degree to which they expand access, their relevance to the needs of potential learners, their cost-effectiveness, their impact on the parent organization, and the knowledge they generate. This is not to suggest that all the criteria suggested must be used in any given circumstance, or that the list should be regarded as exhaustive. Gooler's work simply provides a starting point for identifying and selecting appropriate criteria and moves the discussion beyond the all-too-standard measure of whether the telecommunications system is cost-effective.

The selection of any particular criterion has important implications for all aspects of managing and leading educational telecommunications systems. For example, if opening access is considered to be important, efforts must be made not only to recruit previously underserved learners, but also to collect data that indicate how the learners being served differ from the traditional clientele or how they match with the characteristics of the target group. If a goal is service to minorities, evidence to measure the achievement of that goal must be collected. These differences might include a learner's age, geographic location, background, and job experience. A comparison might then be made between learners served by the system and those served on campus, to point out how the system is meeting its goal. If, on the other hand, the measure for success is the generation of knowledge about educational telecommunications systems, then resources must be devoted to supporting research efforts. The point is that if no criteria for success are agreed upon early in the process, no effort will be made to substantiate that the envisioned impact is being made.

The establishment of criteria for success as a part of the action plan can also provide a means of monitoring movement toward the goal of integrating the system within the organization. One way to measure progress is by identifying a list of benchmarks or pivotal events that might provide an indication of whether progress is being made. In keeping with Tichy's (1980) framework of organizational activity, the list should identify cultural-ideological, political, and technical events of significance. Examples of such benchmarks include:

Cultural-Ideological Benchmarks

- Testimony before a legislative committee by a spokesperson for an underserved group in favor of funding the system because of its potential for opening access to educational opportunity for members of the group
- Endorsement of the system by a consortium of higher education institutions
- Recruitment of learners from previously underserved audiences

Political Benchmarks

- Endorsement of the system by the parent organization's upper administration

- Incorporation of the system into the parent organization's strategic planning documents
- Receipt of proposals to offer educational programs on the educational telecommunications system from additional academic units within the parent organization

Technical Benchmarks

- Support for the technology incorporated within the system from independent consultants
- Completion of a successful pilot project that incorporates the same technology mix as the envisioned system
- Endorsements of the educational effectiveness of the telecommunications system from faculty
- Endorsements from learners

The incorporation of such benchmarks into the action plan can engender a sense of forward movement for the effort and will provide a means of measuring progress. A primary concern for the manager or leader is finding a good fit between the measures of success, the benchmarks, the expectations within the environment, and the characteristics of the system.

Summary

The manager or leader who wishes to integrate an educational telecommunications system within existing educational activities faces a complex and challenging task. Often information describing how other organizations have accomplished the task seems contradictory because it is situation-specific and provides little guidance for bringing about the needed changes within the new environment.

In this chapter the problem of how to put together an action plan has been approached through an examination of change strategies, their characteristics, and the circumstances in which one or another might be appropriate. Once the choice of an overall strategy has been made, the manager can begin to put together a comprehensive action plan for implementing it. Too often such plans are dominated by concerns about the electronics and fail to acknowledge the complexities of organizational life. Tichy's three problem cycles in organizations form the framework for building a comprehensive action plan that accommodates cultural-ideological mix, political allocation, and technical design.

The action plan that fits a particular planning context must be tailored to the setting in which the envisioned change will take place. Yet the basic elements of such a plan will always involve selecting an appropriate change strategy; articulating a vision for the change that includes cultural-ideological, political, and technical-design considerations; defining the elements that will signal success; and establishing benchmarks for measuring progress. With the plan in place, the manager can move on to other considerations. Among those is the challenging step of coming to grips with the actual selection of electronic technologies to incorporate within the technical design. This is the topic of Chapter Four.

Assessing Choices
in Systems Design

Myth: There is a "best" way to package the various educational telecommunications capabilities to make the teaching-learning transaction most effective.

Reality: Numerous combinations of electronic technologies and interactive techniques are as effective as traditional instruction.

The discussion thus far has focused on organizational change that can occur as either a result of or a means to the introduction of telecommunications-based education; the effective management of those changes; and the interrelationship of the organizational mission with the operations, values, and goals of the organizational unit guiding telecommunications-based education. This chapter moves from considerations of institutional readiness and congruence of purpose to the assessment phase. The critical issue now becomes what the nature of the system will be. What types of electronic technology will be used? Who will the system deliver programs to and what kinds of programs will be delivered? How will they be designed? What will be the size of the service area and the number of receive sites?

To establish a process for designing a system and its characteristics and to find answers to the above questions, some thorough planning is in order. Combining a strategic planning process with the discipline of instructional design would seem to incorporate an appropriate mix of analytical and pedagogical elements for good educational telecommunications system design. We will take advantage of these two processes in this chapter to raise many of the key questions that will need to be answered in order to identify major system characteristics. This is also a good opportunity to consider some of the possible solutions to system configuration, hardware, and transport by providing options and examples modeled after existing systems.

Why is system design such a critical and challenging step? There are over forty individual electronic technologies in current use based on voice, computer, or video communications, with the number likely to grow. Some technologies are used independently; some are combined or blended with others. To carry out this activity, nontechnical managers must make a thoughtful study of the options.

Strategic planning will help provide a road map to many of the parameters that specify the system. These specifications comprise the *system design* — that is, the configuration and interrelationship of hardware, software, communications techniques, and approaches to instruction — and will also provide insight into the nature of the infrastructure (technical and instructional support) the organization will require in order to create and sustain the system. Succeeding chapters will examine the primary system components, staffing process, and organizational infrastructure. This chapter will show how three organizational tools — strategic planning, instructional design, and technological preferences — interrelate to provide system design answers.

It is tempting to consider the wholesale adoption of a successful system from another organization. Experience has shown, however, that systems should be uniquely designed for the organization within which they will be used. A manager can only be confident of proceeding with the implementation of a specific system after completion of a systematic development activity such as strategic planning. In the end, the new system may look remarkably similar to the one envisioned before the planning process. Nevertheless, the refining and confirming experience of a detailed planning process will legitimize the design for the manager and others in the organization.

Strategic planning must include the participation of key individuals in the organization, who typically include educators or trainers, organizational leaders, potential system managers, technical representatives, and instructional-design experts if available. The process is a useful tool to facilitate the necessary "buy-in" of the parent organization at large. The fact that many have participated in the vision of the system's significance for the whole organization is preferable to one person's intuitive plan. Finally, this type of group planning process for system design has an advantage over mandated systems, which must create "buy-in" after the fact.

A number of terms related to educational telecommunications systems are given in tables in this chapter. You are encouraged to use the Glossary if you encounter an unfamiliar expression.

A Historical Perspective on Electronic Technologies

The evolution of educational telecommunications systems can be seen as a phased continuum in which new electronic technologies join existing delivery systems, expanding the options available to managers. Five phases bring us from earlier developments to the present:

Phase 1: Print (correspondence)
Phase 2: Print and audio (radio, audioconference, cassette)
Phase 3: Print, audio, and video (television, satellite, video-conference)
Phase 4: Print, audio, video, and computer (computer-assisted instruction, electronic mail [E-mail])
Phase 5: Blend of technologies (audio-video-graphics, compressed video)

The last fifty years of activity have included a constant and intensive search for and introduction of new electronic technologies and applications in order to reach more learners in a more cost-efficient fashion while increasing instructional effectiveness.

In 1979 Curtis and Biedenbach (1979, p. 1) assembled "a reference manual describing the major types of educational telecommunications systems." At that time they reported six major educational telecommunications methodologies:

1. Public broadcasting (radio and television)
2. Instructional Television Fixed Service (ITFS)
3. Teleconferencing-telewriting (via standard telephone lines)
4. FM-broadcast station multiplexing
5. Community antenna television (cable TV)
6. Satellite circuitry

Just nine years later data provided by the National University Continuing Education Association's (NUCEA) Division of Educational Telecommunications showed that twenty-three technologies were in common use by at least 10 percent of the colleges and universities that responded to the association's survey (National University Continuing Education Association, 1988). In total, forty-one different technologies were reported to be in use at that time. The technologies and the percentage of institutions using the technology are shown in Table 4.1.

A number of patterns emerge from a comparative analysis of the institutional uses of these technologies:

1. The evolution of new technologies appears to be continuing at a rapid pace. A new survey would no doubt show that facsimile, audiographics, and computer conferencing, for example, have moved up the utilization list, while compressed video would be a new entry.
2. Each institution uses a unique mix or blend of technologies.
3. No one technology dominates.
4. A recurring theme is the three-pronged thrust that blends audio, video, and computer applications. Rochester Institute of Technology, for example, combines technologies to solve particular instructional or logistic problems. It makes extensive use of videotaped courses, print materials, audioconference discussion sessions, audiotapes, individual phone sessions, and frequent computer-based communications (National University Continuing Education Association, 1988, p. 65).

Table 4.1. Percentage of Institutions Using Electronic Technologies.

Audio	Video	Computer
	Over 50	
None	Broadcast TV, public	None
	Satellite downlink	
	Videoteleconferencing	
	(one-way video)	
	Videocassette	
	25–50	
Audiocassette	Cable TV, one-way	E-mail
Telephone	Closed-circuit TV	
	ITFS	
	Microwave	
	Satellite uplink	
	10–25	
Audioconferencing	Slow-scan TV	Computer-assisted
FM radio, public	Videodisc	instruction
	Videoconferencing	Computer-based instruc-
	(two-way)	tional management
		Computer conferencing
		Bibliographic searches
		Simulation and gaming
	Less than 10	
Audiographics	Broadcast TV, com-	Audio-video-graphic
AM radio	mercial	Computer-assisted design
Cable radio	Cable TV, interactive	Computer graphics
FM radio, commercial	Direct broadcast, satellite	Electronic bulletin board
Facsimile	Low-power TV	Interactive videodisc
Radio talkback	Videotext-teletext	Modeling
SCA radio		
Two-way audio		
Public-address system		

This brief review suggests that there is no one ideal educational telecommunications system. Organizations currently using telecommunications systems to deliver educational programs have designed a wide variety of delivery structures depending on their needs. But how does one proceed to design a new system? Of the three possible paths to an effective system design — trial and error, copying, or planning — good planning is the process of choice.

Strategic Planning

A considerable body of information exists about strategic planning that shows how the process can be applied to various types of organizations including, for example, for-profit companies, the public sector, and postsecondary institutions. The strategic planning process usually involves the following steps:

1. Determine that the new initiative (creation of an educational telecommunications system) is right for the parent organization and assess the internal strengths and weaknesses of the organization relative to the initiative.
2. Assemble the right planning team and planning process to get the job done.
3. Conduct a scan of the environment within which the parent organization functions by looking at past trends, current conditions, and future possibilities.
4. Carry out an external analysis to pinpoint opportunities and potential threats in order to forecast broad goals and specific objectives.
5. Define goals and objectives.
6. Develop a strategy and plan.
7. Implement, evaluate, and update.

Previous chapters considered the issues raised by the first step in the process. Chapter Five will look at the proper planning team and process, as specified by step 2. Environmental scanning, external analysis, and forecasting (steps 3 and 4) will be the basis for our approach to the development of a system design in this chapter. The last three items function like the management by objectives (MBO) process of using goals, objectives, and methods to accomplish objectives, evaluation, and an accompanying repetition of the cycle. These elements are embedded in subsequent chapters.

Keller (1983) and Simerly and Associates (1987) provide a useful review and treatment of the strategic planning process as it relates to postsecondary organizations and continuing education units in particular. These accounts are recommended to readers unfamiliar with the process.

Strategic Planning for System Design

The Environmental Scan

The environmental scan in this case is a comprehensive review of the parent organization's position on providing off-site educational programs. Such a scan takes into account past trends, current conditions, and future possibilities. In the context of educational telecommunications systems, the major purpose of the scan is to select those learners and program possibilities that are relevant to the parent organization's mission and that may also benefit from telecommunications delivery. These selected activities and learner populations embody organizational opportunities and potential threats.

The environmental scan must encompass constantly changing events and trends within the external environment, such as changes in the program needs of various learner groups or in the electronic technologies. The system design issues under consideration will also define the context of the external environment to be analyzed. The external market for programs might be the area you intend to serve, yet you must simultaneously weigh the possibility of other providers entering your service area via their own educational telecommunications system. This is just one of the reasons that decisions based solely on present conditions run a high risk of being ineffectual in the future. External indicators, such as those suggested by Gooler (1977) and discussed in Chapter Three, also serve as benchmarks to identify one's own position relative to other service providers and to provide the basis for meaningful evaluation of system design progress.

The environmental scan is particularly useful in identifying the interrelationships among strategic issues. For educational telecommunications systems we suggest that seven strategic issues must be considered: *type of program, learning situation, service area, receive sites, learner dispersion, system utilization,* and *costs*. These issues (which will be used in the next section of this chapter to demonstrate how to design a system) and the trends affecting each of them must be examined from three perspectives:

1. What has happened in the past, what is the current situation, and what is likely to happen during the time of the development and near-term use of the system?
2. What is happening to the parent organization and its students in the service area? Outside the service area, what are the trends with regard to the development of electronic technologies, their costs, and likely competitive elements?
3. What are the opportunities and constraints? For example, could partnering with another organization to share a system make the use of certain electronic technologies more attractive? On the other hand, do organizational limits on expenditures constrain consideration of specific transport systems or limit the planned service area?

Beyond analyzing past trends, strategic planning must assess future directions. Forecasts permit the identification of potential problems and weaknesses, as well as opportunities and areas of potential future strength; however, they should be used with care because their reliability is not always high.

Finally, the results of the comprehensive environmental scan serve as the basis for selecting the issues of greatest importance to the development of the proposed system. Limiting the number of strategic issues is essential to obtaining the data base, rationale, and commitment needed to implement the new system. This allows the organization to focus on the issues that are pivotal to considerations of purpose and direction and that address wider organizational aspirations.

External Analysis and Forecast

Once the strategic issues have been identified and examined, goals and objectives should be established for each issue. These benchmark statements serve as the framework for further analysis.

Like the environmental scan, external analysis also pinpoints and evaluates major opportunities and threats that the parent organization cannot control but that nevertheless will affect its ability to achieve strategic goals. Major trends pertaining to each strategic issue should be examined in detail. For example, long-term economic and demographic forces should be evaluated in terms of their impact on planned new learner markets; changes in federal and state regulations and the repercussions of those changes on electronic technology must also be considered.

Once they have been identified, the relevant external factors must be prioritized. The two key criteria for prioritization are the likelihood that the event will actually occur and the level of impact that it could have on the plan.

Once your organization has defined the strategic issues through analysis, and agreement has been reached on goals and objectives, it is time to translate those goals and objectives into a system design model for the educational telecommunications activity. If the proposed system involves the entire parent organization and will result in a major change of direction, then the strategic planning process should be comprehensive and is likely to require six to twelve months. If, however, it is only one of many organizational thrusts and affects a minor portion of the parent organization, a few months may be all that is required.

Preferences in System Design and Technology

As the parent organization works through the strategic planning process, certain electronic technologies will emerge as likely candidates for use in the educational telecommunications activity. To assist in understanding this process, we have correlated the seven strategic issues listed in the previous section with the corresponding design characteristics of educational telecommunications systems, charting them against the most common technologies (Tables 4.2–4.8). The tables indicate the "preference" for each technology under the specified characteristic. They do not connote right or wrong approaches; instead they describe the preferred configurations found in the most common systems in use. The characteristics are described below; the first characteristic includes information on how to interpret the tables.

Type of Program

The parent organization's mission, resources, and image normally dictate the learners to be served. Programs for each learner population are often selected as a result of a needs assessment. A simple way to categorize the educational programs to be delivered is to use a continuum that goes from personal growth or avocational workshops, through college coursework and professional development programs, to graduate work. The tables are designed with each technology listed below the most commonly found characteristic situation. A technology that is used across all situations is found in the middle of the chart. In Table 4.2 we see that all but one technology is in common use for the whole continuum of program types. The one exception, on-line bibliographic searches, is used extensively in graduate programs, for example, but is not commonly found in avocational telecommunications-based education programs.

Table 4.2. Technology Preference for Type of Program.

Avocational Short Courses	Used Across All Situations	Graduate Degree Programs
	Cable TV	
	Public TV	
	Compressed video	
	ITFS	
	Point-to-point microwave	
	Satellite downlink	
	Satellite uplink	
	Slow-scan, freeze-frame TV	
	Videocassette	
	Videodisc	
	Audioconferencing	
	Audiocassette	
	Audiographics	
	Public radio	
	Facsimile	
	Computer conferencing	
	E-mail	
		On-line bibliographic searches

Learning Situation

This characteristic presents a continuum that starts with individualized or independent learning at one end. This learning situation usually does not require substantial interaction between an isolated learner and the instructor. Correspondence or contract learning programs would be good examples, as shown in Table 4.3. At the other end of the continuum we have the more traditional group or classroom that has been "wired" for telecommunications-based education. The preferred technologies in this case have the capability for either two-way or student-to-student interaction.

Service Area

A small service area, as used in Table 4.4, is defined as a community or city or a geographical area within which potential

Table 4.3. Technology Preference for Learning Situation.

Learning Independently	Used Across All Situations	Learning in a Group
Cable TV Public TV Videocassette Videodisc Audiocassette Public radio		
	Audioconferencing Computer conferencing E-mail On-line bibliographic searches	
		Compressed video ITFS Point-to-point microwave Satellite downlink Satellite uplink Slow-scan, freeze-frame TV Audiographics Facsimile

Table 4.4. Technology Preference for Service Area.

Small Service Area	Used Across All Situations	Large Service Area
Cable TV		
ITFS		
	Point-to-point microwave	
	Satellite downlink	
	Audiographics	
	Public radio	
	Videocassette	
	Videodisc	
	Audioconferencing	
	Audiocassette	
	Facsimile	
	Computer conferencing	
	E-mail	
	On-line bibliographic searches	
		Public TV
		Compressed video
		Satellite uplink
		Slow-scan, freeze-frame TV

learners are a convenient driving distance from the instructional site. A large service area would most likely be a significant portion of a state, an entire state, or the nation. The introduction of educational telecommunications systems to deliver programs has tended to break down the traditional service areas of organizations. This is a natural consequence of the parent organization's desire to provide increased access to education, which is one of the primary justifications for the introduction of these programs. Chapter Twelve discusses this topic within the concept of universal-access institutions.

Receive Sites

Many receive sites, probably ten or more for the purposes of Table 4.5, could be a significant number of permanent field instructional sites or a variety of sites that change with each program, as is the case with some satellite-delivered programs. System design information can also be derived from an interlinking of two characteristics, for example, receive sites and type of pro-

Table 4.5. Technology Preference for Number of Receive Sites.

One or Few Receive Sites	Used Across All Situations	Many Receive Sites
ITFS Point-to-point microwave Videodisc Facsimile		
	Compressed video Satellite downlink Slow-scan, freeze-frame TV Audioconferencing Audiographics Computer conferencing E-mail	
		Cable TV Public TV Satellite uplink Videocassette Audiocassette Public radio On-line bibliographic searches

gram. The use of cable TV to get to many receive sites, in this case the learner's home, to offer a personal-interest short course, implies that the living room is a perfectly acceptable classroom. Graduate degree programs would tend toward few receive sites with extensive student support services, such as libraries and computer laboratories.

Learner Dispersion

Low density (see Table 4.6) suggests that the learner is isolated from other learners with equivalent needs, in either an urban or rural setting. Although this situation is similar to that of the independent learner, that learner may have chosen to learn alone or may be a disabled student, rather than being physically distant. Designers of educational telecommunications systems normally attempt to bring learners together or "cluster" them to take advantage of the technology in a cost-effective manner.

Table 4.6. Technology Preference for Learner Dispersion.

Low Density of Learners	Used Across All Situations	High Density of Learners
Cable TV		
Public TV		
Satellite uplink		
Videocassette		
Videodisc		
Audiocassette		
Public radio		
Computer conferencing		
E-mail		
On-line bibliographic searches		
	Audioconferencing	
		Audiographics
		Facsimile
		Compressed video
		ITFS
		Point-to-point microwave
		Satellite downlink
		Slow-scan, freeze-frame TV

System Utilization Level

The key issues here seem to be cost of technology and cost of transport (see Table 4.7). On-demand systems can be turned on and off as dictated by use and do not accumulate costs such as dedicated transport when they are not in operation. More expensive systems tend to be used constantly or dedicated in order to be more cost-effective.

Unit Cost

Table 4.8 gives a relative comparison of the costs per program per learner for the same length of program. Technologies may also move across the continuum because of sensitivity to the number of learners per program. Point-to-point microwave, for example, can be relatively low in cost if the system reaches a large number of users. A particular technology that is decreasing

Table 4.7. Technology Preference for System Utilization Level.

On-Demand System	Used Across All Situations	Dedicated System
Cable TV Public TV Public radio		
	Facsimile Computer conferencing E-mail Satellite downlink Videocassette Videodisc Audioconferencing Audiocassette	
		Compressed video ITFS Point-to-point microwave Satellite uplink Slow-scan, freeze-frame TV Audiographics On-line bibliographic searches

Table 4.8. Technology Preference for Unit Cost.

Low Cost per Learner per Program	Used Across All Situations	High Cost per Learner per Program
Cable TV Public TV Videocassette Audioconferencing Audiocassette Public radio Facsimile		
	Satellite downlink Slow-scan, freeze-frame TV Audiographics Computer conferencing E-mail On-line bibliographic searches	
		Videodisc Compressed video ITFS Point-to-point microwave Satellite uplink

in cost (as it is refined or finds greater use) may also move across the continuum. It is likely that compressed video, as a case in point, will become less expensive as the technology improves. The personal computer is another good example of an electronic technology that has become less expensive as it has evolved. You are encouraged to review Chapter Six, which provides a detailed look at budgets and costs for various educational telecommunications systems.

The Role of Instructional Design in System Design

Johnson and Foa (1989) provide a description of instructional design that illustrates the importance of the linkage between that process and the design of educational telecommunications systems. They state: "Instructional design is based on the ideas that (a) the common goal of education and training is the development of human potential; and (b) there is sufficient knowledge about the nature of learning to improve the process of developing that potential. Instructional design, broadly defined, provides a process with which to identify as goals what people need to know and do, to set out to achieve those goals, and to understand whether or when they have been achieved." They maintain that "the purpose of the systematic design approach is that it encourages setting objectives, and provides a way to know when they are met. This process, combined with a growing body of learning theory, provides a set of tools that allow us to maximize individual learning potential" (p. 4).

Instructional design therefore provides us with assistance in the design of educational telecommunications systems at the stages where we consider *program types* and *learning situation*. This mechanism also fits nicely within the MBO structure we suggested earlier with the focus here on objectives, planning, implementation, and evaluation. The instructional-design process therefore has much to offer through the nine-step procedure described in Johnson and Foa (p. 22):

1. *Analysis.* This phase looks at the learners to be served in terms of determining their educational objectives; the or-

ganizations, if any, with which the learners are affiliated; special resources available; and the content of the telecommunications-based programs that will be delivered.

2. *Design.* The design phase represents a series of attempts at creating the specifications of the system's electronic technologies — the use of the tables in this chapter, for example — to define the system.

3. *Development.* A developmental work plan should help move the system design concept from the drawing board to a set of actions.

4. *Pilot test.* It is desirable, if possible, to build the first phase of the educational telecommunications system in order to test the design concepts and assumptions.

5. *Revision.* This is an iterative step along with the pilot test in which recommendations to revise the system design are developed and implemented.

6. *Production.* After satisfactory pilot tests, the complete educational telecommunications system is constructed.

7. *Duplication.* The system becomes the common denominator (as the support and delivery system) for unique telecommunications-based educational programs.

8. *Implementation.* The need remains to monitor and evaluate the long-term effectiveness of the system in light of the original system design criteria.

9. *Maintenance.* As new technologies become available and as the current state of instructional design progresses, the system should be updated.

Finally, Johnson and Foa provide an instructional-design explanation, in the preface of their text, for our statement earlier in this chapter concerning the preference by postsecondary institutions for using a mix or blend of technologies: "In the past decade, advances in the field have centered particularly on developments in communications theory and audio-visual media. The general trend in these areas has been toward greater individual control and power in the use of various media, and a blending of media into a single interactive, visual system. Because learning takes place in each medium in different ways, the task of today's instructional designer is to combine into one seamless product the structure of the information to be learned, what is known of learner characteristics and styles, and knowledge about media production techniques" (1989, p. x). By accident or design, postsecondary institutions have applied this concept in practical ways in the creation of existing educational telecommunications systems.

In the offering of its credit programs, Utah State University, for example, emphasizes instructional design for programs using its COM-NET system, which blends two-way audioteleconferencing, two-way facsimile, and the use of VHS videotape recorders for motion-color video. The Association for Media-Based Continuing Education for Engineers (AMCEE) features noncredit short courses that are videotaped in high-quality studio environments and offered with specially designed study guides and regular textbooks as support material. AMCEE chose this blend to take advantage of the logistic and financial benefits of videotaped classes and the pedagogical and marketing advantages of studio-produced noncredit courses (National University Continuing Education Association, 1988).

Case Study

The following case study shows how strategic planning, thoughtful system design considerations, and the use of opportunities and partnerships can create a successful educational telecommunications initiative. Chapter Eight also contains a two-part case study which, along with issues relevant to that chapter, includes strategic planning and system design components. You may wish to review that case at this time as another example.

In 1979 a university located in the Boston area decided to increase its off-campus continuing education programming. The institution, a young, urban public university less than twenty-five years old at the time, hired its first Continuing Education Unit director in 1980 and charged that person with the design and development of an expanded outreach program. Given the complex nature of the Boston educational environment, the director developed a partnership with the Office of

Adult Learning Services of the College Board for the purpose of conducting an environmental scan, internal and external analysis, and development of a programming forecast.

The new Continuing Education Unit had been created by amalgamating the existing summer session with evening programs. The internal analysis showed that the university was interested in reaching new learner markets and wanted to increase its visibility and recognition in Boston's highly competitive and sophisticated postsecondary educational environment.

The external analysis showed that Boston-area postsecondary education included about fifty institutions. Going two or three miles from an institution in any direction would bring you to another college or university campus. Most of the schools had long-standing continuing education programs with strong ties to just about every learner market imaginable. Independent adult education programs also flourished. What could this university do? The analysis showed that, probably because of the high density of the learner market, traditional face-to-face instruction was still the primary learning format. At that time, eastern Massachusetts lagged behind much of the rest of the country in the use of educational telecommunications systems. The activity that existed was dominated by public television courses and point-to-point microwave that transferred programs from downtown campuses to the suburbs. It was decided that electronic technologies could provide a different approach to serving learners (the analysis phase). If the "right" technology could provide high-visibility programs that both met learner needs and brought the university good press, the Continuing Education Unit could meet the institution's needs and have a good chance for success in a highly competitive continuing education market.

By correlating the university's mission and environment with the preference charts shown in Tables 4.2–4.8, a vision for telecommunications emerged (the design phase). The mission of the university was to serve the metropolitan Boston area, which has a *high density of learners* in a *small service area*. Furthermore, it made sense to consider both a *single-site structure* and a *multiple-site approach* by means of a mass-distribution system across the metropolitan area. Because of the desire for high-visibility programming, short professional development and public service programs seemed most suitable. This last criterion suggested an *on-demand system,* a system that could be turned on or off as needed, allowing programs to be selected and delivered in short, discrete packages. As the tables intimate, some form of teleconferencing made sense for single-site programming, while a TV or radio approach would work for mass-distribution programming. In fact, both were tried and each met with success (development, pilot test, and revision phases). Each approach also took advantage of particular opportunities.

For single-site telecommunications the university chose live-via-satellite videoteleconferencing. The opportunity that presented itself in 1982 was the formation of the National University Teleconference Network (NUTN) as a source of programs and as a support structure to assist an aspiring Continuing Education Unit new to telecommunications-based education. The cost-effective approach the university used in the start-up phase was to rent downlink access from Harvard University, which microwaved the satellite signal to the university campus. In the second year, after a track record of success was established, the Continuing Education Unit rented a portable downlink. By the third year, the university had bought its own portable downlink for use at the campus and at the site of program partners such as chambers of commerce. Videoconferencing filled the programming bill perfectly. The teleconferences consistently brought in nationally known presenters on subjects of major concern. The interactive aspect of the videoconferences also encouraged participant involvement. Both of these characteristics also attracted public attention to the program's "events." The programs were successful from both enrollment and financial perspectives. By 1984, the university had made its mark as a successful teleconference receive site (production, duplication, and implementation phases) and had also originated its own national live-via-satellite videoteleconference to forty-three sites (maintenance phase).

At about the same time as the videoteleconference project got under way the cable television industry presented another opportunity for the Continuing Education Unit. Boston and virtually all the contiguous cities and towns each had their own cable systems, and "public access," or the use of cable facilities by citizens to produce community programs, was being aggressively pursued by community cable-access groups. These groups, represented by cable programmers, often met to share programs and discuss common issues. This local network provided a platform from which the university launched a locally produced cable TV series, "Local Focus," featuring the university and its faculty as presenters and resource people.

The series worked in the following way (a second development phase). A dozen different community cable-access groups each agreed to produce, at no cost, a half-hour program on an issue of local or regional concern, such as urban crime or water quality. The university contributed faculty experts at no cost. The faculty were quite excited about donating their time in exchange for the opportunity to discuss their area of expertise on television. All the programs were produced at about the same time and scheduled as a series so that the same program would air in the same week on all the systems (another example of the pilot testing and revision phases). The job of the Continuing Education Unit, besides coordinating the logistics and arranging for faculty talent, was to have the programs' master tapes duplicated and "bicycled," or circulated to all the cable systems in a timely fashion to meet airing schedules. The net result was a twelve-week educational public service series in twelve different communities covering a population of over a half-million people (production and duplication), and featuring the university and its faculty. The university's goal to provide a public service and be highly visible was met. The costs to the Continuing Education Unit, other than staff time, consisted only of expenditures for blank videotape, duplicating, and postage. The program was not self-supporting, but the cost-benefit ratio for the university was very positive (another way to demonstrate the implementation and maintenance phases).

Summary

This chapter brings together two processes, strategic planning and instructional design. These mechanisms are coupled with the preferences exhibited by commonly used electronic technologies in creating a structure for forecasting educational telecommunications system design. These three parameters — strategic planning, technological preferences, and instructional design — can be visualized and utilized as three interlocking spheres of information. They constitute guiding principles through which the manager responsible for designing the system moves freely but in an orderly manner to ensure that the system meets the unique requirements of the parent organization.

Strategic planning is the road map that assists the parent organization along a series of steps toward an appropriate system design. This design should meet the needs of the whole organization, the learners the organization plans to serve, and the instructional resource personnel who will use the system. Strategic planning reminds us that we need to affirm the full support of the parent organization by assuring that the telecommunications-based education project is consistent with the organization's mission and long-range plan. The next chapter is devoted to assembling a team of staff members for the project's organizational unit who will make the project happen and maximize the probability of its success.

Once the parent organization's commitment is confirmed, a systematic scan of the environment of the service area yields descriptors for the proposed system: the learners and where they are located, likely telecommunications-based programs, and possible competitors. The emergence of vital physical information about the size and shape of the system provides the sphere for defining likely technical parameters. Many educational telecommunications systems currently exist. By studying the preferences others have exhibited in selecting specific technologies, the manager can choose the most appropriate system design options for the parent organization.

The needs of the learners who will make use of the system are considered along with the system's physical characteristics. Instructional-design concepts provide the sphere for creating efficient, effective programs based on an analysis of the learners, the program's content, and the learning environment. Finally, by integrating the technological preferences and instructional-design considerations with the strategic planning sphere, we can continue down the road toward the implementation of a successful educational telecommunications system.

Chapter 5

Management and Staffing Concerns

Myth: Providing leadership and staffing for an educational telecommunications system is a matter of designing the proper structure and staffing it with the best people.

Reality: As an educational telecommunications system evolves from creation to maturity, the leadership and staffing requirements must change to meet the special challenges posed by each new stage of development.

In their attempts to bring order to the ambiguity and change that seem to be the natural state of affairs in organizations, managers often struggle to put in place the perfect structure and staffing pattern, with the hope that order, shared purpose, and productivity will follow. The fallacy in this approach is that forces come from so many angles and with such rapidity that any attempt to impose a vision of order is doomed. Peter B. Vaill (1989) captures a sense of the changing context in which management decisions are made with his metaphor of navigating "permanent white water."

Nowhere is the constant state of change more evident than in attempts to integrate educational telecommunications systems with existing educational activities. Not only is the organizational context for change in a continuing state of flux, but also the rapid advances and refinements of telecommunications technologies themselves present a rapidly moving target for anyone advocating use of a particular technology or even a combination of technologies. Clearly, the management and staffing concerns are significant.

Unfortunately, when we look to organizational theory for guidance in meeting these challenges, we find that much of it fails to take into account the dynamic quality of organizational life (Smith, Mitchell, and Summer, 1985; Kimberly, 1980). However, an emerging body of literature, built on the idea that organizations evolve through identifiable stages during a life cycle, provides an insightful conceptual framework for thinking about management challenges. Although understandably reluctant to wholeheartedly embrace the biological analogy implicit in the life cycle approach, these scholars argue persuasively that "significant insights may emerge through the use of imperfect metaphors" (Kimberly, 1980, p. 9). Even those who reject the idea of developmental stages in any biological sense find that there are predominant thrusts of activity within organizations during particular periods of time (Tichy, 1980). Those who support the life cycle analogy argue that it acknowledges the dynamic quality not only of life within organizations, but also of the interactions between the organization and the environment. Furthermore, it incorporates a recognition that different types of leadership, different types of activities, and, therefore, different staffing patterns are needed at different times.

The failure to perceive and act on insights into an organization's changing needs can have serious consequences. Among them is the inability to move the educational telecommunications system into more mature stages of development. Often the organization fails to evolve because the managers do not recognize the need to change, preferring instead to treat telecommunications efforts as though they are in a continuous stage of creation. In fact, there is a tendency to try to apply successful solutions for management and staffing problems at one stage to similar problems at other stages, even though circumstances may have changed significantly. Solutions generated at one stage often contribute to or even prompt conditions that become problems later (Greiner, 1972; Quinn and Cameron, 1988); what is a strength at one stage may eventually emerge as the very weakness that prompts the need for further change. As Quinn and Cameron (1988) note, the effective management of such apparently paradoxical relationships characterizes successful efforts to create, sustain, and change organizations.

From a life cycle perspective, managing an educational telecommunications system becomes a matter of meeting a series of imperatives, whose nature varies depending on the development of the organization (Smith, Mitchell, and Summer, 1985). In order to effectively meet the management challenge, it is helpful to have a good idea about what stage of development the organization is in, what the characteristic management and staffing problems are likely to be at that stage, and what challenges are likely to be embedded within the strategies being implemented.

In the sections that follow we will examine a model of organizational evolution through a life cycle that can serve as a guide to the manager of an educational telecommunications system. The model highlights the types of activities that are typical during each stage in the organization's life cycle, thereby providing a means of anticipating at least some of the paradoxes that emerge. Without such a conceptual framework, managers seeking to guide the change process will find the effort extremely difficult.

The Organizational Life Cycle Framework

By drawing upon a life cycle model proposed by Quinn and Cameron (1983) and adapted by Cameron and Whetten (1988), we can identify several stages of development based upon the primary characteristics exhibited within an organization at any given time (see Figure 5.1).

The beginning or *entrepreneurial* stage is dominated by the need to secure the resources that will bring the organization into existence and to create a niche for it within the environment.

Figure 5.1. The Organizational Life Cycle.

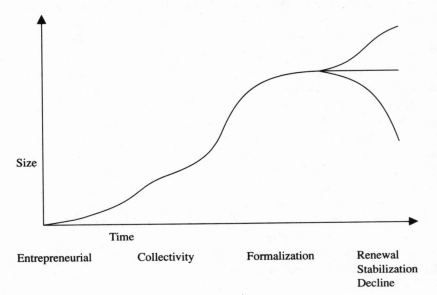

Size

Time

Entrepreneurial   Collectivity   Formalization   Renewal
                                                                     Stabilization
                                                                     Decline

The organization then enters a *collectivity* stage characterized by high individual and group commitment to achieving success. Continued rapid growth during the collectivity stage in turn prompts a move toward *formalization* as the organization attempts to spur efficient production by imposing a greater degree of management control. Finally, the organization reaches a kind of midlife crisis when it can enter a renewal stage, a stagnation stage, or a decline stage (Quinn and Cameron, 1983). Armed with this information about the characteristic concerns that emerge during each stage and with the knowledge that each stage generates different management challenges, the manager of telecommunications-based education can begin to recognize patterns in what previously appeared to be random activity. In order to accomplish this, we must first examine each stage in some depth.

Entrepreneurial Stage

When the integration of telecommunications with an existing education is a new undertaking within a parent organization, the effort will most closely mirror the characteristics of the entrepreneurial stage of development. The literature reveals that in this start-up stage the effort is usually dominated by a single individual, or at most a small group of leaders. A large portion of the leadership's energies are expended in bringing together the resources to create an organization that incorporates a vision about change. Some scholars go so far as to characterize the role of entrepreneurial leaders as the crucial element in determining early success (Kimberly, 1980). They assert that leadership must achieve a survival threshold by successfully assembling the ideological, political, and technical resources needed to launch the new effort (see Chapter Three). This may involve securing resources from within the parent organization through internal reallocation strategies, from external sources such as legislative action, or from grants and donations.

The entrepreneurial stage takes place over an extended period of time and includes a good deal more than the simple articulation of a new idea (Van de Ven, 1980). It usually begins with the initial inception of the idea, then quickly involves the leader in recruiting a small group of people who share the vision. This group of entrepreneurs is most often led by a generalist, and it usually employs a very informal communication system involving little or no structure (Smith, Mitchell, and Summer, 1985). This implies that the person who is attempting to create the new system will need to spend considerable time shaping its vision and selling it to important stakeholders within the parent organization and the surrounding environment. The elements of such an effort are detailed in Chapter Three.

Decisions made at the entrepreneurial stage exert considerable influence throughout the life cycle (Miles and Randolph, 1980). Conclusions about the nature of the clientele to be served or the approach to instructional design to be followed, for example, can become so deeply ingrained in the culture that they can only be changed with great difficulty. For this reason a clear understanding of the founding circumstances of an organization is important to managers who attempt to make changes during the organization's later stages of development. In particular, such knowledge can provide valuable clues as to which values and beliefs are deeply held within the organization and, therefore, might be the most difficult to change. If, for example, an organization is founded on individual efforts in instructional design, a change to a highly formalized structure emphasizing teams might be extremely difficult. When making such a basic change, the manager must be prepared to expend considerable effort, but the key to success lies in knowing and understanding what values are important and in formulating a deliberate strategy for the change.

The literature also indicates that when an organization is in the entrepreneurial stage, the manager and staff engage in considerable activity designed to reduce uncertainty about production of the new product or service (Tichy, 1980). Since the technology and precepts of distance education are often relatively unknown and vary with the specific environment, the manager of an educational telecommunications system can expect to spend a great deal of time and effort surveying the environment to find out how to go about establishing the new program. Environmental scanning activities to secure information about production and distribution issues become a major focus, and considerable learning takes place at the top of the organization, often through interaction between the members of the leadership group and the environment.

Information about ways to fit the envisioned effort within the parent organization is available from many sources. Outside consultants can provide specialized knowledge that may not be available within the management group itself. At the same time, the manager may engage in extensive professional networking activities in an attempt to interact with others engaged in similar efforts. Informal and formal surveys can be used to explore and map potential options and to eliminate unnecessary risks, and literature searches can uncover relevant educational, administrative, financial, and organizational issues.

One of the key elements that influences the likelihood for success during the entrepreneurial stage is the skill with which those in leadership positions use their understanding of the specific institutional setting to assess what is learned from the scanning activities. Unfortunately, managers are often tempted to adopt wholesale systems that have been or are successful elsewhere and introduce them directly into their environment; the result is often a short-lived experiment that remains disconnected from the culture of the parent organization. As we will see when we examine organizational decline, unintegrated change becomes vulnerable to a variety of forces. Ultimately, the manager must rely on his or her own evaluation of the degree of fit between available models and the specific environment. This is the most interesting challenge of the entrepreneurial stage.

The information-gathering effort will generally uncover a number of roles that must be accommodated in some fashion before moving forward. At a minimum, provisions must be made for program development, instruction, administration, marketing, student services, and technical support. Since at first most systems are quite small, staff members may need to fill several of these roles simultaneously. On the other hand, if the new effort is part of an already functioning educational or training organization, some existing staff and structure may be incorporated. For example, a higher education institution may already have in place a student services area geared to support other programs that can be drawn upon to support the telecommunications effort, or existing structures may be used to provide needed administrative support during the creation process. (See Figure 5.2 for an example of how the effort might be organized.)

As the educational telecommunications system is started, it is important for the manager to recognize that beginning a new organization demands change within the parent organization as well as considerable learning within the new organization. One helpful way to conceptualize the change is to see it as a process in which the system's staff must discover and negotiate new roles in working with academic colleges and departments as well as with other units in the parent organization.

The management of telecommunications-based education or training usually involves the creation of complex and interdependent administrative systems that incorporate new, more collaborative ways of working across formal administrative lines. It may be necessary, for example, for elements of a continuing education organization to work in a collaborative manner with staff from the campus telecommunications unit in order to operate

Figure 5.2. Entrepreneurial-Stage Organization Chart.

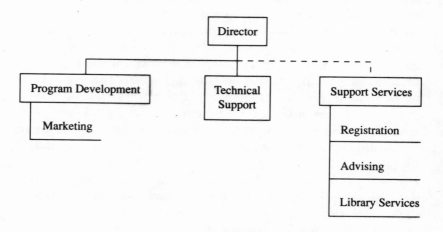

Note: The dashed line indicates indirect reporting responsibilities from another department.

the delivery system. The two units may become extremely inter-dependent but retain their own administrative reporting lines and never have a formalized relationship. On the other hand, in some cases elements of the two organizations may be blended into a new organization. In each case, new roles for both staffs will have to be negotiated and new workable relationships defined. The nature of such agreements becomes a function of the cultures of the specific organizations and the personalities involved.

In addition, educational telecommunications systems often make it desirable to develop new relationships with agencies that are not administratively tied to the parent organization. It may become necessary to negotiate a new set of relationships and understandings between the agency originating the programming and those that will function as receive sites. Successfully negotiating such arrangements requires staff members to understand the setting not only of the parent organization but also of the collaborating agencies. For example, if community colleges are likely to be the relevant receive sites, an important concern may be recruitment of staff who have extensive contacts within the community college ranks or, at the least, a good understanding of the inner workings of those institutions.

However, extensive experience in training within the private sector might be a more appropriate selection criterion if the primary audience for the new system is in the private sector. In the same vein, if the primary product of the system is to be graduate-level educational programming, the structure and staffing patterns must include library support for off-campus locations, provisions for academic advising, access to on-campus facilities such as computers, and a way to proctor examinations. Other types of programming would require a different structure and a different staffing pattern. In any case, the structure, staffing, and resources must support the goals of the program.

Finally, since the staff of an organization in the entrepreneurial stage must work within a highly ambiguous environment and make decisions under circumstances in which there are no easy or straightforward solutions, they must have good negotiation and communication skills and be willing to learn. Above all, they must be able to deal with ambiguity without becoming immobilized by it. The managers and staff must be willing to move forward even though they realize that decisions made now may have unintended or even negative consequences later in the life cycle.

Collectivity Stage

Once the resources have been assembled and the organization has faced the need to produce the new educational product on an ongoing and sustained basis, the effort often moves from the entrepreneurial stage to the collectivity stage. In many cases the movement into this stage is prompted by a kind of crisis caused by entrepreneurial thinking (Greiner, 1972). The pressure placed on the organization to produce quickly in order to meet growing demand for the new product may reveal that the thinking at the entrepreneurial stage was inadequate to sustain production and growth over the long term; this may even prompt a leadership change.

When innovative products or services are the core activity of the organization, there are many unknowns about how to organize effectively. As a result, much must be learned through direct experience with the new processes and products within the specific environment. Since the technology of work involved in integrating telecommunications with continuing education is relatively unfamiliar, each decision is treated as a unique event. New ways to organize resources are formulated and tested. Solutions that show promise are retained; the others are discarded or revised. Those that appear to work are quickly made part of the routine and, over time, become a part of the organizational culture. This pioneering activity is often a source of considerable exhilaration as well as anxiety and stress for all involved.

Fortunately, it is relatively easy to make adjustments during the collectivity stage because the organization is usually small and structurally fluid and because managers have so much direct involvement in day-to-day decisions. A management team whose shared vision includes why the integration of telecommunications-assisted education should be attempted, how it can be accomplished, and what the result might look like has considerable knowledge about the total decision-making context and is in a relatively good position to assess how well the adjustments fit with the overall vision. One of the strengths of the collectivity stage, particularly in the beginning, is the high degree of involvement in the decision-making process by managers and their resulting flexibility to make necessary adjustments in staffing and structure. That flexibility, however, can pass quickly with an increase in the tendency to establish routine solutions.

As an organization grows in size, activity, and complexity, encouraging a shared view of the organization (Nadler, 1988) becomes a crucial task for managers of educational telecommunications systems. Unfortunately, the pressure to meet increasing demands on the organization to engage in a growing array of activities is great, and too often the cultural dimension falls by the wayside. When this happens and the vision remains the sole property of the manager, a growing gap can develop between the organization as it is envisioned and as it actually functions. This gap is known as "organizational drift" (Lodahl and Mitchell, 1980, p. 185). Drift often represents a retreat from the ideals expressed during the entrepreneurial stage as managers come face-to-face with the demands of day-to-day operation during the period of rapid growth and yield to the temptation to give their attention to matters of production to the neglect of cultural concerns. An example is that of an organization that builds elaborate instructional-design models but fails to deal with growing opposition to the system as a whole among key faculty within the parent organization.

Managers can combat drift in a number of ways. Above all, they must act to ensure that others throughout the telecommunications unit and within the parent organization share a common vision about the purpose of the system. This requires managers to assume a leadership role in selling the vision at every opportunity to other organizational members, particularly at the senior management level, and to stakeholders in the parent institution.

The primary means of selling the vision is by extensive personal contact between management and staff throughout the organization. During the early part of the collectivity stage, the selling can be done on an informal basis as a result of direct contact between the manager and the staff and between the manager and the leadership of the parent organization. In fact, staffs of organizations at this stage of development often report a strong sense of family and cooperation, a high level of commitment, and considerable direct contact with management. As Quinn and Cameron (1983) note, these characteristics are associated with human relations criteria; they conclude that elements of the human relations approach to management are more important during collectivity than at any other stage.

Another means of guarding against drift involves giving careful attention to recruiting and incorporating new members into all levels of the organization. Here ideology can be used as a resource in selecting staff as well as in providing the context for staff orientation and training activities. The emphasis must be on ensuring that new members of the organization share the ideological commitment of the leaders and founders. The manager must be willing to expend considerable energy on communicating the vision directly and on creating systems that reinforce its tenets. Extensive orientation of new staff must be a high priority.

The importance of taking special pains to indoctrinate new staff is underscored by studies indicating that the later persons are recruited into an organization, the less likely they are to share the ideological commitment of the leadership (Lodahl and Mitchell, 1980). If little attention is paid to cultural issues within the young organization, new members introduced into highly ambiguous situations find themselves without a set of organizational values for guidance. Left to their own devices, they will develop values that may or may not reflect those of the manager. As time passes and the organization matures, control over the socialization process passes into the hands of colleagues at lower levels of the organization, and the task of maintaining commitment among new members becomes more and more difficult. Because the organizational culture is not yet fully formed, this development can accelerate drift.

An example can quickly illustrate this point. Faculty members who become involved in teaching via telecommunications-assisted delivery systems often approach their first assignment with concerns about the effectiveness of the systems and about their roles as pioneers in the area. During the collectivity stage, these concerns are likely to become the source of much discussion and interaction between individual faculty members and the system's manager; in these interactions the manager, who has a broad organizational perspective, works to develop a shared view of the purpose and promise of the new effort. At a later stage in the organization's development, however, the same activity may involve attendance by a number of faculty members at an orientation session conducted by a specialist, who is likely to reflect a much narrower view of the organization. It is unlikely that the result in terms of conveying an overall vision of the organization will be the same.

Formalization Stage

The transition from collectivity to formalization is often extremely troublesome because it is usually not expected, understood, or managed very well (Quinn and Anderson, 1984). Nor is it possible, except perhaps in retrospect, to delineate the particular point at which formalization starts. Often the beginnings are found in efforts during the collectivity stage. In fact, formalization appears to be a natural outgrowth of evolution through the collectivity stage as more and more tasks are made routine. In other words, elements of formalization may be found in earlier stages, but the formalization stage is reached when the dominant way in which the organization reacts to problems is through established rules and procedures.

The onset of a formalization-and-control stage is usually prompted by a combination of factors, including continued rapid growth in the demand for the product or service, a corresponding growth in the size and complexity of the organization, and growing pressures from external forces to conform to certain practices. Much of the problem rests with the paradoxical nature of formalization processes that, as this discussion will illustrate, appear to have the potential for both positive and negative consequences.

Growth in the size and complexity of an organization results in a reduction in the frequency and comprehensiveness of contact between the staff and the manager. Management teams that were the central focus during the collectivity stage find themselves being pulled apart as each member becomes more and more involved in production issues. The addition of an increasing number of specialists erodes the cohesiveness that dominated the collectivity stage (Quinn and Anderson, 1984). Whereas previously the various staffing functions were likely to be informally conducted by a few people acting in multiple roles, the emerging staffing patterns reflect increasing levels of specialization (see Figure 5.3 for a sample organizational chart).

Managers are often reluctant to release control over the decision-making process and move it to the lower levels of the organization. Whereas during collectivity control was maintained by the manager who personally issued orders and observed their implementation, the size and complexity of the operation now begins to make such an approach impossible. Consequently, there is a strong tendency to institute extensive formalization,

Figure 5.3. Organizational Chart During the Formalization Stage.

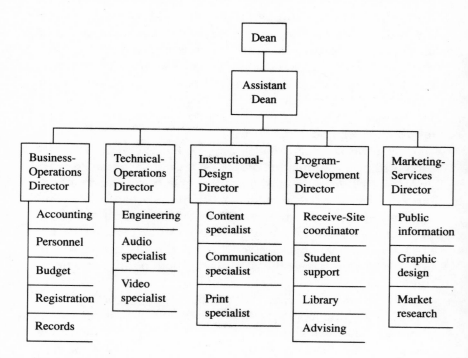

consisting of procedures and rules, as a means of controlling the potentially negative aspects of drift and encouraging efficient production. As a result, managers may pay little attention to securing commitment through cultural means. By instituting formal structures, they attempt to retain enough power to delegate decisions to lower levels in the organization; they have little concern, because the valued decision-making premises are already built into the procedures (Walsh and Dewar, 1987).

Support for formalization also comes from the staff, who want to move beyond the heavy personal demands of the collectivity stage as rapidly as possible. As Quinn and Anderson

(1984) note, one of the negative features of the intense effort found in the collectivity stage is the tendency of managers to burn out as they become deeply involved in matters of production while simultaneously attempting to cope with a variety of ideological and political demands. From this perspective, some of the drive toward formalization must be seen as a survival tactic. Furthermore, the very implementation of formalization leads to further formalization, as the more creative people in the staff are encouraged to leave by the increasing number of tasks that are accomplished through routine solutions. They are, in turn, replaced by staff members who are more willing to use formalization to provide meaning in their work.

Another powerful source of pressure toward formaliza-. tion is the parent organization. As soon as a new organization begins to function, the parent organization will assert pressure on it to act consistently and in accordance with the parent organization's expectations. Often the somewhat informal processes that characterize the collectivity stage are judged to be inadequate by the parent organization, which places a high premium on predictability. Pressure to make procedures and policies conform to those of the parent organization is particularly intense when the parent organization has a bureaucratic structure (Quinn and Anderson, 1984).

Thus, managers of educational telecommunications systems can anticipate intense pressure to conform to a variety of procedural norms that characterize postsecondary educational institutions. For example, a new system that delivers classes on a nontraditional schedule will experience pressure to conform to on-campus class schedules for purposes of record keeping, head counts, financial aid, and overall scheduling. From the perspective of the parent organization, any deviations from the norm are inconsistencies that must be eliminated. However, from the perspective of the telecommunications manager, such deviations may be a key element in defining the market niche. The manager must be prepared to defend the characteristics of the system that are vital to maintaining the niche, while simultaneously mediating the fit with the parent organization.

Another example of pressure that can be exerted by the

parent organization takes the form of demands that the telecommunications organization operate in accordance with political arrangements regarding geographical service areas that were negotiated before telecommunications made such boundaries untenable. Again, much negotiation must take place and considerable effort must be expected to find a balance between the needs of the host institution, the new organization, and learners. The key to success is often a matter of keeping the needs of the clientele paramount in negotiations.

Other sources within the external environment also exert pressure toward formalization. Learners, for example, have certain expectations about educational organizations and exert pressure on the organization to conform. If, for example, a program offers college or university credit, learners will want its courses to meet requirements established by their employer or other funding agencies for reimbursement. They will want to know what sequence of courses will be offered and on what schedule. Furthermore, they are likely to have certain expectations about the support services that should be made available as a part of the learning experience. Accrediting agencies, state departments of education, and other institutions all exert pressure on educational telecommunications systems to conform to a variety of standard practices and to establish formal methods of complying with those expectations.

Excessive formalization can also deprive the organization of the benefits of creative efforts from new members. New people coming into an organization dominated by formalization encounter a highly structured system headed by people who value congruence more than innovation. These newcomers experience formalization as a highly restrictive atmosphere where deviance is punished rather than rewarded and where they are prevented from innovating within their own setting. This contrasts sharply with the situation during the collectivity stage, when there was little experience to draw upon and reliance upon direct communication with the leader provided newcomers with the cultural values to guide decision making. New members often see the organization from outside and want to join because they share its vision; they also bring with them ideas about how to improve upon it. Although they are eager to contribute to the organization's success, they may be restricted from doing so by the very formalization instituted in an effort to protect the vision. Their creativity and flexibility are limited and the organization is deprived of valued sources of energy and ideas. The result often is growing frustration throughout the organization (Lodahl and Mitchell, 1980).

In summary, the temptation to establish rules and procedures as a means of dealing with environmental pressures is great and has a variety of internal and external sources. Unfortunately, although formalization may ensure some control over interactions between the organization and elements in the environment, extensive formalization can inhibit the organization's ability to learn and make needed changes. For this reason, managers of educational telecommunications systems should approach extensive formalization with care. As Walsh and Dewar (1987) note, if formalization is allowed to grow unchecked, it can contribute to organizational decline. It is too easy for the premises for decisions to become frozen and applied without thought to their actual relevance to a particular situation. This is especially true if management begins to use formalization as a tool for maintaining its position of power rather than as a way to deal with pressures from the environment. In these circumstances there is considerable danger that management will begin to equate performance with obeying the rules.

Renewal, Stabilization, or Decline

As Figure 5.1 indicates, organizations that move through the formalization stage often face a kind of midlife crisis that can determine the nature of the next stage of development. For some, formalization is the precursor to a stage of growth and renewal that is followed by formalization at a different level. Others stagnate at the formalization stage. Still others move quickly from formalization into decline and eventually to termination. An examination of the sources of decline provides considerable insight about the long-range impact of decisions made during the earlier stages of development. In addition, as educational telecommunications systems mature, more managers will face the problem of how to renew those that are locked into formalization and that therefore face impending decline. In an attempt to analyze some of the features of these stages, we will first identify factors that can prompt decline, and then turn our attention to how they can be dealt with by moving the organization into a renewal stage.

Decline

The literature dealing with organizational decline and termination shows how the failure to adequately resolve the paradoxical problems of earlier stages can cause problems later (Cameron, Sutton, and Whetten, 1988). Decline and termination are, after all, normal stages in the life cycle of organizations. The primary challenge for the manager is to anticipate the sources of decline and set the stage for renewal. Failure to address the sources of decline can lead to stagnation, further decline, or even termination.

Whetten (1980) has identified four potential sources of decline: loss of legitimacy, vulnerability, environmental entropy, and organizational atrophy. Of the four, three involve the organization's interrelationship with forces in the external environment. *Loss of legitimacy* generally involves a challenge to the organization's right to resources because it is unable to meet the needs it claims to be addressing. For example, the telecommunications system that sets a goal of serving the educational needs of thousands of learners, but registers less than two hundred a year, runs the risk of losing its rights to resources. A system that claims to serve an entire state, but actually serves only one location, faces a similar problem. Loss of legitimacy can often be traced to a failure to adequately and realistically define what constitutes appropriate measures of success (see Chapters Three and Nine).

A second factor that can prompt loss of legitimacy is what Whetten (1980) calls a shift in societal ideology. In other words, the value that society puts on the product or service being produced by the organization may decline. For example, a society may decide that education is less important than defense when it is faced by an external threat. Some scholars go so far as to argue that an organization will fail only when society no longer values its basic objectives. They note that if an organization can establish a strong enough claim to legitimacy, it may be able to survive even when it is not particularly successful in efficiently producing the valued product or service (Kimberly, 1980).

The second source of decline, *vulnerability*, is essentially a political phenomenon. Public institutions in particular are vulnerable to a variety of political threats from within both the specific and general environments. Often these threats have their origins in a failure to deal adequately with public demands and political concerns in an earlier phase of development. Usually the problem is prompted by a failure to manage the expectations of a powerful group of stakeholders or to incorporate appropriate stakeholders in the decision-making processes. The failure to include faculty in the decision-making process of a telecommunications-based effort in higher education, for instance, can be politically disastrous.

The third source of decline, *environmental entropy*, is the reduced capacity of the environment to support the organization (Whetten, 1980). A general downturn in the economy, for example, might prompt society to determine that an effort to create an organization that will provide educational services to the underserved might be less vital than maintaining some already existing educational delivery systems. One factor in the demise of the University of Mid-America, a regional effort to produce and offer television-based undergraduate instruction, was the poor economy of the late 1970s and early 1980s (Van Kekerix, 1986). Similarly, an organization that is unable to anticipate and adjust to demographic changes will also encounter an unsupportive environment.

Loss of legitimacy, vulnerability, and environmental entropy all involve the organization's interaction with factors in the environment and point to the need for the manager to be closely attuned to such factors. Some can be controlled by the organization more easily than others. Loss of legitimacy can be a function of the extent to which the organization operates efficiently within the marketplace and is well within its ability to control, if the actual work involved is a known quality. On the other hand, there is considerable risk when the technology is relatively unknown, because it is not always possible to decide how efficient an organization is when there is nothing to measure it against. In some cases vulnerability becomes a function of how skillfully the manager is able to manage the political environment. Of the three sources, environmental entropy is the least likely to be controllable, although it may be possible to combat some of its effects by scaling back in size or redirecting efforts into new areas as societal values change. In any case, the manager must be alert to any developments within the environment that may signal the onset of decline.

Of the sources of decline, *organizational atrophy*, defined as the inability of an organization to respond to new conditions, is the most clearly internal, and it has important implications for how the organization interacts with the environment. As has already been noted, organizations tend to apply lessons learned during earlier stages of development to new situations, failing to recognize that the characteristics that were an asset can become a liability at a later stage of development. The paradoxical nature of formalization has already been noted, but there are other examples as well. A funding agency may find that opening access to underserved learners is a noble goal worthy of support. During the entrepreneurial stage, the drive to secure resources is paramount and the need to secure the support of the funding agency dominates; thus, the desire to open access may be positively reinforced. However, some stakeholders within the parent organization may be concerned about the impact of such activities on the academic prestige of the institution and raise questions about the lowered academic standards that they feel might result. When the organization reaches the formalization stage, it may experience considerable pressure to conform to institutional norms regarding these standards. At this stage, the desire to open access can become a liability in legitimizing the organization.

The topology of sources for organizational decline formulated by Whetten provides a general framework for analyzing the phenomenon. The key features of this approach are the recognition that sources of decline may originate within either the organization itself or the environment, that the various sources are often interrelated, and that the organization may face a complex series of challenges to its survival arising from the interaction between its internal characteristics and its environment. The manager who does not recognize the complex nature of the sources of decline may fail to take comprehensive actions to realign the stages of the organization to match changes in the environment. If the organization is to remain viable in the long term, the manager must foster the attributes of a learning organization. This is the subject of the next section.

Renewal

As the discussion of decline indicates, its sources often have an environmental referent. This suggests that managers of educational telecommunications systems must find ways to systematically scan and adjust to the environment. Unfortunately, excessive formalization and control makes change difficult (Greiner, 1972). A primary aim of formalization activity is to create an organization whose goals, structure, and technology are congruent. Although highly congruent organizations can be very successful in the short term, they often become extremely resistant to change, shielding themselves from outside influences by insisting on applying routine solutions to problems even when the problems are unique (Nadler, 1988). As a result, stagnation sets in and the organization can function effectively only if the environment remains stable.

To foster renewal, the manager must find ways to make an organization more responsive to environmental developments and more flexible in responding to them. The current literature on organizational renewal or *transformation*, as it is sometimes called (Kilmann, Covin, and Associates, 1987; Tichy and Devanna, 1986), offers some interesting insights into the challenges faced by organizations that function in rapidly changing environments.

Some organizations have successfully applied the strategy of deliberately shifting from a traditional concept of control from above to one of control through high commitment. At the core of this approach is an emphasis on skillfully managing organizational culture. Communication lines are opened within the organization and reciprocal learning is encouraged between levels of the organizations as well as between the organization and its environment (Beer, 1988). The strategy for combatting drift shifts from achieving congruence through formalization to achieving the same result by having the various levels of the organization share common beliefs and visions about the organization and its meaning.

Management plays a key role in the transition, because it must provide meaning for the dramatic change that takes place when the organization is turned upside down (Tichy and Devanna, 1986). The manager must find and articulate a theme into which the new commitment fits. For those involved in managing educational telecommunications systems, this often involves a renewed dedication to providing access to education using new forms of technology. The primary goal is to open the communication and decision-making processes to include the lower levels of the organization where contact with the environment takes place. Furthermore, in order to mobilize energy for the needed change, the manager must provide the staff with training and development, to familiarize them with the opportunities and demands of the new technologies and to help them acquire the information and skills to function effectively. The manager must reinforce these actions by setting high performance standards through personal example and through carefully crafting the staff evaluation and reward processes.

The change in an organization from the formalization stage to one that encourages high commitment through decentralization can be threatening to the existing power structure and may generate considerable resistance. The change affects the reward structure and will prompt a whole series of renegotiations among people on the staff. In addition, considerable tension is caused by the need to continue to function while simultaneously undertaking substantial change (Beckhard, 1988).

Those who wish to revitalize an organization in an effort to reach another stage of renewal must prepare an organizational vision that matches the changes that are needed. The manager of a training unit might, for example, use the current interest and opportunities in telecommunications as the triggering event for redirecting the total organization. To do this, the manager must develop a vision of how integration of telecommunications with the existing unit might better position the newly revitalized organization within its institutional setting, and then strive to gain the commitment of staff to this vision.

A key element in the effort must be careful management of human resource issues within the organization. The leadership must carefully consider what types of individuals are needed to bring the organization through the renewal into its next stage of development. It is not enough simply to restructure the organization to fit the new technology. Instead, the entire process of staffing, appraising, developing, and rewarding the human resources of the organization must be brought into congruence with the new vision. For example, in hiring or promoting staff, the organization may choose those who have desirable academic degrees in areas such as instructional design, those who have demonstrated an interest in and desire to use telecommunications, or those with experience in distance education; these choices send signals to the staff about what is considered important within the renewed organization.

In addition, the leadership must look carefully at staff training needs. Here an important issue is the kind of training opportunities that should be provided for current employees so that they can contribute to the revitalized organization. Staff may be trained in the use of telecommunications-based delivery systems or in a variety of services that are vital to the support of distance education efforts. Furthermore, staff may need training to understand any special requirements of distance learners or of the technologies involved in a delivery system. It is crucial to identify not only what existing expertise might be brought to bear on the revitalization effort, but also what new skills are needed and how they will be brought into the organization.

A strategy that puts a heavy emphasis on managing human resource issues incorporates the understanding that the people in the organization make the transition, that certain skills and talents will be needed both during and after the transition effort, and that opposition to the changes may have to be overcome. Failure to manage these issues encourages resistance. Thus, by putting an emphasis on hiring and developing the types of people needed in the new organization, by providing training in key areas, and by shaping the appraisal and reward systems, leaders can move an organization from formalization into renewal.

The paradoxical nature of change becomes apparent again as an organization nears the end of a renewal stage, when it encounters renewed pressure to formalize many elements of its activities although at a different level than before. In short, the paradox of success continues to follow the organization throughout its life cycle: it must experience a series of formalization and renewal stages in order to continue to thrive and grow in an ever-changing environment (Van de Ven and Poole, 1988).

Summary

The framework of the organizational life cycle offers a useful tool for analyzing management and staffing concerns in establishing and developing an educational telecommunications system. It recognizes the dynamic quality of organizations and draws attention to the fact that they may have different kinds of management and staffing needs at different stages in their development. In addition, this approach recognizes that strategies and tactics that may be successful at one stage are not necessarily appropriate at another. As Smith, Mitchell, and Summer (1985, p. 818) have observed, "managers probably need to change their priorities as their firms move through different stages. If they cannot, they may inhibit the further development of their organizations."

Recognizing and managing the paradoxes involved in making necessary transitions during the life cycle are major challenges. At each stage managers must give considerable attention to the formulation and management of cultural issues as well as production issues. The strategies that can be used successfully vary depending on the stage of development. In addition, the leader must always be aware that a successful strategy often incorporates elements that may inhibit evolution into the next stage.

We have attempted to explore some of the implications of this approach as they apply to organizations involved in telecommunications-assisted education. As Lodahl and Mitchell (1980, p. 203) note, "The organization is a success as an institution to the degree that it exhibits authenticity, functionality, and flexibility across generations." To be authentic the organization must embody its ideals, to function it must operate efficiently, and to be flexible it must be willing to adjust to take advantage of the creativity of its members and the challenges of the environment. This is the goal for which all managers of educational telecommunications systems must strive.

Chapter 6

Ensuring
Fiscal Stability

Myth: Telecommunications-based education is extremely expensive.

Reality: The cost of telecommunications-based education ranges widely depending on the electronic technology used.

Educational telecommunications systems tend to be uniquely designed for the parent organization within which they are developed. In addition, many technologies are available to the organization planning to implement a system to deliver and support telecommunications-based educational programming. Therefore, as no one ideal system exists, there is no one best budget structure. This does not pose a serious fiscal management problem. Once programming goals have been established and the technology has been selected, an effective budget model can be formulated.

The first step in moving toward a viable fiscal structure is to review useful financial assumptions about these systems and their associated electronic technologies. The second step is to analyze the impact of the parent organization's objectives for the telecommunications unit, its placement in the structure of the organization, and the resulting fiscal implications. A review of the most relevant budget components is covered next. The fourth step is to discuss the typical expenditures to be found in the budgets of telecommunications systems and the consequences they can have on the bottom line. A detailed review of revenue sources will follow an examination of expenditure categories. Finally, various expenditure and revenue elements will be linked through budget components that should allow managers to build a complete budget.

In order to get the most out of this chapter, readers should be familiar with the basic techniques of budgeting and financial control, particularly as they relate to the management of self-supporting units (units that must generate the funds they anticipate expending during each budget cycle). An understanding of budgeting in postsecondary educational units such as continuing education or corporate training programs will definitely be of assistance. A helpful resource is Gary W. Matkin's *Effective Budgeting in Continuing Education* (1985).

Financial Assumptions

In general, the cost of an educational telecommunications system will vary as a function of the following factors:

- The nature and number of receive and origination sites
- The quality and complexity of the equipment used to send or receive program signals
- The method of program transport used and the distance required to move programs from origination to receive sites
- The degree of interaction designed into the system
- The nature of the instructional and support staff
- Whether the system is a full-time (dedicated) or part-time operation
- The level of reliability required
- The electronic technology selected

As a useful starting point it can be stated that, in general, nonelectronic systems such as correspondence study are the least expensive. Audio systems are less expensive than computer-based systems, and video systems as a group are the most expensive, with interactive video at the top of the cost hierarchy. Since a system can be created by combining assorted electronic telecommunications components, it is helpful to examine each of the eight factors independently. This process of system design and associated costs is in some ways like buying a component stereo system, where the buyer might ask: What quality of sound do I demand? Do I need the compact disc player? Which size speakers do I require? What can I spend for the system overall? For an educational telecommunications system, for example, it would be informative to consider the relative costs of audio versus video and to determine whether the instructional value of interactivity justifies the expenditure of funds.

Receive Site

The receive site is the system's counterpart to the traditional classroom. The main difference is that the receive site includes the equipment required to transform the program that has been received into a usable form for presentation to the learners. The site may also include the equipment needed to allow participants to communicate with the program's origination site. Once the unit cost per receive site is established, it can be projected to a multiple-site configuration. In general, this results in a direct relationship between the number of receive sites and their total cost to the system. The total cost per site is determined by combining the space costs with the cost of the equipment needed to present the program. This analysis assumes that the organization owns or controls the receive site. One exception would be when the receive site is the learner's home and the equipment is the learner's television set. In this case the learner bears the cost of items such as equipment and cable charges.

In order to provide a feel for relative costs per site for some selected technologies, a hierarchy of receive sites can be created, with the least expensive site to the left in the hierarchy and the most expensive to the right. In this relationship, < means "less than" and < < "much less than." Items separated by a comma have relatively equivalent costs.

[print < audiotape < audio live, videotape < computer
< audiographic < one-way video << two-way video]

Origination Site

The origination site is the location where the program is created
and supervised. Typically, it is a unique operational component of the system. A system that originates programs by producing them at a video studio would be a case in point. In some
cases a system may not have an origination site; origination costs
are instead replaced by the expense of buying and transporting
programming. A system that leases the rights to externally
produced, live-via-satellite video teleconferencing is a good example of one that does not build in an origination component,
purchasing rather than developing programs. In other cases the
origination and receive sites may be equivalent, as in an audioconferencing system, in which origination-site and receive-site
costs are the same. Ultimately, actual costs are determined from
the specific technology used. Applying our cost hierarchy to origination sites we get the following:

[audiotape < audio live < audiographic
< computer << live video]

Send and Receive Equipment

With the exception of video production studios, the most complex part of an educational telecommunications system, for both
technology and the determination of costs, can be the send and
receive equipment. In some cases this can be as simple as a box
in which to pack an audiotape or videotape to send to a receive
site. In other systems, such as a live-via-satellite system that incorporates a satellite uplink and downlink to either send or
receive signals from a satellite, the cost of transmission equipment is a major consideration.

Certain types of telecommunications systems have both
send and receive capabilities as part of the receive-site equipment. Audio and computer conferencing systems are good examples. Low-technology prepackaged systems such as print or

tape form the baseline case; they require only a suitable package prior to distribution. Video programs that are "broadcast" over commercial, public, or cable TV simply require a basic television set. However, specialized equipment becomes a significant cost consideration when the system involves the reception of narrowcast video programming. Narrowcast programming, information electronically transmitted to a specific learner audience rather than the general public, needs special hardware to receive and translate the transmission signal into one that can be viewed on a television set. Video signals that are relayed from a satellite directly to receive sites require a satellite downlink to collect the signals and translate them into a usable form. Although these specialized components can vary in cost from a few thousand to more than ten thousand dollars, they offer unique system, distribution, and programming opportunities. Unique opportunities also exist with compressed-video systems. These systems send video signals over terrestrial lines as well as by satellite. The telecommunications manager is still faced with the need to translate the signal into a usable format with specific CODEC equipment (so-called from its ability to code and decode transported signals). Our cost comparison hierarchy for equipment that receives and processes signals for receive sites is as follows:

[audio live, computer < < video
compression, satellite downlinks]

The equipment for sending programming is related to the previous discussion on receive-site equipment. In many cases the sending capability is built into receive-site equipment, the most familiar example being the telephone that is the basis for audioconference systems. Some notable exceptions are listed in the following hierarchy. These systems represent the more technically sophisticated approaches to educational telecommunications systems.

[broadcast radio < broadcast TV < narrowcast
video, videoconferencing < compressed
video < satellite uplinking]

One variable that should be introduced at this juncture is the possible need for bridging. Audio and video systems that use terrestrial lines and that also have multiple sites may require the addition of a *bridge* (an electronic device, also called a multiple-access unit) to sort and direct program signals. For example, if a number of streets converge at an intersection that is devoid of traffic signals, chaos results. A bridge functions like a traffic cop, directing programs from the origination site, through the complex converging point, to the proper receive site. Bridges can be invaluable in increasing the flexibility of multiple-site systems and are one of the more expensive items in the capital expenditure budget.

Transport

Transport refers to the means by which information, in our case the programming, is moved from one point to another. In non-electronic systems, the transport for prepackaged print and tape programs can be the U.S. Post Office or one of the express delivery services. For electronic transport, cost is proportional to the bandwidth, which is the spread between the highest and lowest frequency a communications channel is capable of carrying. Broader bandwidth means greater cost. Audio and computer systems use one or two telephone lines (narrow bandwidth), compressed video typically varies from one to twenty-four phone lines (moderate bandwidth), and transmissions such as a full-motion video image comparable to the one on your home TV require the equivalent of hundreds of phone lines (broad bandwidth).

Alternative technical approaches and quantity purchases of bandwidth do, however, moderate the cost for broadband systems. For multiple sites, video, broadcast, and narrowcast systems as well as satellite transmission are solutions that result in reasonable transport costs per receive site. Another rule to keep in mind for both electronic and nonelectronic systems is the relationship of distance to cost. The farther you transport the program, the greater the cost. Satellite systems are the obvious exception to the distance rule, since the cost of one transponder (the part of a satellite that receives a signal from an uplink on Earth and then transmits it back to the surface of the Earth for reception by numerous downlinks) provides signal coverage of a large area of the Earth's surface. Our transport hierarchy of costs is summarized below.

[prepackaged < audio, computer < video
compressed < < video full-motion, satellite]

Interactivity

Interactive technologies provide some form of two-way communication between sites in a system. Because interaction is a desirable characteristic, system designers look for cost-effective ways to incorporate it in the learning process. It is often possible to take advantage of much of the equipment for one-way systems in interactive systems. Audioconference systems are interactive systems with equivalent two-way communications, whereas a telecourse with telephone call-in is nonequivalent two-way communication. As a result of such variations, two-way systems are not necessarily double the cost of one-way systems. Nevertheless, a hierarchy can be created as follows.

[noninteractive systems < interactive systems]

Staffing

Staff for educational telecommunications systems can be split into four categories: management, technical, instructional, and support. *Management* staff oversee the system's work plan, facilitate day-to-day activities, and supervise the budget. *Technical* staff select, operate, and maintain equipment. *Instructional* staff design and teach courses or present programs. And *support* staff provide a variety of functions such as training people to use the system, coordinating learners at receive sites, operating receive-site equipment, and carrying out general clerical tasks. The less sophisticated and smaller systems, such as those that receive video teleconferences or audioconference systems, tend to be handled by jack-of-all-trade individuals who fulfill most staff functions. These smaller systems hire instructional support on a project-by-project basis. We can generalize to say that smaller systems have a staffing pattern characterized by a central management position, often an entrepreneurial individual with continuing education experience, who draws on technical and instructional expertise as need dictates. As the system becomes more complex, staff specialization results. Large systems will have management teams, technical teams, and instructional resources that are usually contracted from academic units. Obviously, big systems require a big staff. The best criterion of relative costs would probably be to measure the system on the basis of staff cost per program or per programming hour.

Full-Time and Part-Time Systems

Dedicated systems are designed to operate full-time. The assumption is that the level of program activity will be great enough to keep staff busy at all desirable times and that the financial commitment of dedicated staff, facilities, and possibly transport will be justified by the volume of programming. The alternative to buying a dedicated system is to fund an *on-demand* system, in which all components are structured to be turned on and off as needed. This approach can be cost-effective as an interim step toward a dedicated system. However, system managers will need to think carefully about the commitment of staff and fiscal resources required to implement such a strategy.

System Reliability

Ensuring system reliability is the curse of the telecommunications manager. This problem is typical of units that rely heavily on electronic technology to deliver a product. Any program that depends almost entirely on a complex technical infrastructure is subject to some degree of failure. The way to minimize system failure is to have a good cushion or "fail-safe" margin, which can be maximized in two ways: quality equipment and redundancy. It is wise to purchase equipment with a good record of reliability and repairability, from a company with an excellent service contract. In addition, either built-in redundant hardware or spare parts should be kept on hand for the inevitable breakdown. This back-up strategy will have associated costs (typically 10 to 20 percent of annual capital equipment expenses), but they will be some of the best dollars spent on the system.

At this point a sense of the relative costs of different components of the system, as listed at the beginning of the chapter, should be emerging. The transition from narrowband audio and computer technologies to the various video technologies includes a significant increase in costs caused by the need for more sophisticated equipment, larger staffs, and broadband transport. Nevertheless, these relatively expensive technologies are much in demand and are being used by a substantial number of educational institutions and corporate training units. Video is perceived by many people to be nearly mandatory for instructional effectiveness. Moreover, it is much easier to gain support for telecommunications systems with a video component. This component also opens the system up to more applications.

Just as the computer industry experienced a major decline in costs, we are seeing a similar decline in the costs of delivering video. Research in recent years on delivery of a quality video image over existing telephone lines (compressed video) promises a series of breakthroughs in the 1990s that should drastically cut costs at the same time that image quality improves. The industry has already seen significant strides in the rapidly advancing field of compression technology. Based on data for the period 1982–1990 (Schwartz, 1991), the cost of T-1 transport (bandwidth equivalent to twenty-four individual telephone lines) for compressed videoconferencing dropped 60 percent. If you are in the early stages of implementing an educational telecommunications system, these new developments can be a part of your system. The rapid evolution of this entire field is one of the reasons why actual equipment and transport prices are not provided.

Relating Organizational and Fiscal Objectives

Matkin (1985, p. 13) states that "the budget system must be consistent with the managerial philosophy governing the organization and must be designed with a clear idea of the organizational structure." We believe that this statement also expresses the reciprocity of purpose that must exist between the parent organization housing the telecommunications unit and the educational telecommunications system itself.

Since the creation of the system springs from the needs of the parent organization, the organization should be expected to articulate its goals and objectives for the system, preferably as part of the institutional strategic plan. In turn, the system's manager must keep the unit in tune with the current and long-term vision held by the institution. James C. Votruba expresses this in an effective fashion when he describes the relationship of continuing education units to the parent organization: "Thus the challenge for continuing education leaders, as for the leaders of all other organizational subunits, seems clear. They must relate their activities to the essential priorities of their parent organization if they are to achieve organizational support and centrality. If this is true, then continuing education agencies serve two fundamental and equally important constituencies. They serve adult students, on whom they depend for their credit and noncredit enrollments, and they also serve their parent organization, which they depend on for staffing, budget, program approval, and ultimately, their existence. To lose touch with either constituency is to court disaster" (Simerly and Associates, 1987, pp. 187–188). This synergy of purpose should become the basis for establishing the position of the system in the parent organization. Will the system be a stand-alone service for all units of the parent organization? Or will it be a center within a larger but related functional unit such as a division of continuing education, a corporate training unit, or a media services center?

Once structural issues are settled, budget expectations can be established. If the system will provide core services for the parent organization, it should logically be expected to receive sufficient funding to be a *subsidized system*. The fiscal structure would be an expenditure budget with no revenue expectations. Later in the chapter we will review this situation, as well as others, in some detail. A different set of fiscal expectations exists if the system is intended to expand the organization's programs and services and create its own revenue base. In that case it will necessarily have to be a *self-supporting system*. In some instances the organization may be expected to provide certain basic support to the system such as facilities, a waiver of overhead charges, some equipment, or core staff. This is the compromise situation of *partial subsidy*. The institution may justify a permanent partial subsidy if the system generates services for the organization, or it may provide a temporary partial subsidy in order to give the system an opportunity to establish fiscal stability. In all of these cases, however, the parent organization's structure and management philosophy must be consistent with and supportive of the telecommunications system's fiscal objectives.

Budget Components

This section presents six components of budgets that are relevant to educational telecommunications systems. These budget components can be thought of as "subbudgets," dealing with various formats or purposes. They will be integrated in the summary of this chapter as examples of a master budget. Matkin (1985) provides a useful approach to this concept in his discussion on understanding budgets and establishing budgetary systems:

1. A *program budget* is a line-item budget of expenditures and revenue for a single organized activity that is usually self-supporting.
2. A *program center budget* is a composite of related line-item program budgets under one manager for a specific time period, usually one year.
3. *Service center budgets* include only line-item expenditures that are dependent on the allocation of limited resources during the budget period.
4. The *subsidy budget* is an allocation from a reserve or development fund to the center for a specific purpose, such as purchasing a major piece of equipment or underwriting a new center during the start-up period. In both cases the allocation could be spent over more than one year.

5. A *capital equipment budget* plans for the generation and expenditure of funds for capital items (educational telecommunications system hardware, in our example) that should return value to the system over several budget cycles.
6. The *master budget* is all-inclusive and assembles all budgets from the various centers of the unit or division.

Expenditures

Common expenditures can be grouped into four categories: personnel, capital equipment, current expenses, and programs.

Personnel

Management personnel are primarily responsible for the planning and day-to-day operation of the system. Small on-demand systems probably require only a one-person operation, with the manager also serving as technical troubleshooter and program developer. Other specialists such as technicians are only brought in when the need arises, often on a fee-for-service basis. Dedicated systems, particularly those with multiple sites that cover large geographical service areas, will have one or more part-time or full-time technicians in addition to a manager. If the organization has an audio-video, engineering, or computer center that already has personnel on staff, the possibility of a shared or joint appointment should be explored.

A number of specialized positions exist that may or may not be vital to the system's operation. Systems committed to producing programs may employ production personnel as part of their staff or can hire them on contract from a production facility. Producers of educational programs will also want to consider contracting for instructional-design specialists who are trained to develop the best strategies for teaching and learning. Managers should make use of part-time or flexible personnel opportunities when possible.

Student workers can be a valuable and economical personnel resource. Students find working with educational telecommunications systems to be fun and a useful career development experience. They are capable of operating equipment, serving as receptionists, and performing general office tasks. Coincidentally, many telecommunications staff, surrounded by computers with word processing and electronic mail capabilities, are now doing more of their own paperwork. One of the more challenging personnel considerations is the staffing of receive sites that are distant from the main campus or office. If the receive sites are based at facilities owned and operated by other organizations, it is often useful to establish joint arrangements with those organizations.

Personnel costs (salaries and fringe benefits) for small systems, such as those that function as programming centers in continuing education units through the purchase of programs, usually have salaries in the range of 10 to 15 percent of the budget. For larger multiple-site systems, the personnel budget line item moves into the "big three" of budget expenditures, going as high as 25 to 30 percent of the budget.

Capital Equipment

This item is often the second of the three most significant expenditure categories (transport is the third). The major classifications of capital equipment include receive-site equipment such as computers, television sets, and audioconference and video projection systems; sending and receiving equipment such as CODEC or satellite uplinks and downlinks; and audio or video program production hardware. Expenditures for individual pieces of equipment can range from a few hundred dollars to over one hundred thousand dollars and are made for items with a lifetime greater than the budget period. For these reasons Matkin (1985, p. 356) considers capital equipment budgeting somewhat unique. First, major capital purchases obligate an organization to a long-range plan of action over many years. Second, as discussed previously, it is vital for the parent organization's strategic plan to put the educational telecommunications system at or near the top of its priority list. If ill-defined priorities were to cause a sudden shift away from educational telecommunications, expensive equipment might be shelved.

Thus, the financial issue of committing the outflow of current value (cash) in exchange for future benefits is an important consideration.

Following is an example of one strategy for minimizing the impact of major capital expenditures. Assume that the system's manager has one-time access to reserve or grant funds to purchase a needed major piece of equipment for $60,000. Two fiscal considerations to address are the impact on future budgets and replacement costs. The manufacturer reports that the equipment has an "operating lifetime" of five years. This suggests the need to accumulate $12,000 a year (perhaps through user fees), ideally in an interest-bearing reserve account to help cover likely price increases due to inflation. It could be that simple. Next, assume that the current literature reports that upcoming technical developments will badly date the equipment in three years. Thus, the equipment has a "useful lifetime" of three years. Now is the time to negotiate a trade-in clause in the contract with the seller. Assume that a 25 percent trade-in, or $15,000, is possible after three years. In addition, an annual increase of 8 percent, to take into account new developments and inflation, should cover the cost of the new piece of equipment at $75,000. Subtracting the trade-in of $15,000 yields $60,000, which would require an annual addition of about $20,000 to the system's reserve in order to buy the new model.

By taking advantage of the useful or operating lifetime to pay the system back for major capital purchases, a system manager can level out periodic peaks in expenditures. Nevertheless, capital equipment can account for a significant percentage of the system's total expenditures, perhaps 15 to 30 percent of the capital budget.

Current Expenses

An inventory of current expenses for an educational telecommunications system looks similar to most current expense lists:

> Dues and fees
> Facilities maintenance

Books and periodicals
Postage and freight
Travel
Contract services
Equipment maintenance
Telephone service
Public relations
Equipment, noncapital
Office supplies
Equipment lease
Transport
Computer use
Overhead

Some of these expenditures deserve attention.

Notable on the list is "transport." This has the potential for being the third big expense item, particularly for broadband video systems. Satellite transponder rental, for example, can range from $200 to $600 an hour. If the system uses telephone lines for transport, the rates will vary based on distance and bandwidth. These rates can mount up if dedicated leased lines are used, particularly for compression systems. Transport expenses in the range of 15 to 25 percent are not unusual. "Postage and freight" are also forms of transport. This item should be analyzed if moving significant numbers of tapes or printed material is part of the system activity. Another item of importance to telecommunications systems is "equipment maintenance." Assume about 10 percent for annual upkeep. The "equipment, noncapital" item is only noteworthy in that most hardware inevitably will require special tools for routine maintenance and adjustments.

The other current expenses (often referred to as OCE) are fairly routine. Here are summary comments on these items, pointing out special considerations:

- Dues and fees, books and periodicals, travel, contract services. Fund these items at normal levels to assure that staff can keep current with the field.

- Facilities maintenance. This item can be a consideration if sensitive equipment requires a controlled environment. Most telecommunications equipment, however, is reasonably hardy.
- Equipment lease. This can become substantial if the decision is made to lease or lease-purchase equipment rather than make an outright capital equipment purchase.
- Telephone service. There is a potential for elevated usage if staff need to communicate routinely across a multisite system. Educational telecommunications systems can avoid this cost if they are renting dedicated phone lines, which can be used for fax, phone, or E-mail.
- Computer use. This has a potential for significant expenditures if computer applications are an integral part of the system. Managers should anticipate this early in the planning process.
- Office supplies, public relations, and overhead tend to be routine expenditure items in telecommunications systems.

Without substantial transport expenses, the aggregate of all current expenses can amount to 30 to 45 percent of the budget. If transport is substantial, the total impact on expenses may be 45 to 55 percent.

Programs

Programming activity should be treated as a separate budget center either within the educational telecommunications system or separately from it if telecommunications is intended to be an autonomous support unit. This approach makes it easier to determine the financial success or failure of individual programs. The telecommunications system may or may not be directly responsible for the development and implementation of the programs it delivers. Even if it does not manage the programs directly, its managers will nevertheless work closely with programming centers, since the system is the primary delivery mechanism. If the system is self-supporting, the manager will charge programming units a "user fee" for the services provided.

This revenue source will be discussed in the next section of this chapter.

Since educational telecommunications systems usually serve existing continuing education or training units, which often have resident expertise, it is not necessary to spend much time on program expenditures. The most common program expenditure categories, or line items, are:

Instruction
Promotion
Programmer's time
Program licenses
Facilities
Telecommunications user fee
Program materials
Refreshments

Revenue

This section considers a number of potential revenue sources for educational telecommunications systems. Each organization will be somewhat unique in the revenue mix it will develop to support its system. The probability of developing a given revenue source will vary, depending on the organizational priority for telecommunications, the availability of discretionary funds, the revenue potential of planned programs, and the possibility of secondary sales of program products. In any case, it is likely that the system will run on "montage funding," an approach that uses a variety of revenue sources; ten possible sources are described here. The order of the list is arranged so that systems in the start-up phase should look closely at items 1–4; newly established systems can legitimately consider items 1–5 (item 5 incorporates three options); and mature systems can explore items 1–8.

Item 1. General Funds

These funds are allocated by the parent organization for normal operating expenses. The system's manager can make a case for these funds on an annual basis if the system is a priority in the organization's strategic plan and if it will expand the organization's core programs or activities. Alternatively, if the system is expected to create its own revenue base, managers could ask for a one-time allocation as seed money.

Item 2. Reserve or Development Funds

In addition to general funds, most organizations hold a reserve for special needs or emergency situations. Occasionally funds are also set aside each year in a development fund. Continuing education divisions, for example, usually try to maintain a reserve or development fund of their own. If the system is to be a part of, or closely aligned with, continuing education, it would be logical for the continuing education leadership to commit a portion of these set-aside dollars to help get the system going. Because an often-used general rule in continuing education is that it takes about three years to get a new program running at maximum effectiveness, the manager should make the case for a three-year decreasing level of support from development money.

Item 3. Grants

The manager should explore all options for funding from federal, state, and private grant programs. This possibility can be investigated with the parent organization's grants office, and visits with nearby organizations that have developed an educational telecommunications system can provide the manager with information about their experience. Obtaining a start-up grant to fund equipment is another common approach. If there is no statewide leadership or system in place, the parent organization can take a proactive role in developing an agenda for educational telecommunications to serve rural learners and populations isolated from needed academic programs. If activity is taking place, the manager can see how the parent organization can play a role. This agenda might lead to state funds for the system. A good resource for information on telecommunications activity in the western states, for example, is the Western Interstate Commission on Higher Education (WICHE) in Boulder, Colorado. Chapter Ten provides information on other organizations that can be helpful. Funding from business and industry is also a possibility. Corporations or independent foundations could become interested in the project, especially if the telecommunications system would serve the same people to whom these organizations sell a product or service. The parent organization's library or grants office should carry reference materials that describe the funding priorities for most foundations.

Item 4. Reallocation of Current Expenses

As earlier chapters point out, one of the reasons for the creation of telecommunications systems is to reduce the time and expenses of faculty and staff travel to teach and support off-site programs. A dollar saved is a dollar that can be reallocated. These savings will not cover the cost of a telecommunications system, but it is hard to deny the system's right to request travel savings to cover a portion of its expenditures. Savings can be identified for air and automobile travel, meals, and lodging. For example, if $1,500 is normally needed to cover instructor travel to teach a program across the state, telecommunications-based education can allow the $1,500 to be reallocated to support the system.

Item 5. User Fees for Programs

One of the primary reasons for the creation of educational telecommunications systems is to deliver programs to distant sites or to dispersed locations within an organization. Regardless of who implements the program for the organization, a user fee should be assessed for the right to use the system, which consumes resources such as staff time, equipment wear, and transport. Those resources must be replenished or supported. The main exception is a system that is entirely subsidized by the parent organization.

Two approaches to calculate user fees follow. The simplest method is to assess a "flat charge" determined by dividing the annual budget for the entire educational telecommunications system by the total number of usable operating hours in a year. In the first example, a system has an annual budget of $300,000. The system is available 12 hours a day Monday through Friday and 10 hours on Saturday, totaling 70 hours a week, or 3,500 hours for a fifty-week year. It is impossible to attain 100 percent scheduling of the system, so no more than an 80 percent utilization rate should be projected, yielding 2,800 hours. Spreading the annual budget over the hours utilized ($300,000/2,800 hours) gives an hourly flat charge of $107.14 per program per hour.

A more equitable structure is to create a "rate card" for the services the system provides. In this example each of the system's distinct services is defined; its hourly rate is then established as it was in the earlier example. Suppose the system in the previous example offers five different telecommunications services, one of which is a videoconferencing facility that includes use of a satellite downlink, meeting room, and technical staff support. Of the total budget of $300,000, it is determined that videoconferencing expends $90,000 a year but is available for only 1,200 hours a year. The rate card would then show a charge of $75 per hour ($90,000/1,200 hours) for videoconferencing.

A final consideration in setting rates is the possibility of having a sliding scale of rates dependent on the purpose of the program:

1. The lowest rate is for programs developed by the educational telecommunications system for the system's programming center.
2. The medium rate is for programs done for other units in the parent organization.
3. The highest rate is for programs contracted to external organizations.

How do expenses charged to learners, such as tuition and fees, fit into this discourse on revenue sources? It would be tempting to add "tuition and fees" as a separate entry in the list of revenue sources. Learners, however, pay for the opportunity to participate in an organized learning experience. Tuition and fees are meant to cover the costs of the total program, only one of which is the expense of using the educational telecommunications system. The program manager therefore turns part of the program's revenue over to the system manager as a user fee, even though the funds started out as tuition and fees. In smaller on-demand systems, the program center may be the same as the system and the two budgets can be folded together. However, it is recommended that the two be kept separate in order to better track individual expense demands against revenue. Review the master budget in the summary section for this chapter to see how this is handled.

Item 6. Contracts and Consulting

A relatively small percentage of postsecondary institutions and corporations currently have a significant educational telecommunications capability. In a recent survey, NUCEA reports on eighty-seven colleges and universities that are "using telecommunications technology either to extend instruction to adult learners off campus or to bring instruction to campus" (National University Continuing Education Association, 1988, Foreword). This is about 19 percent of the total membership of NUCEA, an organization that represents the most active cadre of four-year, postsecondary institutions involved in telecommunications-based education across the nation. This suggests that there is an excellent opportunity for the staff of mature educational telecommunications systems to share their knowledge and expertise through contracted work or consulting. If this is done in a systematic fashion, some revenue can accrue as part of the base budget.

Item 7. Research

The significant growth of educational telecommunications systems and applications in addition to the influx of new electronic technologies implies that there are ample research opportunities for staff and faculty involved in instruction on these systems. As with contracts and consulting, system operating costs can be written into funded research projects.

Item 8. Product Sales

Systems involved in producing programs also produce a variety of products such as instructional and application materials, audio- and videotaped courses or lessons, and training guides. Any of these products may have a sales potential, particularly if the content has wide appeal or demand. However, there are some practical considerations in this type of activity. How long will the content be current? The time between program development, production, and marketing can be substantial. Will the program still be salable? Managers should also become familiar with the ownership rules or regulations established by the organization as they start to plan for the development of such products.

Table 6.1 shows how montage funding, over a four-year period, can take advantage of a combination of revenue sources to establish a fiscal base that will support a new educational telecommunications system.

Summary

In this concluding section various components of budgets that have been examined in this chapter are integrated. Examples are given of three master budgets (the all-inclusive budget that aggregates all component budgets) for three educational telecommunications systems: a subsidized service center, part of a self-supporting program center, and a self-supporting centralized service.

Table 6.1. Example of Montage Funding.

| Revenue Source | Percentage of Funding | | | |
	Year 1	Year 2	Year 3	Year 4
Organization's reserve	35	20	10	0
Grant	40	30	10	0
Resource reallocation	5	10	15	20
User fees	20	40	60	70
Product sales	0	0	5	10
	100	100	100	100

The Subsidized Service Center

This kind of educational telecommunications system was defined earlier as one that is essential to the core mission of the parent organization. It provides funding in exchange for the expectation of service to all units in the organization. As a result there is no revenue budget and no program budget.

The subsidized service center may be an autonomous unit in the parent organization, or it may be established as a new function of an existing media services center. This is a common structure found in postsecondary institutions and also in K–12 school districts. Services provided by such a center can include access to audioconferencing equipment or to the parent organization's satellite downlink.

The budget process for a system functioning as a subsidized service center involves the development and submission of the annual budget request to the administration of the parent organization. Following the allocation of general funds to the center, the center's manager oversees the distribution of these resources. The budget planning process can become more involved if the manager also hopes to get a grant funded or proposes to access additional general funds through a reallocation of resources. In these situations the manager should consider submitting a master budget with three sections, each one with its own work plan and budget. In this case the master budget might be summarized in the following example.

Subsidized Service Center Master Budget

Section A. Basic operating budget request
  1.   Personnel expenditures, 25–30 percent of budget
         Management staff
         Technical staff
         Instructional designer
         Student help
  2.   Capital equipment, 15–30 percent of budget
         Current-year purchases
         To Center reserve (from multiyear plan, roll forward funds)

3. Current expenses, 45–55 percent of budget
   Dues
   Facilities maintenance
   Books and periodicals
   Postage and freight
   Travel
   Contract services
   Equipment maintenance
   Telephone service
   Equipment, noncapital
   Office supplies
   Transport
4. Summary page of basic operating budget request

Section B. Grant project budget
   1. Project expenditures (to be listed using format above)
   2. Project grant funds requested in proposal
      Funds requested from funding source
      Matching funds requested from own organization
   3. Summary page of grant project budget

Section C. Reassignment of educational specialist to educational telecommunications to instruct on system (sample of a reallocation of funds project)
   1. Project expenditures
      Instructional salary and benefits
      Special instructional materials
      Computer software for student learning modules
      Reception for community leaders to view project
      Travel to receive sites (for limited face-to-face sessions)
   2. Project funds requested
      Funds from receive sites (4 × 20 percent of expenditures charged per site)
      Twenty percent of expenditures from parent organization
   3. Summary page of educational specialist project

In the educational specialist project, the parent organization pays for 20 percent of the instruction rather than 100 percent and obtains the remaining 80 percent through fees charged to four receive sites.

The Self-Supporting Program Center

Earlier, the relationship of the program budget to the telecommunications budget was reviewed. In this example we will work with a common programming structure. As is frequently the case, a self-supporting program center in a continuing education or corporate training unit sees a need to develop an educational telecommunications system capability to support its current programming options, add new programs, or expand its ability to reach a larger learner market. This type of system is often an on-demand audioconference system or a satellite downlink.

A desirable master budget structure for this situation is attained by combining individual budgets for each program run by the center during the budget period, such as those presented in the "programs" category in the section on budget components. First, the center has budgets for programs that are not using the educational telecommunications system. Second, each program using the system needs to incorporate items such as the appropriate system expenditures, program license, and telecommunications user fees. Third, the center incorporates an annual budget for the telecommunications system itself. The net result is a master budget for the center driven by the three kinds of budgets, which are interrelated to ensure that the sum of the telecommunications-related expenditures from all the programs using the system provides sufficient revenue to run the system each year.

Self-Supporting Program Center Master Budget

Section A. Budget for *X* programs without telecommunications component

1. Expenditures
    Instruction
    Promotion
    Programmer's time
    Facilities

2. Revenue
    Learner tuition and fees or grant, co-sponsor funds, and other sources

Program materials
Refreshments
Overhead

Section B. Budget for *Y* programs with telecommunications component

1. Expenditures
    Instruction
    Promotion
    Programmer's time
    Facilities
    Program materials
    Refreshments
    Program license (if
        required)
    Telecommunications
        user fee
    Overhead

2. Revenue
    Student tuition and
        fees or grant, co-
        sponsor funds, and
        other sources

Section C. Educational telecommunications system annual budget

1. Expenditures (stan-
        dard items)
    Personnel
    Capital equipment
    Current expenses

2. Revenue
    Telecommunications
        user fees from *Y*
        programs

The Self-Supporting Centralized Service

This configuration is a variation of the previous example. The major difference is that the system in this example is designed to serve a number of units. It is probably a stand-alone functional unit representing the category of large, dedicated educational telecommunications systems. In this case the master budget is a more elaborate version of Section C from the preceding example. Many of the budget situations described in this chapter come into play here. The capital budget is probably sizable and requires a multiyear approach. The system is dedicated and will require substantial full-time staff, dedicated facilities, possibly dedicated transport, support of field sites, a variety of services for a mixture of clients, and a montage of revenue sources.

Self-Supporting Centralized Service Master Budget

Section A. Central site budget

1. Expenditures
    Personnel (all types, to support management, production, instructional design, 25–30 percent of budget)
    Capital equipment budget (both current year and roll forward, for entire system, 15–30 percent of budget)
    Current expenses (all categories including dedicated transport, 45–55 percent of budget)

2. Revenue (a montage; see Revenue section)
    General funds
    User fees
    Reserve
    Reallocations
    Contracts and consulting
    Research
    Product sales

Section B. Field site budgets (one per site)

1. Expenditures
    Field site personnel
    Current expenses (site rental and overhead to central budget could be significant)

2. Revenue
    User fees of all types

Educational telecommunications system budgets can only be developed after organizations have decided on the programs to be delivered, the learners to be served, and the system design. The role the system will play in meeting the parent organization's goals will determine where it fits in the organization's future and the degree of institutional financial support versus the amount of external support it will obtain.

Like system design, budget design evolves in a unique fashion. The system manager must balance organizational priorities, learners' needs, and educator preferences when defining the system's technical characteristics and judging its financial viability. Careful integration of these issues should move the manager toward successful introduction and implementation of telecommunications-based education as a growth area for the organization.

Developing
a Marketing Strategy

Myth: Marketing telecommunications-based education involves marketing a universal product to a mass audience.

Reality: Telecommunications-based education is a value-added product for certain segments of the marketplace. Marketing this product requires good strategic marketing principles in terms of product design, price, distribution, and promotion, but also involves some specific considerations related to the nature of telecommunications-based education.

Marketing telecommunications-based education can resemble a trip through a hall of mirrors. Uncertain about how to formulate an overall marketing strategy or promote the product to potential consumers, the system manager may achieve success only by chance. This chapter focuses on applying a marketing philosophy to the integration of telecommunications-based education within an existing educational program. In doing so it draws upon Kotler's definition of marketing as "a social process by which individuals and groups obtain what they need and want through creating and exchanging products and value with others" (1984, p. 4). In this context the term *marketing* encompasses "the overall process of studying, analyzing, and making decisions about how to best serve the consumers" (Simerly and Associates, 1989, p. 10) and includes the selection and design of products as well as the "sale" of the product to the consumer.

Throughout this discussion the term *product* is used to denote the educational programming service, both content and delivery, that is being offered as telecommunications-based education. The term *consumer* or *learner* is used to denote the person who participates in the educational activities, whereas the person who has the responsibility for making decisions related to the system is referred to as the *manager* or *marketer*.

We begin with a description of the evolution of increasingly sophisticated strategies that put concerns about effectively segmenting the marketplace at the forefront of strategic marketing. A suggested framework for segmenting the marketplace provides the backdrop for decisions related to product design, price, distribution, and promotion. Special attention is drawn to identifying the elements of an effective promotional message and to providing quality service.

The Evolution of Marketing Strategy

Marketing strategy has undergone a radical transformation as a result of changes in society and the evolution of technology. The earliest ideas about marketing involved using media to sell a universal product in a mass market. The marketer's dream product was one that no one could resist. The 1950s and 1960s were the heyday of this mass marketing approach; however, the 1970s saw an emphasis on extending product lines by introducing design modifications to meet the specialized needs of increasingly smaller segments of the market. By the end of the 1980s, the days of selling the same product to virtually everyone were gone, and the emphasis had shifted from satisfying general needs to fulfilling the needs and tastes of individual consumers by supplying them with customized products and services.

The development of a marketing strategy for telecommunications-based education parallels the evolution of marketing strategy as a whole. A close examination of the strategies of many early telecommunications efforts reveals a vision of selling a centrally produced product to a large-scale market. Many of the early champions of broadcast television as a delivery system for education, for example, regarded the medium to be the key to providing access for many who had been denied such opportunities in the past (Davis, 1963). They regarded higher education as a universal product that was highly desirable to a vast audience. To these enthusiasts, electronic technology was a means of removing barriers to participation, thereby tapping vast new markets.

Needs-assessment efforts seemed to indicate that large numbers of individuals wanted additional educational opportunities, but the mass marketing strategy met with limited success. Often the product offered did not match what the marketplace desired. Too often it consisted of isolated courses, rather than complete programs leading to a specific educational goal such as a degree or certificate. In addition, various barriers to participation, such as inadequate learning skills, competition for time, and insufficient finances, could not be overcome by technology. In retrospect, these early marketing strategies failed to deliver the desired product and underestimated the barriers to participation. Consequently, the size of the audiences attracted to many early programs was disappointing (Van Kekerix, 1986).

By the 1980s the concept of market segmentation, defined as "the process of partitioning markets into segments of potential customers with similar characteristics who are likely to exhibit similar purchase behavior" (Weinstein, 1987, p. 4), was increasingly being applied to marketing telecommunications-based education. Successful strategies usually offered an extended product line to a highly targeted audience. Complete engineering graduate programs delivered via technology, for example, were marketed within geographic areas where the population density of engineers was high. Similarly, sizable audiences were found for courses delivered via broadcast television to segments of the market who were unable to pursue degree programs through other means. Thus, managers who found a way to segment the market to match a specific product with a specific group greatly improved their chances for success.

Segmenting the Marketplace

Although appropriate segmentation of the potential market is often regarded as the key to marketing success, there is no single correct way to accomplish the task (Tarr, 1989). The potential combinations and permutations of segmentation are virtually limitless, and often the most useful form is based on a combination of several variables. There are, however, some major dimensions that should be considered in a market analysis.

Geographical Analysis

Geographical segmentation of the potential market for a specific system may be approached from very different perspectives depending upon the system's stage of development. If it is still in the design stages, its selection of technologies may be driven by the geographical distribution of a specific potential audience. For example, the professional association that wishes to design a system to provide educational opportunities for its membership will want one that can reach its audience wherever it may be located.

On the other hand, there are circumstances in which the geographical scope of the potential market is predetermined. For example, the selection of a particular form of technology may act as a limiting factor. A manager may have access to an ITFS system, but because these systems provide line-of-sight transmission of television signals over a limited area, they incorporate certain geographical limitations.

Technology may not be the only limiting factor in determining the geographical scope of the potential market. An institution may have a limited service area as set forth by its charter, its governing board, or its leadership. In such a case, the ability of certain forms of technology to reach audiences outside the service area may not be relevant.

Development of an educational telecommunications system can also redefine the geographical scope of the marketplace for a specific product. For example, an educational program offered to a local market in a traditional classroom format can be offered to a wider potential audience with an ITFS broadcast system; access to a statewide television network expands the geographical scope of the potential market to encompass the entire state. By the same token, broadcasting television via satellite can enlarge the geographical scope even further to include a national or even an international audience.

A major consideration in analyzing the potential geographical expansion of the market must be an assessment of the risks involved in offering the program to the expanded audience. Unfortunately, it is often difficult to resist the temptation to focus exclusively on the promise of a greatly expanded market without a careful consideration of other factors. In general, any expansion will increase the costs of promotional activities. For example, if the major promotional effort involves direct mail, the printing and mailing costs will increase because the pieces will need to be dispersed to a wider audience than before. In addition, extension of programming to wider audiences usually increases the complexity of the coordination tasks involved. Materials for learners must be distributed over a wider area, technical coordination may become more complex, and new relationships with receive sites will need to be developed. Each factor increases the cost involved in offering the product.

Expansion of the geographical scope can also affect other marketing considerations. For example, institutional loyalty may be an important factor in marketing success within a restricted area, but it may be a significantly smaller factor at the regional or national level. In fact, in the expanded marketplace the manager must overcome a tendency to look toward local resources for educational programming and must carefully balance the increased risks of market expansion against the potential benefits to both the provider and the consumer.

Demographic Analysis

The demographics of the marketplace must also be taken into account. Demographic segmentation divides the market into groups on the basis of ten variables: age, sex, family size, family life cycle, income, occupation, education, religion, race, and nationality (Tarr, 1989). Its key assumption is that age and stage of life have a direct correlation with certain consumer needs and wants. By becoming familiar with the demographic makeup of the population, the marketer can begin to make assumptions about consumer behavior with a greater degree of accuracy. For example, knowledge about a population's sex composition and marital status can lead to reasonable assumptions about the potential market for telecommunications-based education based on what is known about the needs and habits of similar populations. By analyzing demographic data, the marketer can determine what program benefits are likely to be most valued and can attempt to match those benefits with the characteristics of the proposed system and the content of its programming.

If, for example, the program is restricted to a particular area that includes a large number of young married couples with children, the system might be geared toward offering undergraduate courses via broadcast television, under the assumption that a significant number of women would find such a program attractive as a means of pursuing educational goals while simultaneously fulfilling familial obligations. However, it is not enough simply to know that such a group exists within the market area. The marketer will also want to find out as much as possible about this group through psychographic and behaviorist data in order to more specifically gear the system and its offerings to the characteristics of the group.

Psychographic Analysis

At one time an understanding of the demographic data about a geographical area would allow the marketer to make some reasonably accurate assumptions about the life-style of the people living there. However, American society has become so fragmented that it is no longer possible to make assumptions based on demographics alone. To know the market, the analysis must move beyond demographics to *psychographics* — the use of activities, opinions, and ways of living as a means of describing consumers. Psychographic segmentation is based upon people's beliefs, opinions, hopes, fears, prejudices, needs, desires, and aspirations and is usually expressed in a life-style (Mitchell, 1983).

For example, the psychographic characteristics of engineers make them a particularly attractive market for telecommunications-based education and training. They are unlikely to be intimidated by the technology, they are more likely to be tolerant of occasional delivery system failures, and they frequently have had previous experience with similar systems. Psychographic information can play an important role in reducing the risk in offering telecommunications-based education; however, psychographic analyses also have their shortcomings. Individuals often do not fit into neat categories. The marketer who relies exclusively on data analysis and makes assumptions based on those data may be surprised by the stubborn refusal of people to fit into a particular category.

Behavioristic Analysis

Behavioristic data can also provide valuable information about the potential market for telecommunications-based education, including information regarding volume segmentation, user-status segmentation, benefit segmentation, and loyalty segmentation. *Volume segmentation* involves identifying those clients who are the heaviest users of existing educational programming, finding out as much as possible about them, and then attempting to identify people with similar demographic and psychographic characteristics who could be served by the educational telecommunications system. *User-status segmentation* provides a means for classifying users as nonusers, ex-users, potential users, first-time users, or regular users of a product. Knowledge about the user status of a particular segment provides a means of assessing the potential of additional audiences.

Benefit segmentation is used to identify the specific benefits a consumer might seek from the product. Is he or she seeking job advancement? Is convenience a key factor in a decision to become a consumer? Often the psychographic data discussed above are directly correlated to benefit segmentation. *Loyalty segmentation,* on the other hand, reflects the degree of loyalty a consumer has toward a particular product or provider and has important implications for an institution with a reputation for providing high-quality educational programming in a particular field or within a particular geographical area.

Behavioristic segmentation can be helpful in providing another layer of information regarding a potential audience. For example, if the parent organization has had a traditional role of providing educational programming for teachers, behavioristic data might indicate that certain segments of the potential teacher audience are likely to be regular users, that those who received their undergraduate education from the organization already have some loyalty to it, and that convenience of access ranks high as a benefit.

Taken together, geographical, demographic, psychographic, and behavioristic analysis can provide a great deal of information about the potential market for any educational telecommunications effort. This discussion has used geographical scope as a starting point, but in some cases this may not be appropriate. The best starting point is often determined by the characteristics of the system and by the nature of the parent institution. In any case, the key to success lies in knowing as much as possible about the potential audience and designing an educational product that fits its geographical scope, demographics, psychographics, and behavior. Yet analysis of the potential market is only one step of the process.

Determining an Effective Marketing Mix

The manager of an educational telecommunications system must draw upon the analysis of the potential market to select an appropriate market mix that matches considerations of product, price, distribution, and promotion with the characteristics of that market. In other words, the product must match the needs of both the producer and the consumer and be priced appropriately for them. It also must be distributed so that it is within convenient reach of a sufficient number of consumers, and the producer must be able to communicate its benefits in a way that stimulates its use. Each of these considerations has important implications for the manager.

Product

For a product to be attractive to both the consumer and the producer, there must be a match between what the consumer wants and what the producer wishes or is able to produce. From the manager's perspective, there are several broad criteria by which telecommunications-based educational products and systems can be evaluated. Kotler (1984) suggests that the most important consideration is the degree of fit between the product's characteristics and the mission and purpose of the parent organization, the product's long-range potential, the visibility likely to be generated, and the ability of the organization to successfully mount the effort.

Assume, for example, that the parent organization has a statewide mission to provide professional development programming for nurses. In such a case, a continuing education program for nurses that could reach this audience at many locations would fit within the mission, would have the long-range potential of being a conduit for other types of medical training, and would enhance the visibility of the parent organization. Theoretically, the parent organization should have the academic resources to provide the program, although its existing resources might be insufficient to take on this expanded role. Depending on the technical environment, there might also be some question about whether the needed support for the system itself could be provided. However, the chances of acquiring the needed resources are much better in these circumstances than in one where nursing education is not considered to be a part of the organizational mission.

There are many ways to test the degree of fit between a proposed product and the parent organization. In Chapter Three, for example, the need to align a proposal with the cultural-ideological, political, and technical environment of the parent organization was strongly emphasized. These assessments can be very helpful in evaluating fit. Some suggest that the manager use a grid to plot the degree of match (see Hanna, 1989). If there is no match, the product is unlikely to be successful. The manager must then work to create a more favorable environment for the product or turn to the development of a different product that more closely matches the organization's needs and capabilities.

If there is a match between the product and the parent organization, the analysis should shift to determining how the product is likely to fit within the marketplace. Here the manager can draw extensively upon geographical, demographic, psychographic, and behavioristic data to determine what combination of educational content and system characteristics would have the greatest probability of success. When the target audience is known, one means of reducing risk is to include audience representatives in the design and development stages. Such a group can provide very helpful information early enough in the process so that adjustments can be made in the system and the educational product. Ultimately, however, one must go into the market with the product to find out how well it will be received.

Price

Much information is already available on how to determine the price of an educational product (see Matkin, 1985). In simple terms, competition usually sets the price ceiling, whereas costs determine the price floor. Price, however, may also be influenced by a variety of other factors, including the goals of the parent organization, governing bodies that may regulate certain elements of the price such as tuition rates, and the overall funding patterns of the providing organization. For example, an organization whose goal is to provide an educational service for a widely dispersed audience may find its ability to set a price restricted by a governing board; it may therefore decide to fund the difference from other sources rather than solely through income from program participants.

Since individual programs vary so widely in terms of costs, financing methods, and program goals, this discussion will focus on some of the more common special dimensions of pricing as they relate to telecommunications-based education. One such question is how these programs should be priced in comparison to similar programs conducted in a traditional format. In the earliest discussions of telecommunications-based education, its advocates argued that the potential for reaching a mass market would lead to lower costs and prices for the learner. In practice, however, the high cost of technology and the fragmented nature of the market for any specific educational or training program has made it difficult or impossible to realize a significant savings.

The most common pricing strategy puts the price of telecommunications-based education equal to or somewhat higher than that of traditional classroom instruction. This is particularly true if the product involves college credit, where a governing board sets tuition rates. Often the increased price is justified by the increased production or delivery costs of the telecommunications system or by the value-added nature of the programming. For instance, educational value being provided may be equal to that of the more traditional setting, but the activity may be available at more convenient times or in more convenient locations. If a learner no longer has to commute across a busy metropolitan area during rush hour, the convenience of the program is enhanced and the product has more value. In a similar fashion, education that is delivered directly to the workplace reduces time spent away from the site as well as travel costs, justifying an increased price based on increased benefits. Ultimately the pricing decision rests on a combination of the actual cost of producing and delivering the product, the benefits it provides to the consumer, and the ability of the consumer to pay.

Distribution

Educational telecommunications systems are a way to distribute educational and training opportunities to new and ongoing users of educational products. At one time most companies distributed products to consumers through a single channel — through retailers or sales agents, or by direct mail. In fact, purity of distribution was known for a time as a canon of marketing. However, today the situation is rapidly changing and the use of multiple methods of distribution has become increasingly common (Rapp and Collins, 1987). Thus, Johnson and Murphy Shoes sells its product directly to customers through the mail and through its own retail outlets, while it continues to sell to retailers. From this perspective, telecommunications-based education, along with evening classes, weekend classes, independent study, and conferences, becomes still another means of reaching the consumer of postsecondary education. Furthermore, the increasing array of options available within this field provides even more distribution possibilities.

Promotion

The most wonderful product will not be successful unless potential users become aware of its existence, understand what it will do for them, and know how and where to get it. Effective communication is the key. It is composed of two basic elements: the promotional mix, the way the message is conveyed to the potential user, and the promotional message, what is being said. Each of these will be discussed in turn.

The Promotional Mix. Selecting a promotional mix is primarily a matter of determining which of the many channels for communication might be the most effective in reaching the potential user. Among the most heavily utilized channels are direct mail marketing, paid advertising in the print and telecommunications media, and personal selling. An effective mix usually combines several different channels in an effort to maximize the opportunity to put the promotional message before potential users. (For an extensive discussion of the various elements that can comprise an effective promotional mix, see Simerly and Associates, 1989.) In every case the selection of an appropriate mix should be based on an extensive analysis of the characteristics of the potential consumers.

One unusual element of the promotional mix for many telecommunications-based educational efforts is the opportunity to collaborate with other organizations in marketing activities. Often several institutions provide programs or support services. In such cases marketing efforts are collaborative efforts between the various providers, reflecting the envisioned role of each player and requiring considerable coordination with each entity. There are many advantages to be gained in collaborative marketing efforts, including reduced costs as tasks are consolidated, higher visibility for all involved, better market analysis as the various players bring diverse resources to bear, and good public relations.

The Promotional Message. Promotional messages for telecommunications-based education are more complex than the messages for traditional face-to-face instruction. Effective promotional messages for education emphasize the benefits to be gained by the learner through participation in the learning experience. Since virtually all potential participants have firsthand knowledge of the traditional learning experience, little information about its characteristics needs to be included in the promotional message. The marketer of telecommunications-based education, on the other hand, must design a message that incorporates several additional elements.

Effective promotional messages incorporate an emphasis on the value-added nature of the learning experience being offered. In addition, they must take into account the involvement of multiple players in the decision chain that leads to participation, address questions about the educational effectiveness of the system, and completely and accurately describe the nature of the learning experience being offered.

Emphasizing the Value-Added Nature of the Product. In marketing terms, telecommunications-based education is best thought of as a value-added product — that is, a product to which benefits are added beyond those of the educational experience itself. In most cases the primary value-added characteristics are *access* and *convenience.* A connection must be made between the needs of the potential audience and the characteristics of the learning experience being offered. Here again the information gathered in the market analysis regarding the geographical, demographic, psychographic, and behavioristic characteristics of the potential audience can be very useful in identifying which benefits are likely to have the most appeal to certain segments.

A primary benefit of telecommunications-based education is access where little or none existed before. Persons living in rural areas, for example, gain access to educational opportunities that previously were not available. A person with family obligations finds that it is no longer necessary to choose between fulfilling those obligations and pursuing an educational goal. In each case the product offered is educational opportunity, but the access is made possible by the educational telecommunications system. Too often marketers ask the question: "Would you prefer to participate in a learning situation that involves traditional classroom instruction or telecommunications?" By doing so they fail to recognize the very significant barriers the learner must overcome to participate in traditional instruction. For many learners the choice is to participate via telecommunications or not participate at all.

A second benefit involves convenience to the learner. The telecommunications system may offer a variety of convenience factors. Learners may, for example, save the time they would spend commuting across a large metropolitan area during rush hour. They may also avoid the parking problem often found on campus. With some forms of telecommunications systems, learners can exercise considerable control over the schedule, continuing to meet demands on their time from other sources.

The promotional message must clarify the benefits the telecommunications system offers and explain why they are important to the learner. The primary goal of the message is to assist the learner in making an informed decision about whether the benefits are of significant value, given all the other considerations involved.

Recognizing the Role of Multiple Decision Makers. The promotional message must also take into account the nature of the decision-making process involved in moving a person from a state of awareness to actual participation. In almost every decision, more than one individual influences the outcome. As a result, to be effective, the promotional message must take into account all the concerns that might act as barriers to participation. Furthermore, the message must be tailored toward influencing as many of those who will take part in the decision-making process as possible.

For example, a spouse is often a crucial player in the decision to purchase an educational product. To the extent possible, the promotional message should address the concerns not only of the potential participant but also of others who might attempt to influence the decision. Thus, a promotional message for graduate-level education designed to appeal to both the participant and the spouse might describe the benefits of promotions that might result from completing the program. It might also stress that a minimum amount of time will need to be committed to the activity and that there will be a minimal disruption of family routines. If employers are likely to be involved in the decision-making process, the copy should emphasize that participation will make the employee more valuable. In each case the key to tailoring the promotional message is knowledge about those who make or influence the decision to participate.

Educational Effectiveness. Marketers of telecommunications-based education must address the issue of educational effectiveness in their advertising and promotional efforts. Too many gatekeepers and learners lack familiarity with such programming. Their experience lies in traditional classroom instruction and learning and they find it difficult to believe that telecommunications-based education is as "good" as its more traditional counterparts.

There are a number of ways to deal with this concern. One is to include copy that briefly cites studies substantiating the effectiveness of the system being used. Fortunately, a number of recent studies including those by Clark and Verduin (1989), Verduin and Clark (1991), and Whittington (1987) deal with this issue and can be cited within the promotional message.

Testimonials from learners and teachers who have used the system may also allay any concern about the educational experience being offered. Such endorsements can be extremely effective. If possible, the name and photograph of the person providing the commentary should be included, thereby emphasizing the human side of the system and making the claims of effectiveness more real. It is crucial to select testimonials from persons who are representative of the potential learner group whose participation is being sought. The point to be made with testimonials of this nature is that the teachers and learners who use the system are real people very much like the person who is considering participation.

Conducting focus-group interviews with prospective learners and decision makers can provide valuable guidance about the content of both the testimonials and the promotional copy in general. These interviews should be geared toward identifying the nature of the learners' concerns. For example, the learners may express concern about the amount of access to the instructor they will have during nonclass hours, their ability to fulfill class requirements involving library materials or access to computers, or the testing conditions. These concerns must then be addressed as directly as possible in the promotional copy.

Describing the Learning Experience. The marketer of telecommunications-based education must provide the prospective learner with all the information needed to make an intelligent choice about participation. There is a tendency to describe the learning experience in terms of the technology being used and the way it works rather than in terms of what the learner will actually experience. Elaborate schematic diagrams that indicate the path taken by a video or audio signal, although helpful in explaining the technology, do not describe what the learner will actually experience. Other, more direct means of describing the learning experience should also be used.

Whenever possible, photographs illustrating important aspects of the learning experience should be incorporated with the promotional materials. If, for example, learners will encounter a studio-classroom complete with television cameras and microphones, a photograph of the setting should be included in the promotional piece. If television is the primary delivery technology, a photograph of learners watching an actual presentation might be warranted. The overriding concern should be to describe and illustrate the nature of the experience in such a way that there will be no surprises.

Opportunities can also be provided for learners to observe the system in action. "Open house" demonstrations allow learners to experience the system in a nonthreatening atmosphere. Computer-assisted instruction can be demonstrated for potential learners; if the experience involves "live" television broadcast with two-way video and audio, the learners can be given an opportunity to interact with the instructor as if they were in an actual class. In short, every effort should be made to make the learners as comfortable as possible with the system.

The obligations of the marketer of telecommunications-based education are really no different from those in any other form of education (Offerman, 1987). However, since learners are less likely to have had firsthand experience with the newer forms of telecommunications systems, there is a greater need to provide complete and clear descriptions of the learning experience involved. Promotional pieces must clearly state whether the instruction is live or taped, whether it includes direct interaction with the instructor, and if this interactivity will be audio only or if it will also include two-way video. It is particularly important to avoid jargon when describing the experience since the learner is unlikely to be familiar with the terms being used. Promotional copy should be read by persons unfamiliar with the technology as a means of identifying trouble spots.

Providing Quality Service

Quality service to customers offers a key marketing edge in today's competitive environment. In the case of telecommunications-based education, the need for a service orientation is even more important than in situations where there are greater opportunities for face-to-face interaction with faculty and staff. Naisbitt (1982) and others speculate that as people interact more with technology they want additional human contact as well. Businesses have noted that customers quickly tire of dealing only with computers (Weidemann, 1989). For the manager of an educational telecommunications system, the implication is that there is a need to balance high-tech with high-touch. As many avenues for person-to-person contact should be established as possible.

Fortunately, the new technologies offer a host of options for maintaining close contact between teachers, learners, and others who are a part of the telecommunications system. When the geographical scope of the service area for the system is small, direct contact with learners for registration, advising, and instruction can be used effectively. At a minimum, the instructional staff can set aside certain times when they will be available by telephone to assist learners. Electronic bulletin boards can also be used to provide a convenient flow of information. Where learners might find it difficult to maintain contact, a student-support component can be established and a personal representative can be assigned to act as an on-campus advocate for the learner.

One of the most important elements in assessing the service orientation of the system is an analysis of the total system from the learner's perspective. The learner is followed through each step in the process from the first moment of awareness of the system through completion of the educational activities, with an eye toward eliminating or reducing any barriers or inconveniences. The goal is to try to ensure user friendliness at every step in the process.

In order to provide quality service the manager must learn as much as possible about customers' expectations and then meet or exceed those expectations (Weidemann, 1989). The primary means of learning about expectations is by collecting information at every opportunity. This includes the use of informal discussions with customers, formal interviews, surveys and assessments, and suggestion boxes. The mere presence of such instruments and the activities associated with them indicates a concern for the customer, and the information gathered in this way can be extremely valuable. In addition, the manager must look upon every problem as an opportunity to learn more about customer expectations in order to improve service.

A concern for quality service also carries over to addressing technical failures within the telecommunications system itself. There is, alas, no such thing as a failure-proof technology-based system. The technical mechanisms within these systems are often complex and therefore subject to both human error and mechanical failure. Plans must be made for handling such problems. The manager must prepare both teachers and learners for failures and indicate how the situation should be handled and what responsibilities each person has.

Learners should know how to troubleshoot the system, if that is appropriate. At a minimum they will need a way to contact key individuals if they experience difficulty. Under no circumstances should they be left unaware of what to do and when their responsibilities end. In addition, the manager should be prepared to contact learners in advance of class meetings when problems are anticipated. The emphasis must always be on providing service from the learner's point of view.

Summary

There is every indication that telecommunications-based education will play an increasingly important role in meeting the educational and training needs of people living in a learning society. This should not be understood to mean that it will supplant more traditional forms of education. From a marketing perspective, its emergence is best understood as a way to extend the educational product line to meet the special needs of additional market segments. Thus, to the managers of educational telecommunications systems, the advent of telecommunications technologies simply expands the range of choices available to match products and consumers.

The highest priority for these managers is to carefully analyze the marketplace to find matches between products that the parent organization wishes to produce and those the learner wishes to have. Skillful analysis of available geographical, demographic, psychographic, and behavioristic data can lead to the identification of promising market segments. Products must be identified, priced, distributed, and promoted by using an appropriate marketing mix of communication tools and an effective promotional message. In the promotional process, the manager must strive to empower providers and learners to choose wisely among the many available options (Cross, 1985). By clearly describing the nature of the learning experience being offered and by providing quality service that matches high-tech with high-touch, the managers of telecommunications systems can achieve strategic marketing success.

●●●●●●●●●● *Chapter* 8

Integrating Telecommunications-Based Education into the Organization

Myth: Telecommunications can be successfully integrated into existing educational programming by assigning it to a self-starter who knows how to market programming.

Reality: A sustained effort in telecommunications-based education requires collaboration across divisional lines and has less to do with marketing than with the transformation of working relationships and organizational change.

Following are two examples of initial experiences organizations might have when integrating telecommunications-based education.

A few years ago a staff member at a corporate training center decided to investigate the possibility of receiving a live-via-satellite videoconference. She had heard about satellite receiving dishes (downlinks) but had never really explored what was needed to do the job. The content of the program looked perfect for providing information related to one of the corporation's new product initiatives. And wouldn't it be terrific to be the first person in the company to arrange a satellite-delivered videoconference! The company's media center did not know much more about downlinks and teleconferences than the trainer. After some work with the telephone book and a few telephone calls the trainer found a local satellite downlink vendor who rented a portable dish on a daily basis. The vendor could do the videoconference but also pointed out the need to run cable to the meeting room and asked the distance to the room. "And by the way," the vendor asked, "do you have TV monitors?"

Back at the media center the trainer asked about monitors with the media specialist, whose background was audio and video production. She also asked where they might position the downlink. Who would know the best place? The vendor, of course. Inspiration! The trainer asked the vendor to pay a visit to the company site and put the vendor and the media specialist together to work it out. Problem solved. The trainer then called the organization presenting the videoconference and made the commitment to be a receive site. One of the items of information the trainer obtained was the phone number for calling questions in to the presenters at the origination site. Did the meeting room have a telephone jack? No. Off the trainer went to talk to the company's communications office. Clearly, the company was not prepared for videoconferencing. Although the pieces existed to do the job, there was no interrelationship between them.

A different scenario involves a state university that was in the first phase of implementing its multisite, two-way video telecommunications system. The university had chosen a compressed-video system, which uses a computer to compress and code video images for transport through telephone lines to a distant site, where the signal is decoded and viewed. Since both sites are technically equivalent, video and audio travel in both directions.

A special university event provided the continuing education unit with an opportunity to demonstrate the new system for the university's trustees and top administrators. The two sites chosen were about fifty miles apart. The continuing education office was puzzling over what activity to put on the system during the event to demonstrate its capabilities. Fortunately the college of education included instructional-design faculty, one of whom was asked to come up with a short demonstration using elementary school children. The result was a demonstration in which a music teacher at one site directed children at the other site in a round of songs. Before long the instructor had the administrators and trustees, who were with the teacher, singing along with the children. The demonstration was a huge success that looked simple to the observers.

Behind the scenes, however, the university's media services unit had been brought in to set up and operate special cameras, a computer center staff member was on hand to be sure the microcomputer platform and telephone-line multiplexers did not cause a problem, and a technician from the telephone company was ready to troubleshoot the transport system.

Do these events, which are true stories, sound familiar? If you have begun to offer telecommunications-based education, these incidents should ring true. If you are in the conceptual stage for a system, your turn may be coming. The purpose of this chapter is to show that many existing but separate organizational resources need to be coordinated or unified to serve these systems, as well as other instructional situations that will or should make use of new electronic technologies.

The development of new approaches to telecommunications-based education typically requires more than one electronic technology to be blended and thus compels organizations to rethink what media and distance-related instructional services they should provide. They must ask how those services should relate to each other to minimize the operational challenges educators will face in successfully delivering their programs.

This chapter will first review the recent history and current practices of media and technical support units in typical postsecondary institutions and will then discuss the forces that are impinging on these units. The dynamics of evolution and revolution caused by changes in the culture or growth of the parent organization will also be explored.

Finally, the case will be made for the creation of what will generically be called an *instructional-design unit*. Such a unit recognizes the convergence of electronic technologies and their applications, integrating them so that they will support broad-based instructional and training functions such as educational telecommunications systems.

Technological Functions and Common Organizational Structures

The examples in the previous section suggest that a developmental and evolutionary tension is building in many educational organizations that contain a number of traditional media, communications, computer and instructional training, or continuing education functions. This tension, which develops as a result of changing organizational needs within units that have not adapted to meet the new demands, needs to be recognized by the organization in order to avoid conflict and to take advantage of new program opportunities. The introduction of telecommunications-based education appears to be a programmatic catalyst that is forcing educators to raise questions about an apparently disjointed relationship between functions that now need to be integrated.

Traditional audio-video (AV) service units grew out of the need to provide centralized engineering support for laboratory equipment and control and maintenance of common instructional tools such as film, slide, and overhead projectors. Another frequent function is operation of radio and TV studios and editing facilities. This general description would probably characterize a majority of the AV units of the early 1960s. During the middle of the 1980s, the proliferation of videocassette recorders (VCRs) and hand-held, VCR-compatible cameras (videocams) created a new challenge and possible opportunities for AV units.

Users of the new video technology wanted quick and often daily access plus greater control of the equipment. The new equipment was easy to operate, reliable, and gave satisfactory results for most day-to-day applications. The VCR and video-cam combination was a self-contained package that was easily transported and stored, and hardware costs were within the reach of most departmental and training-unit operating budgets. This led to a decentralization of video production services. Educational units were doing their own videos in a convenient, cost-effective fashion. AV units were now being asked to service mini–video centers spread across the organization. They were also seeing a decline in the use of their own video studios. Some AV units adapted to this change and found ways to be supportive of this distributive transition. Other units have not adjusted well and still struggle with centralization versus decentralization of AV services.

A similar story can be told about the introduction of computers. Mainframe computers were well-established resources in educational and corporate environments by the early 1970s, with computer centers providing a centralized service. The advent of microcomputers put computer centers in the same situation as AV centers are in today, and managers frequently expressed concern about decentralization and duplication. However, a solution was arrived at in the form of "local area networks," which allowed users to operate their personal computer workstations as stand-alone systems or switch over to the network and access the mainframe. This development also aligned the computer center with the organization's communications unit, because of the need for copper wire to transport data and information between sites and mainframe systems. Consequently, computer centers and telephone functions became close working partners.

The last strand in the evolution of instructional support systems is the development of the discipline of instructional design. Instructional design, as summarized in Chapter Four, asks questions about what the learner currently knows, what he or she needs to know, what conditions or functions will assist in learning, and how to assess when and what has been learned.

There is a notable distinction, however, between AV services and computing functions on the one hand and instructional design on the other. Instructional design deals directly with the design and management of the learning process, whereas AV services and computers are tools to assist in the learning process itself. In addition, instructional design provides for the application or use of these tools within the discipline's process of analyzing and evaluating learners, content, and the learning environment.

Johnson and Foa (1989, p. 4) have described the basis of instructional design: "The foundations of instructional design are in the behavioral and social sciences — in particular in behavioral, developmental, social, and cognitive psychologies. Instructional design also draws upon the management sciences and engineering, having been influenced by such fields as systems analysis, operations research, management theory, and organizational development. Finally, instructional design has roots in information science, broadly interpreted to include communications, audiovisual media, information management, and computer science." The foundations of instructional design go back at least to 1900; however, the past thirty to forty years have seen a significant maturing of the field.

Currently most organizations create telecommunications-based educational programs in an ad hoc fashion. In the absence of instructional design as a resource for instructional environments, and in particular for educational telecommunications systems, learning packages tend to be created by (1) an AV specialist who translates traditional instruction to fit the medium, (2) an educator who directs the AV specialist to accommodate the instructional style demanded, or (3) a tense fusion of the two. The track record for this ad hoc approach in past programs shows a mix of successes and failures.

In addition, educators working in this ad hoc situation have been doing something for which they were not hired or trained. They may do a perfectly creditable job; nevertheless, the organization's incentive system was not devised to reward them for such a task. Subject-matter experts are also deflected from their primary job objective, and there is little incentive to get involved and to do a thorough job. Nevertheless, ad hoc approaches have worked on a limited short-term basis. Many organizations have already had the experience related at the beginning of this chapter. Perhaps it is time to consider a more productive and beneficial solution.

It is clear that by including the instructional-design discipline in the program development model, a superior product will result. Nevertheless, the creation of an instructional-design structure may require a substantial change in the organization or organizational unit. Far-sighted leadership can make the change incremental. However, if demands for suitable telecommunications-based educational programs to serve new learner markets are ignored or programs are suddenly thrust upon the organization, a more revolutionary framebreaking approach may be necessary. Whether an organization is contemplating a simple on-site system or a major, multisite regional system, instructional design has much to offer to assist the unit in meeting its program objectives.

Is it time for organizations to also consider new operational relationships between traditional units that are critical to the development and success of telecommunications systems? Perhaps what is required is a broader assessment of these related functions as suggested by an instructional-design-services model. Clearly, even without such an assessment, projects that require telecommunications-based education will force the issue, as suggested at the beginning of the chapter. Is a quiet revolution at hand?

Organizational Development and Distance-Learning Systems

In Chapter Three we considered the two basic types of change strategies: *incremental* and *framebreaking*. One element of change and change strategies not discussed as yet is *time* and the role it plays in leading to a period of substantial transformation. In the 1950s, for example, there were relatively few educational telecommunications systems, and program delivery options were limited. Correspondence study (basically a print-based system), radio schools of the air, and broadcast television courses dominated the telecommunications-based education that existed at the time. Few organizations were involved, and media centers supported the needs of the traditional classroom instructor or trainer. Other technical options were essentially nonexistent. Nontraditional learners, except for those enrolled on campus at some inner-city postsecondary institutions, were relatively small in number. During the intervening decades the student mix has changed, the technical possibilities have geometrically expanded, and institutional priorities have shifted to enfranchise the off-campus, part-time learner.

These shifting priorities and new opportunities illustrate a basic organizational principle: that management problems are rooted in time. Changing priorities and new opportunities normally call for *incremental* adjustments to the evolving environment. If incremental change does not take place, a tension develops in the organization. Tension can also occur if a sudden event has an unforeseen impact on the organization. As described in Chapter Three, this tension can be relieved through a revolutionary or *framebreaking* change.

There is a growing body of evidence (Greiner, 1972) that suggests that growing organizations and major organizational units move through similar phases of development, consisting of two components: (1) extended periods of growth or *evolution* with no major upheavals, separated by (2) periods of substantial turmoil in organizational life, labeled *revolutions*. It is important for organizational leaders to know that each phase is both an effect of the previous phase and a cause of the next phase. Moreover, evolutionary periods tend to be relatively short in fast-growing sectors such as business and industry. Longer evolutionary periods occur in mature or slower-growing sectors such as educational organizations.

The critical task for management in each revolutionary period is to find new organizational practices that will become the basis for managing the next period of evolutionary growth. An awareness of the overall evolutionary-revolutionary effect should help organizations evaluate their problems with greater historical understanding instead of pointing at a new development as the source of the problem. Better yet, organizational leadership will be in a position to predict future problems and prepare solutions in advance.

A Case for the Instructional-Design Unit

Most organizations have not yet adapted the structures and functions of their operating units to accommodate the opportunities and impact of electronic technologies. It may be time for these organizations, as part of their internal analysis, to determine their need and readiness for a redefinition of the role and function of media services and computer services; for example, they might consider merging one or both of these units with an existing or new academic instructional-design component in order to effectively support new educational or training initiatives such as an educational telecommunications system.

Because the discipline is relatively young, the literature of instructional-design systems is not extensive (Briggs and Wager, 1981; Carkhuff and others, 1984; Hannum and Hansen, 1989; Langdon, 1973; Richey, 1986; Romiszowski, 1981). Johnson and Foa (1989) have assembled a number of excellent case studies showing how the discipline of instructional design has functioned as a planning and management tool, been instrumental in the international development of telecommunications-based education, and served as the basis for an interactive-video center designed to serve industry. Keep in mind that the following selected examples represent model or large-scale projects and by no means imply that all organizations need to immerse themselves in instructional design. The first example, however, does demonstrate how a small-scale project can blossom.

Whitaker and Elsner (Johnson and Foa, 1989) review the role of instructional design as a template for change at the seven Maricopa Community College campuses. The instructional-design unit, which initially was a small center supporting the off-campus locations of the existing campuses, grew to influence the curriculum and planning mechanism of the entire system. Instructional design continues to be a catalyst for incremental change, allowing the Maricopa Community College system to remain current and relevant.

Calvert (Johnson and Foa, 1989, pp. 92–103) provides

a look at the Open University of the United Kingdom, which established a model design unit that others have followed — Everyman's University in Israel, Athabasca University in Canada, and Sukhothai Thammathirat Open University in Thailand, to name a few. Faculty members participate in course development teams with instructional designers, editors, media specialists, and educational technologists. Multimedia instructional packages include national television and radio, home experiment kits, regular regional tutorials, and a residential component at university campuses.

Finally, Doulton (in Johnson and Foa, 1989) describes the establishment in 1984 of the National Interactive Video Centre (NIVC) in Britain, which functions as an independent focal point for all organizations in the country involved in interactive video. At about the same time as the creation of NIVC, a number of corporations, Lloyds Bank, British Telecom, and IBM-England, for example, began to produce interactive video. The number of companies involved has since grown steadily.

The work of NIVC also includes corporate case studies from which a set of common problems emerged:

- Organizations need substantial help to determine whether their training objectives meet company objectives.
- Few organizations start with a detailed analysis of training needs.
- Organizations try to create their own theory of instructional design as part of a project.

Given the infancy of the instructional-design field, these problems were compounded in the middle of the 1980s by a lack of sufficient expertise in the marketplace to provide consulting. Nevertheless, NIVC reports that after two years of development efforts in the field, very satisfactory interactive-video products are available (Johnson and Foa, 1989, pp. 106–119).

In summarizing the efforts of organizations to incorporate instructional design, Doulton (Johnson and Foa, 1989, p. 111) observes that "what is now needed is a concerted effort to ensure that organizations, beginning to assess these techniques for the first time, do not all have to go through the same two-year assault course — where the winners reach the end bruised, gasping, and unsure whether it was all worth it, while the losers drop rapidly from sight."

Options for Instructional-Design Units

Instructional design can be a valuable and integral part of telecommunications-based education. The maturity of the organization's existing educational telecommunications system need not be a critical factor relative to the introduction of instructional design. If it has been determined that it can be a valuable component, then the sooner the system incorporates it, the better off the organization will become as its programs benefit from the design and management elements inherent in the instructional-design discipline. A more important issue is the degree of need for instructional design based on the type of telecommunications-based education activity being proposed.

The organization's internal analysis can be helpful in assessing the need for instructional-design support; it will suggest the mix of program *origination* and program *reception* as well as the kinds of programs that will use electronic technologies. In general, the greater the involvement of the organization in the development and delivery (origination) of the program, the greater the potential role for instructional-design support. In other words, "program origination and development" will benefit more from instructional design than "program reception support."

Likewise, the more sophisticated and extended the nature of the individual programs being proposed, the greater the benefits of instructional design. Complete degree programs, for example, offered over multiple terms, ought to benefit to a greater degree than ad hoc short courses, although it can be argued that the benefits to both will be substantial. On the other hand, instructional design is vital for organizations that are originating a large number of ad hoc programs. This discussion leads us to three questions:

1. Should the organization create an instructional-design unit or contract for those services on a project basis?

2. How can instructional design be used to maximize its benefits?
3. What is the nature of an instructional-design unit?

Following are three options for obtaining instructional-design resources.

Extending the Ad Hoc Approach

There is much to be said for continuing the ad hoc approach for some telecommunications-based education. If an organization is primarily involved in the reception of programs on demand, this approach still may be the best strategy.

The reception of satellite programs by means of a downlink located at an organization's facility is an excellent example. Instructional design is normally not a major consideration at the receive site. Most satellite program originators build instructional-design principles into both the origination and receive-site program components. Managers of educational telecommunications systems should discuss this with originators prior to committing to a program. The manager can then lead a well-coordinated effort between existing but independent organizational units to get the job done in a reliable and effective manner for short-term receive-only programs.

Once the organization has experienced a few programs, a pattern for arranging events will probably have emerged. The continuing education unit is likely to be the focus for coordinating program selection with faculty or staff units and it works with the organization originating the program. The AV services unit is now familiar with satellite downlinking, preparing the meeting room, and arranging the telephone for call-backs. The funding for each program may also include an allocation for support of the AV unit and maintenance of hardware, as described in Chapter Six. Nevertheless, extensive use of on-demand programs can put a strain on ad hoc systems and a more structured approach may be required.

Contracting Instructional-Design Services on a Project Basis

Lent (Johnson and Foa, 1989, p. 126) suggests three reasons for using outside sources for instructional-design services: flexibility, speed, and quality control. Two items that can be added to the list are (1) infrequent need and (2) the possibility of using outside talent in an assessment phase as a prelude to creating an instructional-design unit. There is a clear advantage and inherent flexibility to buying only the services that are required, particularly for infrequent projects, because the alternative of maintaining a productive instructional-design unit full-time can be financially substantial. A team that can bring in fresh ideas and apply considerable resources to solve the problems of telecommunications-based education for the system manager can enhance creativity and speed. Last, the external team is focused only on the project at hand and is not distracted by other issues within the organization.

An organization that is experienced in receiving video teleconferences but that wants to produce its own "first origination" is a good example of this situation. An educational institution that has offered telecourses for years and feels prepared to create its first telecourse for national distribution might also consider this approach. In both examples, outside consultants could continue to be retained to guide future programs. Alternatively the organization may have evaluated the work of the outside sources, in addition to getting the contracted service, as a prologue to committing to the formation of an in-house instructional-design unit. Once the need for instructional design becomes frequent, the case can be made for creating an instructional-design unit. This would be preferable to constantly hiring and reorienting outside sources.

Creating an Instructional-Design Unit

There are a number of attractive and productive reasons for considering the formation of an instructional-design unit. As mentioned earlier, diverting subject-matter specialists from instruction to design work is very likely not the best use of valuable resources. An instructional-design unit brings allies into the project and frees the content specialists to do their job. This team approach can induce a creative environment for the development of programs to meet unique criteria. It also encourages professional development by the content specialists, who may begin to see their discipline differently.

In addition, some of the basic elements of an instructional-design unit, such as the organization's media center, may already be in place. If a new instructional-design structure will both provide a needed resource for the organization and allow existing service units to be even more serviceable through their redefined role, then the value-added aspect of the concept can be magnified. At the same time, integration of new and existing service units will produce a unit very much in tune with the organizational culture, which also can become operational in a relatively short period of time.

Finally, control of both quality and proprietary information, as Lent (Johnson and Foa, 1989) emphasizes, is of considerable importance. Proprietary information can often provide a competitive edge. Contracted parties may put control of such information in jeopardy. Internal instructional-design units will also introduce a product consistency into the project stream of the organization that would not be possible if a series of contracted agencies were used. Therefore, the products the organization delivers to its constituents will be more clearly seen as part of a unified whole. Finally, as the Maricopa Community College example demonstrates, the instructional-design unit's value extends beyond its formal role and function to that of being a catalyst for change in other segments of the organization.

Elements of an Instructional-Design Unit

Considering the development of an instructional-design unit implies that the organization will need such a unit to support a number of substantial projects over an extended period of time. This may mean that the educational telecommunications system is a large-scale enterprise that will require instructional-design services for a steady stream of projects. In this case, it would be expected that the design unit could be one operational component of the division that manages educational telecommunications projects of all kinds, and that the unit will be accountable only for such projects.

In the case of the Maricopa Community College campuses, however, instructional design was soon interacting with a variety of projects across the organization. In this alternative structure, the unit should be a centralized function that is available to all divisions of the organization. While our purpose here is not to analyze the overall organizational role and function of instructional-design units but rather to see how they can benefit the proposed systems, the probability that such units could ultimately become organization-wide utilities suggests the need to mention the broader role of instructional-design units.

As one example, in 1990 the Texas State Board of Education established the Texas Center for Educational Technology at the University of North Texas (Brumbaugh and Crossland, 1991). A statewide survey of public school districts served as the environmental scan to assist the center in developing its work plan of instructional-design services. The service fell under five major categories:

1. In-service training on educational technology
2. Research on educational technology
3. Creation of educational technology products
4. Creation of educational technology services
5. Dissemination of findings in educational technology

It is evident that telecommunications-based education projects have awakened in a number of organizations the need to restructure their instructional support services. Nevertheless, in both centralized and decentralized structures, utilization of the instructional-design unit can be viewed similarly by the educational telecommunications system — that is, as a unique resource for the design and management of the learning process.

Lent (Johnson and Foa, 1989, pp. 121–136) discusses a number of structures and strategies for building an instructional-design organization. Based on the typical needs of a dedicated telecommunications system, the essential functional elements of an instructional-design unit should include the following:

- Video and audio production
- Electrical engineering
- Graphics
- Computers and software engineering
- Telecommunications
- Instructional design

Many of the basic technical functions necessary to create an instructional-design unit probably already exist but as separate resources in the organization. The first three functions listed usually exist in the traditional AV center and would benefit in most organizations from affiliation with or integration into an instructional-design unit. The majority of organizations now have in-house computer expertise, which is usually affiliated with information management functions or located within the content-specialist base of educational institutions—that is, the faculty or staff. Likewise, telecommunications expertise often resides within the office responsible for the selection and management of its communications systems. The discipline of instructional design, the sixth area, is usually based in colleges of education. Organizations without this resource need to identify the best way to develop a capability in this area.

Operationally, each of the five technical functions constitutes a section or division of the instructional-design unit. These sections are peers in an organizational diagram. The instructional-design staff takes the role of project manager for each program assigned to the unit. As project manager, the instructional-design specialist cuts across all the sections or divisions of the unit, using individual subunits or integrating subunits to accomplish the objectives of the project. As with the integration of an educational telecommunications system into the organization, a thoughtful analysis of how change will be managed in the creation of an instructional-design unit is a key element in the successful development of such an enterprise.

As suggested earlier, if an organization is not prepared to create an instructional-design unit because it is not justified by the project load, it is still possible to apply instructional-design principles to projects in an ad hoc manner. As program opportunities appear, the project manager assesses the instructional-design needs and assembles an ad hoc work group made up of staff from the appropriate independent centers to discuss the nature of the project and decide how each center can contribute to the project's success. Once agreement is reached on the involvement of the various centers, a work plan and commitment of the necessary resources are arranged. Depending on the scope of the project, this may also require allocation of funds to the support centers.

Summary

This chapter and the preceding four chapters together present a number of guidelines, strategies, and examples of ways in which an educational telecommunications system can be nurtured into existence within an organization. It bears repeating that a majority of the time and energy needed to implement telecommunications-based education, as exemplified by the preceding chapters, involves relationships rather than technology.

The assumptions presented in Chapter Two have been woven into the fabric of Chapters Three through Seven in a practical fashion. This has allowed them to be brought into the workplace to see how they function in facilitating planning, program development, and system design and implementation.

Environmental scanning triggers a learner-centered approach to the first steps in system design. Once learner needs are identified, the organization's internal analysis uses the instructional-design discipline to empower educators and trainers associated with programming.

The necessity of consistency of purpose between telecommunications-based programs and the mission of the organization leads to the realization that programs that are in concert with the priorities of the organization stand a greater chance of acceptance, support, and participation. Continuing education faculty and trainers who have successfully integrated these programs have found that this has indeed moved them toward the center of the organization's value system. One fringe benefit of being a locus of activity is an increased ability to secure financial support for telecommunications-based education when organizational leaders recognize its ability to expand the organization's service area and capability to respond to urgent educational needs.

Finally, success will be achieved through (1) congruence of purpose between telecommunications-based programming and the organizational mission through strategic planning of the system's configuration, (2) bonding to learners who ultimately feel like a part of the organization through proper programs and support, and (3) a sensitivity and concern for the traditional teaching environment and the way the telecommunications-based instructional environment is affected.

•••••••••• *Chapter* 9

Assessing
and Maintaining Quality

Myth: Quality in telecommunications-based education is a matter of combining traditional instructional standards with assessments of technical accessibility, reliability, and interactivity.

Reality: The potential reach and instructional impact of educational telecommunications systems require measures of quality that speak to values underlying new relationships with learners.

Many new and evolving fields proceed without agreement on standards of quality. Telecommunications-based education is no exception. The historic pattern in postsecondary education has been to weigh the quality of nontraditional education by how closely it mirrors the format and content of education in a traditional classroom. The shortcomings of this approach have been noted in the literature on postsecondary education, distance education, and adult learning. As one observation phrases it, "The fact that very few [postsecondary] institutions have

187

sought to measure learning apart from the time expended suggests that higher education is too easily satisfied with surrogate measures of its performance" (Pew Higher Education Research Program, 1992, p. 6A).

Electronic technologies create an educational context that offers an instructional experience that has no counterpart in a traditional classroom and that significantly alters the nature and level of interaction between learners, educators, and the educational material. Individual learning differences regarded as unremarkable in traditional instruction are often a primary consideration when electronic technology is applied to teaching and learning.

How can managers of telecommunications-based education determine how well they are doing and how far they have to go to reach progressively higher standards of quality? Looking to typical measures of success can be misleading. Telecommunications-based education can be successful financially, yet lack many characteristics that a knowledgeable person would consider fundamental to good quality. Conversely, programs that downplay quality and achieve successful cost efficiency can be educationally disappointing. But what characteristics should distinguish programmatic quality? Approaches to quality that are used in business — for example, W. Edwards Deming's fourteen-point philosophy of management and the concept of Total Quality Management (TQM) — hold promise for telecommunications-based education. These approaches contain elements that can be transferred to many contexts and used to introduce or improve standards of quality.

This chapter suggests that quality can be considered at functional, managerial, or ethical levels. The ethical level is the least acknowledged in most parent organizations, yet it is the most likely to be the focus of critical debate when electronic technologies make education disproportionately accessible to particular groups of learners. Establishing standards that operationalize values through measures of program outcomes allows managers to anticipate issues that may accompany the introduction of new systems. This chapter examines a set of values and considers their relationship to the kinds of questions telecommunications-based education raises about setting standards.

Approaches to Quality by Business

It can be useful to compare the measures of quality proposed in this chapter to those in other fields. Two of the most influential approaches to quality currently used by American business are Deming's fourteen obligations of management (1986) and Total Quality Management (TQM). Deming, a statistics professor, is revered in Japan as the father of that country's postwar economic revival. Since 1952, Japan has annually awarded the Deming Prize as its highest honor to firms that have improved product quality.

Among Deming's fourteen obligations of management, paraphrased here, several require managers to:

- Create constancy of purpose for the improvement of products and services
- Adopt a new philosophy that accepts the challenge, responsibilities, and leadership requirements of a new economic age
- Cease dependence on inspection to achieve quality and instead build quality into the product in the first place
- Improve quality continually in terms of systems of production
- Drive out fear so that everyone can work effectively
- Break down barriers between organizational units
- Put everybody to work to accomplish this transformation

Deming's call for constancy of purpose, adoption of a new philosophy for a new economic age, breaking down barriers within the parent organization, and involving everyone in the transformation to improve quality speaks to consensus, inclusiveness, and reciprocity, and to such outcomes as long-term relationships and a more ethnically sensitive climate. His requirements of ceasing dependence on inspection and continually improving the quality of systems, as well as services, are obligations that can readily be adapted to an emphasis on supporting and promoting learner autonomy and new kinds of relationships.

For example, managers who focus on improving relationships and autonomy as proposed later in this chapter will at the same time potentially be addressing Deming's obligation to cease dependence on inspection. Less inspection of results is needed when all managerial processes reflect key components of quality. Similarly, managers who include reciprocity and altruism in an orienting framework that guides their decisions can also be said to be addressing Deming's obligation to drive out fear (of failure) to enable everyone, including learners, to work effectively.

Total quality management is a comprehensive system designed to produce a fundamental transformation in organizations. Users of TQM characterize it as creating a new organizational culture emphasizing five key points:

1. Customer focus
2. Systematic improvement of operations
3. Development of human resources
4. Long-term thinking
5. Commitment to quality

Some of the ways in which postsecondary education is applying Deming's thinking and TQM are summarized along with a useful annotated bibliography in a pamphlet titled *Total Quality Management: A Guide for the North Dakota University System.* For users of TQM, among them higher education institutions, the term *customer* refers to anyone who receives one's work: faculty, students, colleagues, support staff, and so on. Work can only be improved by delivering high-quality products to customers. *High quality* in TQM refers to meeting the customers' real needs, usually determined by asking them what they want. For example, do learners say they want managers to enforce rules or to ensure that learning differences are taken into account?

A mark of quality for users of TQM is to review and improve processes at every step, not at the end, and to recognize that all work occurs within a process. Many employees lack understanding of their importance to the parent organization and cannot see how their work fits into the total process.

TQM-related definitions of quality share several characteristics. First, they focus on meeting or exceeding the needs and expectations of the customer. Second, constantly seeking and getting closer to quality is critically important. Third, everyone in the organization must be involved in the effort to improve quality. Fourth, quality outcomes require quality at every step of the process. Managers who adopt TQM principles view quality as multifaceted and impermanent. No single definition fits all conditions; instead, TQM is proposed as an approach and a set of tools with different applications for different circumstances.

This brief overview of some aspects of TQM cannot do justice to the understanding and phases of activity that TQM seeks to inspire in organizational management. TQM can, however, be useful to managers who adopt the orienting framework proposed in this chapter that emphasizes reciprocity, consensus, altruism, autonomy, and inclusiveness. Managers will find parallels between these components and TQM's focus on processes that involve everyone in the parent organization, the centrality of individuals' needs and expectations, the view that an emphasis on quality must be continual, and the recognition that quality is multifaceted. The definition of quality is nevertheless impermanent and will vary with different applications and conditions.

Implications of the Absence of Standards

There is no single area of telecommunications-based education that offers managers a greater opportunity for leadership than quality and standards. This is an area where universally accepted measures do not exist. Even where documentation of outcomes can offer a basis from which to develop approaches to quality assurance, this information is routinely dismissed in favor of long-held views about how education is best conducted. Because this is an area where attitudes play a major role, being in command of the facts, and even being right, can be less important than being skilled in interpersonal relations and attitudinal change.

Few topics are more emotionally charged than the subject of quality. Yet despite the need for knowledge and guidance in this sensitive area, relatively little basic research has been done on measures of effectiveness either in telecommunications-based education or in nontraditional, distance, or continuing education, nor is there agreement on what those measures should be. Any approach adopted by a manager will be challenged. However, managers who develop a considered position on this subject will have given more systematic, objective thought to the topic than most others in the parent organization.

Moreover, managers who use a multilevel approach to considerations of quality can also begin to correct the view that telecommunications-based education is primarily concerned with equipment issues and thus can direct organizational attention to its larger ramifications. Among the wider issues in using these systems are their effects on interactivity in the instructional and learning processes and on the use of resources.

Acceptance of Marginal Standards

Telecommunications-based education presents particularly sharp dilemmas for managers. First, experience has shown that while adult learners are often dependent on it to access educational resources, they will also accept, perhaps unknowingly, marginal standards of quality. Managers who for financial or other reasons cannot deliver higher-quality telecommunications-based education may reason that marginally adequate access is better than no access at all. Yet in an educational setting, these managers function within a context that is assumed to be educationally sound in all respects. Thus for many members of the public, shoddy standards of quality are taken to be adequate because the programming is presented under the auspices of a reputable organization.

On the other hand, quality is often defined as "what the customer says it is." Learners' only reference point with regard to quality is, for the most part, a traditional classroom experience that puts a premium on face-to-face instruction. While under some circumstances this definition can be useful to educators and business organizations as well, the educational community usually prefers an educative role; such a role implies that one's own program is an exemplar of good standards by which the public can judge excellence. This offers the opportunity to educate the public by raising levels of expectation among users of services who are not themselves in a position to know precisely how "good" those services can or should be.

Lack of Benchmarks

Managers of telecommunications-based education who have the resources to achieve high standards of quality wrestle with another dilemma as well. There is no widely recognized description of what these standards should look like. Accrediting organizations may refer to quality, but such references are usually stated in terms of general organizational obligations to assure quality. They do not propose specific guidelines against which telecommunications-based education can index performance or measure progress. Such agencies typically hold nontraditional education and training to the unspecified standards of traditional education, whether or not they are appropriate.

Professional associations such as the National University Continuing Education Association (NUCEA) and the National University Teleconference Network (NUTN) have attempted for a number of years to specify the meaning of quality in telecommunications-based education. The latter association adopted a set of standards on an experimental basis in 1991, though these standards focus on just one form of telecommunications-based education, live videoconferencing. NUCEA continues to strive to reach agreement on broadly applicable guidelines for good practices in telecommunications-based postsecondary distance and continuing education. These efforts have not resulted in a widely accepted set of standards.

There has been no systematic consideration of whether the search for standards is intended to yield a list of specifications or more generic guidelines. The latter would result in different applications according to conditions, yet all applications would bear some shared hallmarks of quality. The following sections propose a number of expectations of quality that together comprise a set of hallmarks that can apply to all circumstances.

Clusters of Concern About Quality

Clusters of interest in quality are reflected in the literature in several areas, including learner satisfaction with the method of instruction; learner achievement (which in nontraditional education has not been found to be related to satisfaction); the presence of a site facilitator and appropriate, functioning equipment; teaching behaviors; effectiveness measures relating to cost; learner-faculty attitudes; technical quality; instructional feedback; levels and types of learner interaction in the instructional context; and the extent to which learner autonomy and independence are supported. Policy statements dealing with quality in higher education usually rely on parity with on-campus procedures and evaluation measures as the standard against which nontraditional activities are evaluated. Such statements rarely take into account the likelihood that parity may have little practical relevance for the context and most desirable outcomes of telecommunications-based education.

These policy statements frequently contain ad hoc checklists of items to be addressed that may offer only superficial guidance for telecommunications-based education. They may highlight areas such as instructional feedback or specify what interactive sessions are expected to achieve, such as orientation, review, instruction, advice, or consultation. Statements may point to concerns about programs in which there may be too many participants for practical interaction, and they may specify that access to all academic support services (libraries, tutoring, financial aid, advising, and counseling) be provided to nontraditional learners studying at a distance from these services.

Some commentators group these concerns into those that are instructional, technical, or related to use of resources (Dively, 1987, p. 36). But standards to achieve these goals are not usually specified. Ironically, most of the areas highlighted in policy statements are those in which traditional education struggles to reach the exemplary standards needed as a model.

Certain types of outcomes and values can offer a common language and a shared perspective on quality across program variations around the country. Scattered through the literature of distance education, continuing education, educational technology, adult learning, and organizational management are many of the elements managers need to assemble to know where they stand and to see what is needed to achieve higher levels of quality. Moore and others (1990) present a useful compendium on telecommunications that draws together the literature on distance learning and discusses its implications for a number of areas. Among the topics covered are planning, teaching, learning, choice of media, organizational systems, policy, research, and instructional interaction. While this publication indirectly addresses concerns that can bear on quality in a general way, instructional interaction is specifically addressed as a matter of quality.

Levels of Quality-Related Activity

The characteristics of quality in telecommunications-based education are described throughout this book. This chapter offers a perspective on these characteristics, but not a checklist. No single model or checklist can apply universally to the varying combinations of equipment, subject matter, staffing, learner needs and expectations, and organizational history, circumstances, mission, and resources.

It is important to look at issues of quality as a combination of at least three levels of activity. These levels are roughly parallel to the three components of an action plan described in Chapter Three: technical, political, and cultural-ideological. The levels of activity, termed *functional, managerial,* and *ethical,* require managers to give multifaceted consideration to quality. Although the levels are not mutually exclusive, each has a distinct focus that becomes the dominant consideration when questions of quality are addressed.

No single answer to the issues surrounding quality in telecommunications-based education will be universally satisfactory either within or beyond the organization. Managers will encounter strong differences of opinion on definitions of quality and on many aspects of operationalizing this type of education. They can, however, prepare for this aspect of management by determining a balance among the three levels of quality considerations that will (1) best support the current developmental stage of their program and (2) best advance the future of the program within the parent organization.

The levels at which quality is considered in this chapter—its functional, managerial, and ethical outcomes—are analogous to braids of wire. Each strand is individually strong; together they remain distinct but can support a much larger structure. The *functional* level is associated with technical-design activities that concern equipment requirements and specifications. This level also deals with the skilled technical support staff who ensure that facilities and equipment reflect the quality that a manager either implies or specifies in functional and other program and managerial goals. In other words, the functional level of quality cannot be considered apart from its effects on managerial processes and program outcomes for educators, learners, and the parent organization. Similarly, the quality of the program's outcomes cannot be achieved in isolation from functional and managerial levels of quality. These components together form the immediate, physical context within which education occurs.

The second level on which questions of quality often focus is *managerial*. At this level, the focus is on how successfully the relationships that telecommunications-based education requires within and outside the parent organization are fostered and managed. These relationships include those with other organizational units as well as with faculty, learners, and the other individuals who are essential to carrying out the program.

The third level at which quality is weighed is often termed *instructional*. This level is concerned with measures of program outcomes; our focus here is on ethical outcomes. The compendium by Moore and others (1990) summarizes the literature on the effects of telecommunications-based distance learning in a number of selected areas alluded to earlier. It does not propose a list of instructional outcomes or suggest that managers search out such a list as a gauge of quality. Indeed, the compendium's conclusion suggests that there is a lack of basic research findings on which to do more than make ad hoc recommendations regarding instructional quality. It states: "Now is the time to move on from a period of small scale, uncoordinated and not well designed experimentation, too little coordinated planning of courses, too little cooperation in using delivery systems" (Moore and others, 1990, p. 45).

We Become What We Measure

Ethical outcomes are the key to knowing where a manager stands on issues of quality. This level of quality also says a great deal about the character of a manager's program. Quality, by one definition, is what we choose to measure; another way of stating this is that we become what we measure. Consequently, what a manager chooses *not* to measure indicates which outcomes are less valued. None of the other levels at which quality considerations are commonly addressed is so clear an indicator of the quality of managerial thinking as are outcomes that represent managers' values.

Success should be distinguished from quality. For example, if a program admits only those who graduated at the top of their class, it is likely that all learners will complete the program and do so with high grades. As measured by completion, the program is successful. Do its outcomes also reflect quality? If serving diverse learners is specified as a mark of quality, the reported success of the program must be tempered by other measures of quality that have not been met.

Since there are few national precedents to impede a manager's choice of outcomes to be measured, these choices consequently reveal much about the values of the parent organization. For that reason, this level potentially offers the greatest opportunity for managerial leadership. What managers choose to measure can, for example, revitalize neglected values or establish, advance, and validate values that might otherwise be difficult to introduce. In the absence of widely accepted national standards, these measures also establish a needed set of benchmarks; such benchmarks provide a manager with a baseline for the program and a focus for achieving greater quality in terms of the relationship between fundamental values and outcomes.

Functional Quality

Functional, and to some extent managerial, measurements of quality are often predominant in the standard-setting activities of newly established telecommunications-based educational and training programs. Chapter Four provides an orientation to many considerations that are potentially a basis for setting useful measurements of quality at the functional level. Functionality implies finding a fit between the technical features of particular electronic technologies and their integrated technical power. The technical level of quality may also take into account the teaching-learning requirements of particular educators and learners and the nature of the subject matter, as well as the parent organization's mission and resources and the external forces that affect all decision making.

The degree of simplicity of technical access to educational resources, for example, can be a functionally based mark of quality. Such technically based services can also be weighed for quality in terms of their organizational convenience versus their convenience for learners. Services made possible only by electronic technology and the skills of functional specialists also contribute to the climate of telecommunications-based teaching and learning. Therefore these services can be evaluated not merely for their flexibility but also for their contribution of flexibility to a learning context that is hospitable to individual differences.

Managerial Quality

According to Chapter Three, a manager who seeks to achieve managerial quality will have a plan that incorporates a multifaceted managerial process. These two elements thus become measures of managerial quality and also foster quality. Chapter Two suggests that managerial responses need to reflect three desirable characteristics: clarity, flexibility, and consistency with the parent organization's values. All three characteristics can usefully be included among measurements to guide efforts toward managerial quality and to determine when it has been achieved.

There is an extensive literature on management and leadership that offers useful concepts of organizational stages of development and the relationship of managerial strategies to these stages and to the dynamics of behavior in organizations. For example, Greiner (1972) proposes desirable managerial attributes such as flexibility, speedy responsiveness, simplicity, and resourcefulness. Similar lists of desirable attributes are found in numerous writings and can be usefully applied to the management of telecommunications-based education.

There is a place for such lists in telecommunications activities, although their limitations must be kept in mind. A manager might know and display the attributes suggested by Greiner (1972), yet managerial quality could be diminished by a failure to read and respond to the overall requirements of the environment. In addition, measures of quality suggested by lists of personal attributes are likely to overemphasize managerial and functional elements and underemphasize factors such as consistency between program outcomes and the values that are the core of the parent organization's long-range goals.

Ethical Outcomes as a Measure of Quality

Several characteristics of the ethical dimension of quality are proposed as measures of outcomes in telecommunications-based education. None of these characteristics — equity, climate, autonomy, and relationships — is at present applied widely enough to determine the degree of quality they might seek to achieve. The measures are introduced here as a potential complement to more traditional evaluative concepts that focus, for example, on student retention, rates of program completion, or academic grades achieved. They are also proposed as a means of introducing and monitoring consistency between values and program outcomes.

Evaluation in continuing and distance education was conceived prior to the advent of electronic technologies and their widespread application to education; these technologies now face public demands to address socioeconomic problems. While earlier measurement concepts did not focus on issues of multiculturalism, at present the importance of multiculturalism is widely acknowledged in the organizational priorities of business, government, and education.

The characteristics of quality that are proposed here for inclusion among more traditional instructional measures for education and training can add balance to concepts of quality and can assist in operationalizing organizational values. Additionally, managers who incorporate one or more of these or similar criteria in their measures of outcomes will also be establishing developmental benchmarks for programming that can both guide and validate future decision making.

Are the characteristics proposed here — equity, climate, autonomy, and relationships — measurable? This question raises the valid and long-standing concern about any evaluative criteria that stray from readily quantifiable measures. While qualitative approaches can be difficult to conceptualize and apply meaningfully and appropriately, they can yield information that is obtainable in no other way. Moreover, they invite the more reflective inquiry that is expected of a maturing professional field concerned with education.

Inclusion of one or more of the following measures of telecommunications-based education will result in a richer, more broadly informative portrayal of quality.

Equity

Use of a measure of quality such as equity enables managers to take a fresh look at less-examined structural and managerial impediments to greater, more culturally diverse participation in telecommunications-based education. Accessibility to educational resources is one of the most commonly employed rationales for the introduction of telecommunications; it is important, however, to ask: accessibility for whom? Approached in this way, accessibility becomes a more meaningful, more value-laden component.

In postsecondary education, for example, the composition of the adult audience that is served by nontraditional programming in general has been essentially the same for decades: urban, middle-income, Caucasian, well educated, and, more recently, female. Yet a significant portion of our national population consists of people of color, people who speak English as a second language, lower-income people, and others who are educationally underserved by virtue of their physical condition, geographical location, or other "disabling" features of their status. It is not difficult under the present circumstances to anticipate the unintended emergence of an adult population that can be characterized by technological haves and have-nots.

Some would make the case that an educational telecommunications system is merely a delivery system and therefore is an inappropriate tool to deal with concerns arising from cultural diversity and socioeconomic disparities. Nevertheless, an unprecedented level of criticism is presently being directed at education at all levels, as well as at corporate training, for a perceived failure to include and educate a diverse population for today's work life. In short, public expectations of education are changing in ways that require new responses.

It is commonplace for education at every level to use a "damaged goods" response to explain educational shortcomings. Each educational level suggests that the preceding level sent them damaged goods — that is, ill-prepared learners. At the lowest educational level the source of the damaged goods is said to be learners' parents. No level of education and training can be wholly responsible for student preparation, nor can it be entirely without accountability for the adoption of practices that respond to social, economic, and cultural imperatives.

It might be said that all educational levels are better indicators of where our culture has been than where it is going. Yet electronic technology is bringing with it unforeseen transformations that extend to work life, family life, teaching, learning, the geographical reach of educational activities, the meaning of what defines an eligible "resident" student, and much else.

Earlier in this century the construction of a network of national highways was viewed as a technical feat. The network wasn't heralded as a solution to socioeconomic and cultural problems or as a catalyst for cultural transformation, although the highways fostered or contributed to all of these conditions. An educational telecommunications system, narrowly conceived, is merely a delivery mechanism that has no relationship to the cultural and other problems associated with the education of a diverse population. Yet electronic technologies can both exacerbate and modify the inequities associated with the educationally underserved. Introducing even modest goals to alter the composition of the learners who participate in telecommunications-based education will lend credibility to its promised access.

Climate

Merriam and Caffarella (1991) observe in *Learning in Adulthood: A Comprehensive Guide* that few authors have looked in-depth at precisely what constitutes a positive environment for learning (p. 22). They also note, however, that of the three major factors affecting the learning environment — people, structure, and culture (p. 30) — the two least often studied are the interplay of people in the learning setting and the overall culture of the organizations that provide the setting (p. 40). Attention to these components is made even more complex when the three factors are in an educational context created in part by electronic technologies, because this context places learners and educators at a distance from each other and requires adaptation by all participants to the strengths and limitations of the system.

As daunting as it appears to be to develop measures of learning climate, managers of telecommunications-based education are in a good position to begin to characterize and evaluate the tone of the teaching-learning transaction as well as the overall climate of the context in which teaching and learning occur. Managers who introduce such measures will find much in common with those who write the literature of adult development and cognition and will also open up a promising area of quality measurement that is virtually untouched.

Autonomy

Another potential measure of quality is the degree to which programming supports and advances differences and self-direction among learners. Telecommunications-based education can be used to inspire and support autonomy. Managers who look at programming from this perspective can begin to adjust functional, managerial, and ethical components of their operations that might unintentionally and unnecessarily impede this autonomy.

Adjusting functional, managerial, and ethical activities to support autonomy has another advantage: this approach anticipates the inevitable outcome of current trends that will ultimately require greater recognition of learning differences. Garrison and Baynton (1987, p. 6) quoted Moore (1983a, p. 86), who observed that "since autonomous behavior is adult, the very nature of good adult education is the restoration and support of learners' autonomy. . . . " According to Moore (1983b, p. 30), "It is important that we not only design and teach good programs, but that we think, write and argue for learner autonomy, to ensure that distance education works in the interests of learners, not of teachers alone, nor institutions, nor is used as a means of state control and social direction."

Relationships

In higher education, the language that develops relationships between adult learners and managers of nontraditional programs has recently been almost exclusively entrepreneurial. Entrepreneurism brought a needed corrective to educational programming by introducing a customer service perspective that has improved the treatment of students by institutions. Entrepreneurism also seemed to many managers of nontraditional education to be a matter of economic necessity as programming for adults evolved into a national, highly competitive seminar industry.

On the other hand, an emphasis on the buyer-seller relationship may have more limited usefulness for attracting a greater diversity of learners to telecommunications-based education. It might even be said that entrepreneurial language is a barrier to wider participation in such education. For example, searching for "markets" among the underserved is conceptually less powerful than searching for affiliation with neglected constituencies. If affiliation became the focus, managers would need to employ a vocabulary less bent on selling and better tuned to multicultural sensibilities. As a consequence, managers would also need to turn their attention to new funding patterns that recognize and are responsive to the circumstances of underserved constituencies.

By developing measures that look at program quality and by obtaining success, at least in part in terms of establishing relationships with learners beyond that of customer and seller, a manager can begin a commitment to service that reconceptualizes relationships with learners. This also introduces the possibility of fresh thinking about alternatives to current methods of financing education and training.

Values That Speak to Quality

In Plato's time it was radical to use the written word. Plato feared that the practice of reading would weaken memory by making it unnecessary to remember. In the mid-nineteenth century it was radical to believe that the future of America lay with the railroads and industry and not with plantation-based agriculture. Today's managers of nontraditional telecommunications-based education are well placed to put "radical" ideas in perspective.

Managers need to look at the future of programming and ask what funding mechanisms will be most appropriate. They also need to ask what values should be included among the measures of quality in telecommunications-based education that is designed to serve the multicultural audience of the future. The functional, managerial, and ethical features of programming can be weighed differently with an orienting framework comprised of these five values: reciprocity, consensus, altruism, autonomy, and inclusiveness.

Reciprocity

Control and dependency are far more difficult to distinguish in telecommunications-based education than in a traditional classroom, where lines of authority are relatively clear because they rest on shared understandings that go back over time. Telecommunications-based education is a surprisingly reciprocal process between learners, educators, and managers and support staff. For example, educators are dependent on technicians and educational technologists in order to use electronic technologies in the most educationally effective way. There is striking, though undocumented, evidence that learners feel and act differently from those in a traditional classroom. Faculty and learners alike are more conscious of being part of a "process."

Learners form cohort groups that can greatly influence the instructional climate and teaching methodology. Learners are known to rebel as a group, for example, when they are not forewarned of the ways in which a traditional classroom format will be altered when it is replaced by a telecommunications-based format. A distinguishing feature of telecommunications-based teaching and learning is the learners' sense of being a distinct group that can make its wishes known as a group. Faculty are less "independent" of learners under these conditions. Conversely, students are in some respects more independent of their instructors and are more able to decide how instruction will proceed.

Managers, too, are in a more directly reciprocal relationship with students and instructors. Telecommunications-based education requires managerial as well as instructional attention to differences among students. For managers, this means working more closely with learners and faculty on the interaction that will take place between them. One way that managers can begin to focus on the quality of the changed relationships between themselves, faculty, and learners is by conceptualizing the relationship in terms of achieving reciprocity.

Consensus

Underserved constituencies need organizational champions. Managers of telecommunications-based education are in a position to mobilize opinion on behalf of the underserved. When the managerial task is considered to be consensus building, the linkages between programming, relationships with learners, and values of the parent organization can begin to emerge in operational ways. The process of consensus building also affects the parent organization's culture in ways that can make it more welcoming to a greater diversity of learners. Moreover, distinctions between managerial choices can be made according to their contribution to consensus building on behalf of the underserved.

Altruism

Terms such as "social justice" are jarring in the current entrepreneurial atmosphere of educational and business organizations. Yet the growing concern that ethnic differences must be valued and built upon as strengths rather than impediments to education and training will increasingly affect the present entrepreneurial climate of telecommunications-based education.

Altruism suggests that measures of quality need to reflect acts valued not only because they are fiscally sound, responsive, speedy, or resourceful, but because they also address the interests of educationally neglected populations. What is, in fact, socially just and equitable for the underserved? Can some decisions, services, and structures be based solely on grounds of social justice, termed here *altruism,* in order to suggest that this "return on investment" is also valid in nontraditional education?

Autonomy

Autonomy as a value in an orienting framework can counterbalance the view that individual differences indicate deficiencies. When diversity is linked to the pursuit of learner autonomy, it can be transformed from a problem to be overcome into a compelling force that encourages and supports change. Autonomy can also have positive effects on learning. As Davie and Wells (1991, p. 16) note, "Empowerment is the expectation and enabling of a student to take a visible and meaningful role in the electronic classroom. . . . There are two elements which support the development of personal power. They are: (a) a sense of mastery, and (b) a sense of community."

Inclusiveness

All of the values making up this framework are directed to broadening the inclusiveness of the constituencies served by telecommunications-based education. Within the framework, inclusiveness refers to reaching learners who are more diverse in ethnicity and in socioeconomic, gender, physical, and geographical status. Consistency between managerial decision making and the values of the parent organization will be more attainable when a higher proportion of the underserved are included in programming. One result is greater institutionalization of attention to their needs and desires.

Other Perspectives on Standards

How can the measures suggested here be related to the extensive literature on assessment in nontraditional, distance, and continuing education? Can this literature be a point of departure for the development of standards of quality that acknowledge and use the dynamic character of telecommunications-based education? In Chapter Three, Gooler's (1977) criteria for evaluating programs in nontraditional postsecondary education were briefly summarized (p. 91). These components of assessment were developed for telecommunications-based education and might now be extended and elaborated in light of the measures proposed in this chapter.

Ten years later, Gooler (1987, p. 67) wrote: "What is impressive about the new information technologies is their capacity to present to the learner information resources of many kinds or from many sources and to enable the learner to integrate those various forms of information into learning programs that make sense." One way to read the quality implications of such technical integration is in terms of the advancement of learner autonomy; in other words, the greater the integrative capacity of the programming, the higher its level of quality, not in technical terms but because integration advances and supports autonomy.

Moore (1989, p. 100) proposes three types of interaction that need to be distinguished by those who are engaged in providing distance education: learner-to-content, learner-to-instructor, and learner-to-learner. In light of the measures proposed in this chapter, achieving these forms of interaction can be seen as operationalizing the relationships educational telecommunications systems inspire and help sustain. Moreover, instead of being seen as a technology-induced dimension of program design and a technical achievement, interactivity can be reframed as a mark of learner-centeredness. Thus interactivity connotes a level of quality to be achieved in terms of relationships, not technology.

Summary

Two major dilemmas encountered by managers of telecommunications-based education are the absence of widely accepted standards and the inclination of learners using electronic technologies to adapt uncritically to whatever is offered. Some aspects of contemporary thinking on quality in business settings help point the way to overcoming these dilemmas. W. Edwards Deming and the Total Quality Management process both emphasize the centrality of the individual's needs in shaping quality-related practices, the necessity for continuous improvement, and the involvement of the whole organization in the perspective brought to issues of quality.

Quality must be considered at three levels: functional, managerial, and ethical. These levels are drawn together by the development of credible standards of quality grounded in benchmarks for a set of core managerial concerns. These concerns encompass learner satisfaction and achievement, skillfulness of instruction, effectiveness of facilitation and support services, and operationalization of organizational values. A checklist of standards would not be appropriate for every circumstance even if such a list existed. Instead, five benchmark values are proposed — reciprocity, consensus, altruism, autonomy, and inclusiveness — as a framework for standards that introduce continuous improvement centered on learners' needs. Measures of quality that incorporate equity, climate, autonomy, and relationships are also proposed to set standards that extend more traditional measures.

The absence of agreement on how to define quality or decide what aspects of telecommunications-based education are central to it makes this area promising for vision and leadership. Moreover, the development of an orienting framework that links this type of education to the principles that underlie the parent organization's mission offers managers the opportunity to formalize a commitment to fundamental organizational values. This approach supports the development of functional, managerial, and ethical practices that go beyond lip service to incorporate values into measures of program outcomes.

The measures of quality that are considered important reveal a great deal about programmatic priorities, managerial sensibilities, and the goals of the parent organization. The set of standards ultimately adopted not only will measure programmatic elements but also will be a bellwether for consistency between the values of the parent organization and the outcomes sought by telecommunications-based education.

A useful next step is to consider planning and marketing, described in Chapters Three and Seven, respectively, from the perspective of Deming's fourteen points and the approach to quality proposed in this chapter. Quality considerations bring a consistency to a manager's point of view that can improve the likelihood of achieving desirable outcomes in every managerial area.

●●●●●●●●●● *Chapter* 10

Sources of
Information About
Telecommunications

Myth: Seeking references from technical experts is the best way to become knowledgeable and stay abreast of developments in telecommunications-based education.

Reality: Professionals in telecommunications-based education remain current primarily by following nontechnical issues and trends through a small selection of periodicals and conferences from which networks of professional associates are developed.

No field is more dependent on information sharing than is telecommunications-based education. The rapidity of technical change, the variations among applications of electronic technologies to education and the workplace, and the absence of a profile of professional qualifications for management in this field are major obstacles to remaining informed. One way that newcomers to the field can overcome these obstacles is by creating a network of knowledgeable colleagues and assembling selected sources of information to help guide their efforts.

This chapter emphasizes ways to build a selective personal repertoire of information. Lesser-known resources are preferred to a more global approach. A rationale is offered for starting with only a few selected resources, and these resources are described. Because applications of electronic technologies to education and training evolve so rapidly, the emerging literature in the field is somewhat ephemeral. Much good writing is found in unpublished papers presented at meetings or exchanged informally, whose distribution goes no farther. Sources of these less accessible resources are described, along with those that are more readily available.

A dilemma for newcomers to the field is where to start. What information is needed first, and where is it located? Are periodicals and books the most reliable sources, or should more time be spent at conferences talking to expert individuals? How is the information best organized? This chapter centers around the activities that motivate managers to seek out sources and strategies in order to acquire a grounding in the field, build personal networks, and follow trends. Key managerial concerns are presented according to their links to particular sources of information.

Getting Started

Certain preliminary steps are useful in conceptualizing the task of information gathering. The most effective strategy centers on organizing sources of information around the core concerns of managing telecommunications-based education.

Preliminary Steps

Newcomers can begin to catch up with developments by first taking steps to:

1. Clarify and prioritize the specific purposes that telecom-
    munications-based education is to serve for the parent or-
    ganization
2. Specify the fundamental values that are intended to be
    advanced
3. Determine how the purposes, priorities, and values that are
    to be supported and advanced relate to the parent organi-
    zation's mission, its underlying values, and its image
4. Develop measures of quality and success that reflect these
    purposes, priorities, and values and ensure that they will
    guide decision making and provide a basis for tracking the
    program's status and progress

Narrowing the Search

A manager's preliminary responses to these tasks will allow the
search for information to become more focused. Managers who
first clarify a program's purposes, priorities, values, and consistency with the parent organization's mission, values, and image are able to frame their approach to information gathering
more confidently and meaningfully. The search can be more
systematically narrowed to a core of knowledge related to the
stage of development of a manager's program, to factors unique
to the environment, and to external forces. The clarification
process also prepares managers to develop the most useful contacts of all: knowledgeable individuals who can offer advice
tailored to specific circumstances.

Core Concerns

First, however, managers need to become knowledgeable about
the most useful sources of information and learn how these
sources can be related to specific concerns. A good way to approach the accumulation of a reliable set of resources is by considering various facets of managerial responsibility. Delineation
of responsibilities into a core set of concerns will differ from one
program to another depending on circumstances, the developmental stage of a program, and other variations in conditions.

Yet by identifying these core concerns, a manager can search out sources of information with more probability of success.

Following are some of the concerns that will occupy the attention of most managers of telecommunications-based education:

- Discerning key environmental factors that will shape the process of telecommunications-based education over time
- Introducing partnerships that can advance a program's purposes, priorities, and values
- Integrating technical equipment in combination with arrangements for facilities in ways that will improve teaching and learning
- Projecting costs that take into account a program's long-term needs and purposes
- Managing change that accompanies the development of telecommunications-based education
- Putting programming on a sound financial and conceptual basis while adhering to its purposes, priorities, and inherent values
- Introducing and sustaining valid principles of quality
- Anticipating developments and trends in the field
- Interpreting and applying the newest findings that affect managerial practices and teaching-learning outcomes

What sources can tell managers the most about these core concerns? No single organization, periodical, publication, or network of people is sufficient for all of them, or for every stage of development. Nevertheless, managers can develop a combination of selected resources that can be tailored to personal and situational tasks as programming evolves over time.

A Manageable Approach to Resources

A great number of bibliographies are available that encompass nearly every aspect of this field. Some of the most useful are acknowledged in this chapter. For the most part, however, bibliographies lack annotation or are insufficiently annotated to be readily useful even to seasoned managers. This chapter organizes

recommended sources around a number of the major professional development tasks of a manager: gaining a grounding
in the field, personal networking, tracking trends, and linking
sources of information to key managerial concerns. This section on linking resources to managerial concerns suggests how
to connect the sources proposed as most useful to the list of core
concerns introduced earlier.

Each area in telecommunications-based education is affected by the others. Consequently, managers have responsibilities in many areas in which they are unlikely to become
specialists. Under such circumstances, the first question to ask
in gathering information is not "How do I get started?" but rather
"Why are we involving ourselves in telecommunications-based
education?" and "What are the fundamental outcomes and values
we are pursuing?" Such reflection provides perspective for tasks
such as the introduction of new partnerships and the acquisition of equipment.

For example, most managers are attentive to the concern
of putting programming on a sound financial and conceptual
basis. To search out sources of information to address that concern, however, managers must first know for whom they are
programming, and why. Similarly, the newest findings in the
field are of interest to everyone, but managers who develop a
focus based on the learners they intend to serve will be in a better position to specify which aspect of new developments to follow closely. If learners' interactivity in the educational process
is a manager's focus, that emphasis will lead to a combination
of resources that will look different from those used by a manager whose circumstances require another emphasis.

A workable personal assemblage of information resources
will include professional associations, conferences, professional
peers, and regular reading in selected periodicals and books
directed to:

- Approaches to management
- Nontraditional and distance education and adult learning
- National and international forces of change
- New developments in telecommunications-based education

Acquiring a Grounding in the Field

The sources of information suggested below provide useful starting points and selected information intended for nontechnical
managers in any setting.

History

Saettler's history of educational technology (1990) is approachable for managers who are not specialists in electronic technology and instructional design. Titled *The Evolution of American
Educational Technology,* this is a basic reference for managers new
to the field. It also enables seasoned managers to see developments in telecommunications-based education in a broader perspective. The extensive footnotes and references accompanying
each chapter make this text one of the most useful single sources
of bibliographical information in the field.

Conceptualization

The introductory text by Cowan (1984) is a more specialized
overview of telecommunications and its origins. This text has
worn well over time and remains one of the most readable and
insightful commentaries in the field. Written conversationally,
it describes electronic technologies of various kinds and explains
how they function. The development of human potential through
electronic technology is central to Cowan's thinking. This discerning approach is the single best general introduction available for nontechnical managers; it also deserves the attention
of experienced managers of telecommunications-based education.

Issues

The U.S. Congress, Office of Technology Assessment (1989),
has published a compendium of current thinking on educational
telecommunications systems and distance education in this country. If a newcomer to the field could read only one book, *Linking for Learning: A New Course for Education* would be high on the

list of key sources of information. The emphasis is on developments at the K–12 educational level, but the views and findings that are cited are applicable to all educators and managers engaged in telecommunications-based education. The book's broad orientation to electronic technology is not intended for equipment specialists, but excellent information is provided on the subject of electronic technologies and their comparative advantages and disadvantages, all of it in language accessible to non-specialists. Appendixes contain sample costs of systems in nontechnical terms and a brief glossary of technical terms. A more extensive glossary of terminology is found in *The Emerging Role of Telecommunications in Higher Education — Improving Teaching at a Distance: A Guide to Resources,* by Dillon, Blanchard, and Price (1990, pp. 33–43).

A paperback series of sourcebooks titled "New Directions for Adult and Continuing Education" contains a succinct reader edited by Niemi and Gooler (1987) that covers selected areas of educational telecommunications. Titled *Technologies for Learning Outside the Classroom,* the book includes a final chapter on major themes and issues in telecommunications-based education for adults and an overview of major issues that provides grounding for new managers.

Comparative Merits

Most managers of telecommunications-based education, particularly those in postsecondary education, will encounter questions about the relative merits of traditional and telecommunications-based education. Chapter Three pointed out that there is a long history of research on this subject. Studies have consistently shown that there are few discernable differences for measures of outcomes such as grades for coursework. Whittington (1987) provides a summary of such studies and their findings. Verduin and Clark (1991) offer an extensive annotated introductory comparative review of studies of educational achievement related to distance and telecommunications-based education (pp. 213–239). This text also provides a succinct introduction to the history and concerns of distance education and contains a comprehensive bibliography.

Researchers generally recognize that such factors as individual and cultural differences, differences in subject matter, and other considerations have not been exhaustively explored with regard to the comparative outcomes of telecommunications-based education and traditional instruction. The outcomes themselves have often been rather narrowly conceived around measures such as grades, although some studies explore learners' attitudes and feelings as well.

A good example of the caution exhibited by researchers, even when they present evidence of more favorable outcomes for technology-based education, is provided in an unpublished report by H. R. Stone in a letter to Glen Martin, June 8, 1989, that is focused on engineering students. Stone points out that the comparative results, reported in terms of grades, may be influenced by such individual differences as whether a student is studying for a degree or simply taking a course.

For several decades, managers have found themselves citing such studies while encountering continual skepticism as to the efficacy of educational telecommunications systems. In today's more telecommunications-saturated environment, there is perhaps more to be feared from overselling what telecommunications systems can accomplish than from having to show that they yield results indistinguishable from traditional education under many circumstances. As Chapter One indicates, the reluctance expressed by today's skeptics is likely to have more to do with issues of personal control of the instructional process than with learning outcomes.

Surveys and Guides

A series of surveys of educational telecommunications systems in business environments was undertaken in 1974 and was continued roughly every four years through 1986. In what are known as the Brush reports, Brush and Brush (1986) examined how decisions are made to use electronic technologies, by whom these decisions are made, and for what purposes. Operating budgets are reported along with data on staffing and structuring private educational telecommunications systems. For managers outside business, these reports offer an unusually detailed look at some of the operational realities of telecommunications-based education in corporations together with such details as the specific job responsibilities of every member of the business telecommunications team.

The National School Board Association and US West Communications' publication *Planning for Telecommunications: A School Leader's Primer* (Kitchen, Wagner, and Ward, 1989) is a brief guide for planners at the K–12 educational level. Its overview of practical considerations for the introduction of telecommunications-based education can be adapted to other educational and nonschool contexts. The booklet contains rules of thumb for costs and a comparison of selected technologies in terms that nontechnical managers can readily grasp. An example of a feasibility study for a two-way interactive video system and an overview of models and methodologies of instructional design are useful introductions to these subjects for nonspecialists.

Values

Significant sources on values and telecommunications-based education have yet to emerge. However, there is useful information on multiculturalism and other value considerations in continuing education that can enable managers of telecommunications-based education to compare and evaluate their own thinking with regard to value-laden issues. One of the best books on issues in multiculturalism, edited by Ross-Gordon, Martin, and Briscoe (1990), is a practical guide to current criteria considered desirable in programs intended to meet the needs of culturally diverse learners. Researchers and practitioners can use this book as a reference and point of departure from which to apply some of the criteria denoting good practices in multiculturalism. Including theoretical perspectives with an analysis of common barriers to participation by diverse constituencies in continuing education, this book offers a realistic approach for managers of telecommunications-based education at all levels.

The study of participation in nontraditional education in general has been a major focus in the adult education literature since the mid 1960s, when the first major national study of participation was undertaken. Merriam and Caffarella (1991) provide a comprehensive introduction to present knowledge in the field of adult learning. They devote an entire chapter to findings concerned with the reasons why adults may or may not participate in learning opportunities (pp. 79–95).

Among the best texts that draw together value considerations of many kinds for managers of continuing education is *Visions for the Future of Continuing Professional Education* (Cervero, Azzaretto, and Associates, 1990). This is a compendium of perspectives on values that professionals are urged to regard as vital to continuing professional education. The book's summary by Knox (1990), "Emerging Imperatives for the Continuing Professional Educator," is an excellent starting point for managers who intend to include values in the management and outcomes of telecommunications-based education.

An earlier work that is also among the most useful sources for addressing values in continuing education is *Ethical Issues in Adult Education* (Brockett, 1988), especially the first chapter, "Ethics and the Adult Educator." Two articles written from a perspective of ethics and management in business offer sound grounding for all managers of telecommunications-based education: Carroll's "In Search of the Moral Manager" (1987) and Hosmer's "Managerial Ethics and Normative Philosophy" (1987).

Personal Networking

Numerous national conferences are held in telecommunications-based education. Their addresses are provided at the end of the chapter. One of the most approachable activities for a newcomer to the field is the annual Conference on Distance Teaching and Learning in Madison, Wisconsin. This conference bridges business and education at all levels. Sponsored by several organizational units of the University of Wisconsin as well as by state agencies, the conference is organized in tracks: learners' needs, instructional design, research, evaluation, international models, and professional development. Highly focused workshop sessions emphasize interaction among the participants. The relatively small size of the conference (under five hundred) and its reputation for quality and internationalism have given this event a unique place among general conferences for professionals in this field. The conference papers are available for purchase.

Any manager in the field needs to become an active member of at least one professional association in continuing education, distance education, or telecommunications-based education. One of the oldest such associations in higher education is the National University Continuing Education Association (NUCEA), which requires institutional membership before an individual can join. For managers working in universities, NUCEA's Division of Educational Telecommunications and its Independent Study Division are key sources of contact with leaders in telecommunications-based education.

The Community College Satellite Network of the American Association of Community and Junior Colleges, like the National University Teleconference Network (NUTN), focuses on videoconferencing production and reception. The latter, however, is unique in that it is one of the few associations that brings together universities and community colleges to work together on a daily basis. NUTN's annual conference is open to nonmembers. A third leading national association is the International Teleconferencing Association. This association draws individuals from education, business, and government and covers a range of mutual concerns that, despite the association's name, focus primarily on this country.

Regional associations in various parts of the country gather and exchange information on telecommunications, among a number of other issues. One such association is the Western Interstate Commission for Higher Education (WICHE), where the interests of educational policy makers have been the focus for many years. WICHE's Western Cooperative for Educational Telecommunications deals with issues, research, and practices of concern to specialists and nonspecialists at all educational levels and in other organizational settings. Internationally, the major organization is the International Council on Distance Education. This long-established organization, which holds conferences every two years in various parts of the world, is worldwide in structure, focus, and governance. It is headquartered in Norway.

Participation by managers of telecommunications-based education and training in a regional, national, or international association can be a key to the personal contacts that lead to reliable sources of expertise on technical, operational, conceptual, and policy considerations. Such associations can also be a primary avenue for becoming professionally active as a writer and presenter while gaining a sound grounding in the field.

Tracking Trends

Several useful sources exist that follow trends in policy, statewide planning, research on issues in continuing and distance education and telecommunications, business applications of telecommunications, and selected learner-centered issues.

Policy

Regional associations of educators are a good source of reports that track policy issues concerned with telecommunications. Another source of information on policy matters that can affect all educational levels is the association of State Higher Education Executive Officers (SHEEO) and the Education Commission of the States (ECS). Lenth (1990), for example, prepared a report on state priorities in higher education, published jointly by SHEEO and ECS, that enables managers to better understand the place of electronic technologies in the thinking of state planners.

Statewide Planning

Statewide activities regarding educational telecommunications systems throughout the nation have been followed for a number of years by the Annenberg/Corporation for Public Broadcasting Project. Written under the authorship of Hezel Associates (1990), these are descriptive rather than analytical reports. They contain useful listings of resource people for each state.

Research

Several bibliographies in texts have been noted earlier. From 1986 to 1989, NUCEA's Independent Study Division prepared an annual, annotated selected bibliography of applications of electronic technologies to distance education. These excellent bibliographies were informally distributed and were discontinued with the inclusion of this information in the electronic data base of the national Educational Resources Information Center (ERIC).

A key research-oriented periodical is the *American Journal for Distance Education.* This journal is useful to general readers as well as specialists. Its topics range widely and encompass many issues related to telecommunications-based education and training in educational and noneducational settings, both in this country and abroad. Its two close counterparts internationally are *Distance Education,* published in Australia, and the Canadian Association for Distance Education's *Journal of Distance Education.*

Another educational journal, *Continuing Higher Education Review,* is published by NUCEA and directed to professionals in university continuing and distance education. While this periodical does not emphasize telecommunications-based education, it is a reliable source of writing on topics of interest to professionals working in distance and continuing education. For example, Apps (1990) examines beliefs and values as they apply to adults as learners. A framework is proposed that any manager of telecommunications-based education should consider when relating values to programming aims and purposes. Apps's article represents a trend in conceptualization that places increasing importance on the place of values in managerial decision making.

One of the most useful periodicals that track trends in the application of electronic technologies to education at all levels is *T.H.E. Journal* (Technological Horizons in Education). While not strictly a research-based journal, this periodical offers data-based, thought-provoking, and balanced writing that focuses on the practical applications of various technologies to education and training.

The Pew Higher Education Research Program publishes a research-based periodical, *Policy Perspectives,* that addresses themes of importance to managers of nontraditional education. While the orientation of this periodical is the improvement of postsecondary education, the issues it covers — educational costs and outcomes, partnerships, cultural diversity, and the teaching-learning exchange, among others — speak to many of the responsibilities of managers of telecommunications-based education. For example, *Policy Perspectives* explores educational reform in terms of a need to "provide instruction to a diverse constituency . . . [and] to develop and apply appropriate standards for measuring results . . . [directed at] improving quality and access. Postsecondary educators are encouraged to "build more effective partnerships . . . and make better use of technology" (Pew Higher Education Research Program, 1992, pp. 5A-6A).

The American Symposium on Research in Distance Education is an invitational meeting that commenced in 1988. Numerous articles, papers, and books have been produced that, among other issues, explore applications of electronic technologies to education. A bibliography containing sources of the growing literature from the symposium is available from the American Center for the Study of Distance Education at Pennsylvania State University.

Corporate Telecommunications

Trends in business applications of telecommunications are covered in *Business TV,* a popularly written and reliable nontechnical periodical. Its articles bring together information regarding developments in business applications of electronic technologies and provide useful interpretations of trends in educational telecommunications systems in corporate environments.

Compilations of Sources

Trends in sources themselves and ways to access them are among the most difficult to track. By identifying an outstanding "source on sources," managers can become aware of less easily located resources, particularly those that are unpublished. The states that are pioneers in educational telecommunications systems are among the best sources of reports that compile lists of information resources.

For example, Oklahoma is among states that have pioneered in statewide educational applications of electronic technologies. The University of Oklahoma has been particularly active in exploring and reporting on uses of telecommunications-based education at all educational levels. A publication from the University of Oklahoma (Dillon, Blanchard, and Price, 1990), *The Emerging Role of Telecommunications in Higher Education — Improving Teaching at a Distance: A Guide to Resources,* is an excellent compendium of information for managers of telecommunications-based education at all educational levels. The guide contains annotations that include addresses and phone numbers for sources across the country, vendors of equipment, major national associations, conferences, and books, journals, directories, and other publications in the field. A glossary of terms and costs of typical equipment are included in this usefully organized publication.

Student-Centered Issues

Tracking the work of a specialist can guide managers through a maze of literature. For example, Gunawardena (1988) prepared an award-winning unpublished doctoral dissertation on the integration of video-based instruction and distance education, and its implications for learners. This researcher continues to focus on instructional design with an approach that is accessible to managers who are not instructional designers but who wish to become more knowledgeable about how new technologies affect learning.

A conference paper by Gunawardena and Saito (1989) provides an introduction for nonspecialists to the thinking of leaders in instructional design on the application of electronic technology to learning. Dillon and Gunawardena (1990) have prepared a report on another learner-centered concern, *Learner*

Support as the Critical Link in Distance Education, which offers practical guidance to managers on a vital learner-focused topic. None of this research is easily accessed; it either remains unpublished or is published noncommercially. Thus personal networking with authors such as these in order to follow their work is often the best method of staying informed over time.

A learner-centered issue that receives a great deal of attention in research on electronic technologies is interactivity in teaching and learning. Interactivity can be student-to-student, student-to-instructor, or student-with-content. The term also refers to group or individual dialogue, either verbal, electronic, or written, that occurs during an instructional session, at another time, or in connection with a specific instructional event, such as feedback on coursework and examinations.

An unpublished paper by Threlkeld, Behm, and Shiflett (1991) is indicative of some of the research on student interactivity being undertaken singly and in partnership with other postsecondary institutions. The Distance Learning Center at California State Polytechnic University, Pomona, conducts research among high school and adult students in corporate, home, and educational settings where a variety of one-way video and two-way audio technologies are used.

One set of preliminary findings suggests that interaction by high school students during instructional sessions is highly related to good student performance and positive attitudes, as well as to students' feelings of inclusion in the class. Other findings comparing adult students with high school students in several contexts suggest that adults place less importance than do younger learners on in-class interaction and put more importance on other forms of interaction, such as prompt feedback on coursework.

These findings do not constitute a major introduction to work on interactivity and its numerous complexities. They do, however, introduce managers to a center of research on student interactivity in telecommunications-based education and to some of the issues being studied. Other long-standing research of this kind is conducted at postsecondary institutions in this country and abroad, especially at institutions that have been conducting distance education activities for some time. This research is reported regularly in journals such as the *American Journal of Distance Education;* it suggests a starting point for networking with colleagues on educational telecommunications systems, a topic that has long interested distance educators and is now being studied by many researchers.

For managers of telecommunications-based education in any context who are intrigued by the possible effects of technology on human behavior and interaction, the work of Johansen (1988) and his group of researchers at the Institute for the Future in Menlo Park, California, is important. This group's thinking has for some years been at the forefront of what might be termed the sociology and psychology of interactive electronic technologies.

Linking Resources to Managerial Concerns

How can the resources described in this chapter be linked to the list of core managerial concerns presented earlier? There is no single correct way to assemble these resources in relation to the core concerns. One possible approach is the following:

1. *Environmental concerns.* The U.S. Congress, Office of Technology Assessment's *Linking for Learning: A New Course for Education* (1989) and Niemi and Gooler's *Technologies for Learning Outside the Classroom* (1987) are good starting points for any manager of telecommunications-based education.
2. *Partnerships.* Look to membership associations and conferences as the most likely sources of timely, practical information. The University of Wisconsin's Conference on Distance Teaching and Learning is a starting point.
3. *Technologies.* Starting with the U.S. Congress, Office of Technology Assessment's *Linking for Learning: A New Course for Education* (1989) will enable a nontechnical manager to gain a working vocabulary related to electronic technology and an overview of how various electronic technologies apply to particular conditions.
4. *Costs.* The U.S. Congress, Office of Technology Assessment's *Linking for Learning: A New Course for Education* (1989); Kitchen, Wagner, and Ward's *Planning for Telecommunica-*

tions: A School Leader's Primer (1989); and Dillon, Blanchard, and Price's *The Emerging Role of Telecommunications in Higher Education — Improving Teaching at a Distance: A Guide to Resources* (1990) offer an introduction to the costs of equipment that can be a starting point from which to proceed to the other cost management sources recommended in Chapter Six.

5. *Managing change.* Membership associations are a key ongoing source of new perspectives on the management of change in this field. Together with the references cited in Chapters Three and Five, some good starting points from which to approach the vast literature on management and leadership are Bolman and Deal's *Reframing Organizations* (1991), Morgan's *Images of Organization* (1986), and Bennis's often-cited article, "The Four Competencies of Leadership" (1984).

6. *Revenue.* Look to regional and national membership associations for new ideas and success stories that address ways to generate program income.

7. *Quality.* No basic literature on standards of quality in telecommunications-based education proposes universally accepted measures. An initial perspective on this topic can be gained by reading Apps's "Beliefs, Values and Vision Making for Continuing Higher Education" (1990); Cervero, Azzaretto, and Associates' *Visions for the Future of Continuing Professional Education* (1990); and Ross-Gordon, Martin, and Briscoe's *Serving Culturally Diverse Populations* (1990). A useful way to track thinking on quality and standards over time is through the *American Journal of Distance Education* and unpublished papers, particularly those focused on learner-centered developments.

8. *Trends.* Newcomers can get a grounding in trends through the U.S. Congress, Office of Technology Assessment's *Linking for Learning: A New Course for Education* (1989) and by becoming active in membership associations regionally and nationally.

9. *Interpreting and applying findings.* The *Continuing Higher Education Review* and the *American Journal of Distance Education* are two of the most useful broad-brush resources related to this area of concern. Regional and national membership associations provide opportunities for focus in this area.

Associations and Conferences

The following is a selected list of associations, conferences, periodicals, and reports that can be combined differently depending on the perspective, context, and developmental stage of telecommunications-based activities.

American Association of Community and Junior Colleges (AACJC), Community College Satellite Network, One DuPont Circle, N.W., Suite 410, Washington, DC 20036-1176.

Conference on Distance Teaching and Learning, Madison Education Extension Programs, University of Wisconsin, Madison, 159 Education Building, 1000 Bascom Hall, Madison, WI 53776-1385.

Education Commission of the States (ECS), 1860 Lincoln Street, Suite 300, Denver, CO 80295.

Educational Resources Information Center (ERIC), U.S. Department of Education, Office of Educational Research and Improvement, 555 New Jersey Avenue NW, Washington, DC 20208-5720.

International Council on Distance Education (ICDE), Gjerdrums vei 12, N-0486, Oslo 4, Norway.

International Teleconferencing Association (ITCA), 1299 Woodside Drive, McLean, VA 22102.

National University Continuing Education Association (NUCEA), One DuPont Circle, Suite 615, Washington, DC 20036.

National University Teleconference Network (NUTN), Oklahoma State University, 210 Public Information Building, Stillwater, OK 74078-0653.

Western Interstate Commission for Higher Education (WICHE), Western Cooperative for Educational Telecommunications, P.O. Drawer P, Boulder, CO 80301-9752.

Periodicals and Reports and Their Sources

American Center for the Study of Distance Education, College of Education, Pennsylvania State University,

403 South Allen Street, Suite 206, University Park, PA 16801-5202.

American Journal of Distance Education, 403 South Allen Street, Suite 206, Pennsylvania State University, University Park, PA 16801-5202.

Annenberg/Corporation for Public Broadcasting Research Reports, 1111 Sixteenth Street N.W., Washington, DC 20036.

Branhorst, T., and Eustace, J. (eds.). *Directory of ERIC Information Providers.* Washington, D.C.: Educational Resources Information Center, 1986.

Business TV, Telespan Publishing Corporation, P.O. Box 6250, Altadena, CA 91001.

Continuing Higher Education Review, National University Continuing Education Association, One DuPont Circle, Suite 615, Washington, DC 20036.

Distance Education, USQ Press, University College of Southern Queensland, P.O. Darling Heights, Toowoomba, Queensland 4350, Australia.

Journal of Distance Education, Canadian Association for Distance Education (CADE) Secretariat, 151 Slater Street, Ottawa, Ontario KIP 5N2, Canada.

Policy Perspectives, Institute for Research on Higher Education, The Pew Higher Education Research Program, University of Pennsylvania, 4200 Pine Street, 5A, Philadelphia, PA 19104-4090.

T.H.E. Journal, 150 El Camino Real, Suite 112, Tustin, CA 92680-9833.

Summary

Program purposes, priorities, and values are the primary guides to useful sources of information at each stage of the development of telecommunications-based education. The process of becoming knowledgeable and remaining informed requires systematically narrowing the pool of possible resources to a trusted set of publications, associations, and professional peers. Well-informed individuals have achieved that status by turning to a relatively small group of resources that can be reliably consulted over time.

Regional and national associations are excellent sources of mainstream telecommunications-based educational developments. Periodicals are more likely to introduce new perspectives and present more in-depth findings on sensitive topics such as quality, multiculturalism, and values. Books are the most likely sources of detailed accounts of such concerns as managing costs or comparing equipment specifications. Learner-centered research directed to nontechnical managers is more often found in unpublished, less accessible sources.

Those who stay on top of the field continually use new information, which they synthesize and resynthesize by presenting it regularly to audiences whose level of professionalism varies. Opportunities to publish and consult are needed to sustain an information-rich professional environment. Sources of information are combined and recombined in a process that tailors resources to evolving personal and situational tasks. Managers who begin with a perspective that takes its cue from core managerial concerns can put together a small, workable combination of resources that will bring two essential qualities to information gathering: balance and focus.

Policy Issues
in the New Telesphere

Myth: The managers of educational telecommunications systems need to have
little interest in policy development beyond finding ways to provide adequate
funding for the specific effort under their
direction.

Reality: If left without a solution to a pressing problem, the political system will
create one. Consequently, managers of
educational telecommunications systems
must be prepared to take an active role
in shaping educational policy at the institutional, state, regional, and federal
levels.

The day-to-day operational challenges of telecommunications-
based programming are often so demanding that managers find
it difficult to give proper attention to the many larger policy issues raised by the introduction of technology into educational

settings. Some of the dangers of focusing solely on operations to the neglect of political issues have already been noted in previous chapters. This chapter extends the discussion into the policy arena and argues that managers of these systems must become articulate participants in policy development at a variety of levels within the change environment.

The emergence of telecommunications-based education is taking place within the context of a fundamental debate about the content and quality of education, and its clientele. The need for a highly educated society in order to meet the challenges of today's world is widely recognized. Virtually everyone regards the development of human resources as a key ingredient in fostering economic competitiveness within the emerging global economy. But traditional education and training are under heavy attack. Critics within and outside the academy demand not only improvement in the quality of public and private education, but also greater access to educational opportunity in order to meet the need for a highly trained and motivated work force.

On the one hand, vocal critics of current educational practices in the United States decry the declining quality of education at all levels, point to a variety of measures to substantiate their claims, and call for a return to the basics. Some propose innovation as a means of meeting the growing demand for improved quality. Others note that quality is by no means the only problem. Certain segments of the population have been and remain notoriously underserved and therefore find it difficult to compete with the more privileged. Racial and ethnic minorities, women, older students, and people living in rural areas of the nation, for example, find it difficult to participate even though access to education is increasingly seen as a key ingredient in improving their quality of life and promoting economic development. Thus, many national problems are reflected in increased demands for improved quality and access to education to meet society's needs.

This chapter is based on the premise that managers of educational telecommunications systems must become knowledgeable and articulate advocates within the public policy arena if telecommunications-based education is to reach its full potential as a solution to problems of access. Among the most important policy issues of concern to managers are who will have access to the programming, what will be taught, who will teach it, how will the content of the program be regarded and who will pay for it. Much existing educational policy was formulated before current forms of telecommunications technology existed. Consequently, some existing policies actually hinder rather than promote the application of telecommunications technologies to societal problems. It is vital that managers familiarize themselves with the issues, attempt to influence the decisions that are made by educating those who are directly involved, and apply their expertise in the field to enlighten the policy makers at every opportunity.

If managers fail to make themselves a factor in these matters, telecommunications-based education may not be advanced as a potential solution to problems of educational access and equity or may be unrealistically advanced as a complete solution to these problems. In either case the stakes are high: failure has important implications for how well the challenges of an emerging global society will be met. Given the complexity of the topic, this chapter should be regarded as an initial foray into a field where issues are still being identified and debated rather than as a definitive statement. Nevertheless, it is a call to action for managers of educational telecommunications systems.

Determining Who Will Benefit

One of the primary ideological appeals of those who champion the integration of telecommunications with existing educational programming has been the possibility of providing the underserved with access to educational opportunity. There are many underserved groups. There is, for example, a growing need for educational programming to upgrade the skills of the work force in an economy where job requirements are constantly changing and where the composition of the work force is shifting toward women, immigrants, and minorities. At both the individual and collective levels, there is an increasing recognition of the need and demand for additional educational and training opportunities. Yet significant barriers to participation remain in place at all levels of education. Therefore, the issue of access quickly becomes a discussion about equity.

It is well known that many contemporary adult education programs do not adequately serve minority populations. Those who do participate tend to be younger, with a higher educational level and a higher income. Many minority individuals find that they are unable to participate in traditional higher education programs because the attendance requirements conflict with other demands on their time and attention. Others do not participate because they have not been successful in past educational endeavors and see little hope for change in the future. To a large degree minorities have never found the educational environment hospitable to their needs because they do not fit the typical student profile, and some simply cannot afford the costs involved.

Managers must become familiar with the various elements of this discussion because telecommunications-based education is one potential solution to concerns about access. As its champions point out, technology can be used to overcome many barriers of time and place. The ability of telecommunications systems to serve the needs of the geographically isolated or place-bound learner has been well demonstrated, allowing individuals who live hundreds or even thousands of miles from the provider of needed education or training to participate in programming.

Time barriers can also be overcome through the use of certain forms of technology. People who have a job or home commitments that prevent them from meeting the rigid attendance requirements of on-campus instruction may participate via television or videotaped instruction at a time that is more convenient for them. Other forms of telecommunications-based education, such as those that rely on computer-assisted instruction, allow students to pace themselves, thereby removing many of the time barriers to participation. Integration of telecommunications with existing educational efforts offers much promise as a means of meeting the needs of the underserved. Managers must bring this type of education to the forefront whenever the educational access of these groups is discussed.

Serving the Underserved

The ability of telecommunications-based education to overcome barriers of time and place is of considerable interest for groups such as women, the physically challenged, and those who live in rural areas. Telecourses, which combine television presentations with extensive printed materials, are heavily used by women, who may be unable to leave their homes and attend traditional classes due to the demands of parenting. Television segments can be broadcast directly to the home or can be made available via videotape. Furthermore, recording the programs off the air allows the participant to view them while working around an unpredictable schedule. Managers must become involved in discussions in this area since they can be a factor in successfully opening access to this routinely underserved group.

The ability of telecommunications-based education to remove time and place constraints is important for other underserved groups as well. Many of the physically challenged can utilize some forms of telecommunications-based education more readily than they can on-campus classroom instruction. Persons who are confined for health or other reasons can also have access to previously denied opportunities. An array of technical systems that can be matched to the needs of the learner can significantly reduce barriers to educational opportunity.

The need to open access for minorities is great. The increasing reliance upon the development of a highly skilled work force as a way to keep the nation competitive in the global economy necessitates acknowledging the demographic reality that minorities will constitute over half of the total U.S. population by the year 2050 (Moe, 1990). In the future, workers will come from populations that have traditionally been discriminated against and who have been left unprepared for any but the most menial labor. These populations present a significant challenge to educators and human resource professionals, who typically work within systems that have long neglected the learning needs of minorities (Martin and Ross-Gordon, 1990).

Nor is higher education's hospitality to diversity very encouraging. Of all the demographic groups it serves, the minority adult population is the least accommodated (Moe, 1989). Studies tend to agree that increasing minority participation in higher education is a matter of financially and educationally implementing programs that involve academic assessment, adequate tutorial and mentoring services, visible minority leadership, and a commitment to an academic and social environment that support learning in a multicultural setting (Moe, 1989).

To alleviate social problems, institutions of postsecondary education will need to find ways to reduce existing barriers to promoting student diversity. The primary way to achieve this goal is through altering existing patterns of delivering education in an attempt to reach the previously underserved (Moe, 1990). When the parent organization is slow to make changes, a manager of an educational telecommunications system who is committed to serving the underserved can play a vital role as a change agent. In order to do so, he or she must make educational programs more relevant, accessible, sensitive, and acceptable to the underserved. For instance, the manager has an obligation to develop educational programs that provide participants with knowledge and skills, while at the same time maintaining respect for the cultural legacies and histories of individuals and groups (Moe, 1990). In fact, one of the future challenges faced by educators is the need to provide programs that address sensitive and potentially explosive issues in the workplace itself (Martin and Ross-Gordon, 1990). Examples of such programs include education for managers designed to help them remove mixed messages from their communications, programs for employees in a pluralistic work force to correct deficiencies in communication skills, and programs that specifically deal with organizational problems and issues resulting from inattention to the needs of a culturally diverse workplace (Martin and Ross-Gordon, 1990).

Where service to a rural constituency is a part of the parent organization's mission, the manager of an educational telecommunications system has a clear and direct interest in policy making related to service to rural areas. People who live in these areas have well-documented needs for education and training (McCannon and Crom, 1988). However, the low population density and low income levels in many rural areas constitute considerable barriers to participation. Rural areas also have a considerable need to provide opportunities for people to retrain themselves for new employment opportunities and new careers. Opportunities for lifelong learning are crucial to the survival of rural populations, whose problems of technological advances, displacement from agricultural occupations, and unemployment all require educational solutions. In addition, whereas new populations continue to come into urban areas, providing fresh human capital, rural areas often experience negative population growth and must rely on a diminished, aging population whose retraining and educational retrofitting are the only means of promoting economic growth.

Both highly specialized and more general educational opportunities are needed. Their absence can adversely affect the ability of companies to recruit and retain the highly skilled professionals and workers needed to promote and sustain economic growth. A company that is an important element in a local economy, for example, may find it difficult to recruit recently graduated professionals into a particular geographical region because it offers no opportunities to pursue appropriate advanced degrees. Highly qualified potential employees might elect not to relocate to such an area, fearing the long-range implications for their professional advancement. These key individuals play a vital role in providing and maintaining economic opportunities for a considerable portion of the population within a given community and therefore exert an influence on the local economy that is not reflected in numbers alone.

The argument that impact must be assessed can be made in health care, engineering, education, and many other areas. In each case, the professionals involved are widely dispersed in rural areas but need ongoing access to continuing education and training if they are to maintain a high quality of service to the population. Failure to provide a means of access can result in an unacceptably poor quality of life for rural populations as a whole. Thus, providing access to educational and training opportunities for rural areas is not only a matter of serving the needs of large numbers of people; it may also provide access for individuals who have the ability to significantly affect the quality of life for entire communities.

The absence of educational and training opportunities within a rural area can also determine the willingness of a company to locate in or remain in an area. Increasingly, the competitive demands of the global economy can only be met through ongoing training of the available work force. If resources for that training are readily available, the economic possibilities are dramatically increased. Access to education and training therefore becomes a key consideration in promoting economic development.

The Equity Dimension

It is clear that technology is a potential solution to many problems related to access to educational and training opportunities and that managers of educational telecommunications systems must seize the initiative to become articulate participants in the policy- and decision-making processes. However, for those who examine the issue of access closely, there is a corollary concern about equity. Providing access to education and training for additional representatives of the same or similar groups of people does not really deal with the issue of access. The paradox is that the same technologies that empower some disempower others.

It is important for the manager to recognize that all forms of technology involve trade-offs. Successful technology usually supports the status quo because it is introduced in support of existing programs and therefore provides ever-greater access to people who already have considerable access (Jacobson, 1991). In addition, technology is often expensive, ensuring that it is likely to be made available first to those who can best afford it. A key concern for the policy maker must be the extent to which the technology might be exploited to favor one group over another. This is of particular concern when access for ethnic minorities and the economically disadvantaged is at stake.

Since telecommunications-based education offers a potential solution to a number of concerns related to access, it is important for those who have expertise in the area to become a part of the decision-making process. Managers must do more than simply advocate telecommunications as a solution to problems of access, however. More important is the need to help all concerned articulate a realizable vision for telecommunications in discussions related to access. In short, the manager has an interest wherever a policy-making decision can have an impact on the parent organization's ability to serve the underserved, and he or she must be prepared to address the embedded equity issues.

Financing Telecommunications-Based Education

One of the most important equity issues facing the manager of telecommunications-based education is how to finance its operation. A consistent claim of early champions of technology was that such systems offered a relatively inexpensive means of providing access to education, particularly to widely dispersed audiences. Unfortunately, distributing education over a wide geographical area is not inexpensive, and operating costs are often higher than the costs of providing the same educational program on terms more convenient to the organization.

Because of the considerable costs of telecommunications-based education, a key policy issue for managers concerns the question of who should pay for the service. When programs are provided to the general public, some portion of the total cost can be recovered through tuition and other student fees. If the potential student density is sufficiently high or the specific clientele has the ability to pay relatively high tuition and fees, the potential for recovering all costs directly from the learners may be good.

One means of recovering costs is to impose a relatively high tuition and fee structure. However, this severely limits access to those who can afford to pay or whose employee benefits include reimbursement for such expenses. As a result, the needs of more highly paid professionals are more likely to be served than those of nonprofessionals. When the developmental costs of a telecommunications system are underwritten by a private company, the system is driven by the needs of that company. Often this results in systems that are only available to larger and more profitable companies, who can afford the costs. In each case the net result is an increase in educational opportunities for those who already have considerable advantage.

Even when the primary audience is a highly paid professional group, low population density may make it impossible
to operate the system solely on the basis of the income generated from tuition and fees. In addition, when the provider is
a public institution charged with offering instruction to the
citizens of the state, tuition and fee structures that differentiate
between on- and off-campus learners may be resisted by potential participants who argue that they already provide support
for the institution in the form of taxes. Interestingly, states that
are willing to subsidize higher education in an on-campus setting often require the costs of off-campus instruction to be paid
fully by the participants. The fact that no other group of students is required to do this raises a basic policy issue related
to payment: how much of the cost of telecommunications-based
education should participants be required to pay?

The problem is related to what McCannon and Crom
(1988, p. 9) characterize as "the volume driven model of self-
support" for continuing education. Continued use of this model
results in denying access to those who are most in need. McCannon and Crom contend that unless this approach to funding is
changed, access will be denied to underserved learners in rural
areas; this argument can be extended to include a variety of
other underserved groups as well. Supporters of changing this
policy argue that "the costs of such developments [educational
telecommunications systems] are minimal compared with the
accumulated costs to placebound students who would otherwise
encounter the significantly higher costs of relocation — and lost
opportunities" (Enarson, Widmayer, and Trendler, 1990, p. 64).

Arguments concerning cost-effectiveness for educational
telecommunications systems are difficult to make in many cases
because most analyses ignore the savings involved. Items such
as the amount of time saved by participants who do not have
to commute long distances are rarely included. No value is put
on the amount of time away from work or family that is reduced
by more accessible educational activities, nor are the costs of
relocation taken into account. How much is it worth to an individual, a family, or a community to avoid the disruption of
moving to another location in order to pursue a desired educa-

tional goal? Finally, what are the lost opportunity costs for a company or community when the net result of failing to provide educational access is the loss of highly skilled and motivated workers? Unfortunately the savings involved are indirect, difficult to estimate accurately, and therefore often ignored.

The volume-driven model of self-support for educational telecommunications systems is also a cause for concern for those who wish to assure equal access to the latest educational technologies for minority adults (Ross-Gordon, Martin, and Briscoe, 1990). Reliance upon this model ensures that the communities, school systems, companies, and individuals with the most resources will be the first to receive emerging educational services. Those with fewer resources may lag far behind in acquiring the benefits of the new technologies.

Thus, under the self-support model, a significant barrier to participation for many of the underserved is the lack of financial resources needed to pay for the desired educational activity (O'Brien, 1990). Policy often accentuates this problem. Current federal policy, for example, makes it difficult for those who pursue education on a part-time basis to get financial aid. In addition, it further discriminates against those who pursue nontraditional educational opportunities, especially when the activities do not conform closely in all respects to on-campus instruction. Therefore, the volume-driven model must be replaced by more innovative approaches or the net result will be an intolerable gap between the haves and have-nots based on who can afford to gain access to needed educational and training opportunities (Apps, 1988).

Issues of equity must be carefully considered when decisions regarding financing are made by the managers of educational telecommunications systems. Jacobson (1991) points out, for example, that in Alaska some communities have toll-free access to a statewide computer network, whereas the majority of communities must pay a toll to achieve the same level of access. The result is a growing gap between empowered and newly disempowered groups. Similar inequities characterize systems that only serve the more populous areas in predominantly rural states. In still another example of inequity, the level of technology is unevenly distributed throughout the system. What are the implications of providing some learners on a system with two-way video and audio, while others only have access to one-way video and two-way audio? The manager must be aware of the need for policy that more closely ties together funding and equity.

Influencing the Internal Decision-Making Process

The manager must also work to make telecommunications a factor in decisions related to a variety of institutional policies. More than at any time in the past, postsecondary institutions are being asked to provide lifelong learning opportunities to an increasingly diverse learner population. Prominent voices within the literature on higher education are calling for a redefinition of public service and a closer alliance between societal needs and university activities (Apps, 1988; Lynton and Elman, 1987). They note the increasing blurring of traditional distinctions between teaching, research, and outreach or extension activities (Apps, 1988). In this view, institutions of postsecondary education can no longer serve only young people just out of high school. They must also respond to the needs of adult students for both credit and noncredit offerings, to calls by industry and business for better-trained employees, and to the needs of communities for assistance in solving local problems (Apps, 1988).

Within the emerging telesphere, the question of what is the most economical method of providing educational or training opportunities to the greatest number must be brought to the forefront. The advocate of integrating telecommunications with education becomes an important voice in discussions and decisions related to the changing mission of the institution and the place of telecommunications-based education. Too often such decisions have been and continue to be made on the basis of traditional criteria that ignore new opportunities and challenges.

In many cases the manager must become a spokesperson for a shift in focus to a wider consideration of the wise use of resources for the greater good, rather than maintaining a narrowly defined self-interest. The discussion must shift from a strictly parochial view to include statewide, regional, national, or even international considerations. Telecommunications systems often provide a means of reaching beyond the immediate geographical vicinity, but few of the groups empowered to make decisions are inclined to look very far beyond their own service area. For example, institutional boards are likely to build a program that is under their sole control and is dedicated to servicing needs within an immediate geographical area. Yet if the maximum benefits are to be achieved, collaborative efforts must reach across existing authority lines and develop telecommunications systems with other providers. The advocate of telecommunications must become an articulate spokesperson for the wider view and, to the extent possible, play an educational leadership role. A wider perspective is especially important when the discussion of policy moves beyond the institutional level.

At the same time, there are a variety of policy issues at the institutional level that must be of concern to the advocate of integrating telecommunications and continuing education. Too often emphasis on technology overshadows any discussion of changes in internal academic policies to accommodate distance education efforts (Olcott, 1991). This is unfortunate because the policy issues raised include such basic matters as residency, academic standards, faculty compensation, promotion and tenure, and student and faculty support services. The manager must be cognizant of these issues and their ramifications since the goal is to bring about, in Olcott's words, "an equilibrium that fuses proven traditional academic instructional systems with new learning systems" (1991, p. 52).

Many of the institutional issues concern traditional measures of quality for telecommunications-based education. As was noted in Chapter Three, numerous studies over the years have confirmed that students using distance education formats achieve on a par with students involved in traditional classroom instruction; however, there remain questions about the intellectual equivalency of these experiences. At one time much of the discussion centered on the provision of equivalent support services such as advising and library access, but various forms of technology are increasingly providing alternatives to traditional face-to-face physical contact.

Students participating in distance learning, for example, can access library services through electronic means. Advising may be accomplished through occasional travel to the originating institution or at a variety of dispersed sites, and, in many cases, by telephone and fax. While some concerns have been alleviated, others centering around the relationship between the learner and the scholarly community remain.

Most often these concerns are manifested in policies related to residency. Residency typically refers to the number of credit hours a student must complete in residence (on campus) to complete a degree program. These requirements were initiated as a means of ensuring that a learner who earned a degree from an institution had in fact acquired a substantial portion of the coursework from the degree-granting institution. Traditionally, resident status was denied to any courses that deviated from traditional classroom instruction. In some institutions courses delivered by telecommunications have been denied resident status on that basis. Those who hold to a traditional definition of residency generally stress the total learning experience provided in an on-campus setting, including involvement in the cultural life of the campus and opportunities for interaction with peers, faculty, and administrators. Those engaged in distance education degree programs most often point to the considerable barrier such policies put in the way of place-bound adults whose responsibilities preclude attendance. They also point out that the learners in these programs are likely to be adults for whom the degree is the primary motivation and who have less need for on-campus experiences, which are often more suited to eighteen-year-olds. Thus, policies concerning residency often have a direct bearing on the accessibility to underserved groups.

The issue of residency is often made extremely complicated by traditionalists. The primary concerns are not only how much of a program of study must be completed as resident credit, but also how a particular course is classified. In the strictest definition, a resident course is one that is taught on campus as part of the regular campus program by full-time faculty. Others define residency in terms of who teaches rather than where the teaching takes place, or certain geographical locations may be declared resident sites to the exclusion of others. Some definitions put an emphasis on adherence to the schedule of the on-campus program. Thus, if a course is taught off campus but meets on the same schedule as if it were on campus, it is a resident course. Other institutions have removed all distinctions concerning residency, regarding any credit generated by an institution as simply credit toward whatever program is being pursued.

Since matters of residency can have an important impact on telecommunications-based educational programs, the manager will benefit from familiarity with the existing definition as well as with the circumstances under which policy decisions are made. He or she can attempt to influence the process toward more liberal interpretations of residency but must be sensitive to the institutional values embedded in such questions. Advocating a position that is too extreme in view of the existing culture can undermine the advocate's credibility.

Another set of issues at the institutional level centers around providing the instructional staff with the resources, including time, that are needed to effectively provide instruction. All modes of distance education require some additional effort by the instructional faculty, who must modify their conventional instructional approach to meet the demands of the technology involved and the clientele being served. These modifications might be minor or extensive. For example, an instructor who wished to take an exercise that was traditionally presented in a group setting and make it available and viable in a computer-assisted independent-study mode would undoubtedly face a considerable challenge involving much creativity and effort. On the other hand, a "live" presentation delivered to off-campus locations might require only minor modifications.

The manager must be aware of such concerns and be prepared to accommodate them. The specific approach is likely to vary depending on the institutional context. One means of providing support for faculty involvement is by supporting individual academic units in gaining recognition for efforts that involve telecommunications; the manager might, for example, support an academic unit's request for additional faculty or other

resources. If such a strategy is not available, one that compen-
sates individual faculty directly for their efforts might be pursued. In addition, the telecommunications unit might make a
variety of faculty support services available only to those teaching on the telecommunications system.

Two additional policy areas are of critical importance to
the advocate of telecommunications: the extent to which the
teaching faculty have their efforts recognized in the promotion
and tenure process and the extent to which their efforts are integrated into the teaching assignments of the academic unit.
The manager should strive to integrate the telecommunications
effort into the total compensation, reward, and promotion system. Such assignments are established by the academic unit;
the degree to which teaching via telecommunications is integrated into the system is an indication of its integration into the
unit's mission.

Influencing the External Decision-Making Process

A variety of other policy-making agencies beyond the institution influence telecommunications-based education and, therefore, are of interest to managers. Some directly regulate telecommunications activities; others contain a variety of policy
makers who indirectly affect this type of education. One of the
primary reasons why regulation is complex is the ease with which
telecommunications efforts can cross conventional political
boundaries.

At the state level, one of the primary questions in the area
of public regulation is how to balance protection of the consumer
with access and its corollary, equity (Sobol, 1990). All too often
state-level regulatory efforts are inconsistent, unclear, and le-
gally untested, particularly in regard to out-of-state activities
by an institution. One aspect of regulation concerns how to decide when a distance education effort falls within the regulatory
jurisdiction of that state. Reilly (1990) reports that his review
of state regulations for distance education indicates little consistency about how this matter is addressed, although a number of states apply tests of physical presence as a deciding fac-

tor. Some states define physical presence to include student recruiters, a facility, a class, or an office. The presence of any of these within a state's boundaries could bring an organization offering distance-learning programs under that state's regulations. This means, in some cases, that if an institution pays a monitor or class facilitator for services in support of its distance education, it falls under state jurisdiction and must gain approval to continue operation.

State agencies are legitimately concerned with protecting citizens from fraud, and activities designed to provide consumer protection are readily accepted. But, other, more controversial considerations may also come into play in the guise of regulation. In some cases the regulatory effort may be driven not by the desire to ensure quality but rather by a wish to shelter local institutions from healthy competition. Some argue that their goal is to protect a state's considerable investment in its own institutions, but the net result can be harmful to citizenry by reducing access to educational opportunity (Grieder, 1990). There is always a need to balance such competing interests.

Even where one political entity clearly has undisputed jurisdiction, as in monitoring the actions of a state institution within the state's boundaries, regulators also decide which institutions, and which programs, should be provided to a particular audience. Among the most common criteria for selecting which program to make available are (1) the number of students served, (2) the economic impact of the group served, (3) the nature of the offering, and (4) the balance of the particular offering with those available from other providers. On the surface, identifying unwarranted duplication of programming would seem to be a rather straightforward proposition. However, when telecommunications-based education is involved, the issues can become very complex. The difficulty reflects the richly diverse nature of educational programming in the United States.

An example will illustrate the nature of this complexity. If an institution is the sole provider of engineering education at the graduate level, it meets the criterion of exclusivity. The effort might also meet the criterion of economic impact, because it serves a group of people who are often key to the productivity of many others. Credence is lent to this argument if numerous industries within the state report difficulty in recruiting and retaining engineers because access to continuing education is difficult or impossible to achieve in those communities.

However, the engineering field is highly specialized and the number of people within the total field of engineering is not large. When individual specializations are taken into account, the number of people who are likely to pursue individual graduate programs is very small, even when telecommunications delivery is able to reach all or most of the communities where there is a concentration of engineers. The question becomes how to balance the potential impact on the economic development of the state of providing graduate-level engineering education against the more financially desirable impact of reaching larger numbers with other types of programs.

Another illustration of the complexity involved in making decisions about what should be offered relates to graduate-level business education. Different types of institutions offer programs with unique characteristics. Although several institutions within an area may offer a degree with the same name, the programs often incorporate significant differences. All M.B.A. programs, for example, are not the same. Where one institution is accredited by the American Association of Colleges and Schools of Business and one is not, should access be provided only to the accredited program? On the surface this might seem like a straightforward decision in favor of the accredited institution, but there are other factors to consider. A major consideration may be the numbers of people who will be served. The accredited program is likely to be much more selective in admitting students and will require more extensive prerequisites. As a result, many people who express an interest in pursuing an M.B.A. will find that they do not qualify for acceptance into the accredited program. In addition, many of those interested in the program may not be concerned about the accreditation issue and may be able to achieve their educational goal through the unaccredited program. In these circumstances the decision to offer only the accredited program will deny access to a large segment of the total group expressing a need.

Managers of educational telecommunications systems must gain the ear of members of decision-making bodies and attempt to educate them about the many considerations involved. It is important for such groups to have a good grasp of the issues involved, and the manager can often play an important role in laying out alternatives. From an institutional perspective, the key is for the parent organization to have a clear picture of its own priorities in the area and to be able to articulate them. Careful attention must be given to framing these priorities as a part of decision making.

The manager must also be aware of the political nature of the decision-making process in the public arena. Often the process is complicated by demands from interest groups for a particular educational service or program. Whereas the regulatory body may consider the primary concern to be the prevention of duplication, the potential clientele may regard significantly increased access as the primary issue. Clearly such a dilemma presents a significant problem for the institution, which is placed directly between the demand to achieve and retain the highest levels of quality and the demand to expand access to educational opportunity, often with very little in the way of additional resources.

The advocate will need to monitor the decision-making processes of regulating bodies carefully in order to fit the priorities of the educational telecommunications system within the decision-making framework being followed. Above all, the manager must recognize the extreme complexity of such processes and their political nature.

Summary

The integration of educational telecommunications systems with existing education and training raises many interesting policy issues. Managers of these systems must become familiar not only with the issues involved, but also with the implications of each issue in order to influence policy development. Telecommunications-based education is often seen as a means of providing greater access to educational opportunities at all levels, but issues related to the equity of access loom large in the political arena.

The manager must be concerned about these ramifications. At some point a grass-roots movement may demand access to telecommunications-based education as a right and necessity in a democratic society in much the same manner that citizens demand access to roads and libraries today. In the meantime, the manager must become an articulate advocate of the role telecommunications-based education can play as a means to that end.

An important aspect of this role is the need to shape the public debate along the lines of a shared, realistic vision of a future in which educational equity will be measured largely by access to electronically delivered information and education. Thus, the manager must provide leadership in the policy arena at the institutional, state, regional, and federal levels if the full potential of telecommunications-based education is to be achieved.

Chapter 12

Moving Toward
Education for All

Myth: Learners prefer face-to-face instruction over all other forms of instruction.

Reality: Learners will select a variety of instructional formats depending on a number of factors including personal learning style and degree of fit between the
requirements of the delivery and the life
circumstances of the learner.

William Oscar Johnson (1991) wrote an article for *Sports Illustrated* envisioning life for the typical armchair sports fan of the
twenty-first century (just a decade away) who is following sports
at home by means of an interactive video system. Sports is the
primary motivation for creating the telecommunications system
that Johnson visualizes. Education, however, will probably not
be far behind in adopting and adapting these systems to its own
purposes. With acknowledgment to Mr. Johnson for the inspiration, here is how we believe that educational telecommunications systems might look soon after the turn of the century
as innovations and improvements in electronic technology and

the new information age provide educators with a virtual reality — *universal-access education.*

Linda Learner, a middle-aged, African American stockbroker with two children living in Rochester, Minnesota, settled down in her favorite chair in the Learner family room. Taking up one wall of the room in front of Linda was the family Home Telecommunications Services System (HT2S). Linda had been aggravated when Leonard, her husband, first suggested they buy the HT2S. It was a major purchase, although easily within the financial reach of the average family, but she was only thinking of all the sports events Leonard would watch. Then she realized that she could use the system to take the courses she needed to earn her master's degree; her boss wanted her to complete her degree in health and human services finance. Now it was time for one of the two courses she was taking this term, SIHCS 605, "Stock Investing in the Health Care Sector," to start its first session.

Actually Linda had sports to thank for many of the educational programs that were now available to people living anywhere in the country. First, leading universities like Notre Dame and athletic conferences such as the Big Ten had created their own broadcast systems, selling their major sports events to existing commercial networks. A few years later the conferences, through a partnership, formed the University and College Network to broadcast college sports full-time on their own network. Then, following the examples of the National Technological University and Mind Extension University, the colleges and universities started developing and providing a variety of national degree and personal development programs. It was wonderful for Linda that Minnesota Mass University (MMU) had decided to produce the health sector M.A. degrees, through which she custom-designed the health and human services finance degree program with her adviser.

HT2S is easy to use and really something to watch — sixteen small TV monitors and a console used to select pictures and sounds for projection on a central eight-foot, high-definition TV screen. In addition to receiving multiple video signals, a big-screen image, and interactive feedback by means of a write board, HT2S is a videophone with conference-call capability, a computer, a family finance and management tool, and a home security system.

With the universal interface, all these functions are operative at once. While Linda was "in class," stock market quotes, weather reports, and a call from her mother were coming through. In tape storage were all of yesterday's fifth-grade classes for review work by Linda's son, Larry, who had remained home sick.

As Linda keyed in the information to receive SIHCS 605, she couldn't help recalling that just ten years ago the Rochester city fathers had complained that their city was the largest in the nation without a public college or university. Now Rochester, and every other town in the country, had equal access to almost any postsecondary program. Not only was it convenient for Linda to learn at home, but it had taken only about sixty seconds to register for the class, by keying in the Learner family access code, Linda's student number, the MMU course number, and the pay-for-view authorization. It was so handy — paying for the entertainment, sports, and educational programs on one bill, not to mention all the personal finance transactions and video buying services.

Leonard, who went into military service after high school, was also taking a class to complete his two-year certificate at North Central Universal Access University. Linda had been impressed by the way NCUAU managed classes with thousands of students, and Leonard was happy with the instructors. The National Education Accreditation Council, a federal review agency, also gave the course and NCUAU high marks for academic quality. In fact, the next session of Leonard's class was now being downloaded to tape for Leonard to review after Linda logged off the system.

Linda, now ten minutes into her 605 class, noticed that the instructor was asking for questions. She had a minute, more than enough time, to use the write board to transmit what was on her mind. It always amazed her that, even though hundreds of people from all over the country took classes like this, when questions were transmitted every few minutes, the computer consensus question was almost always exactly what she had asked. She wondered if it would be the same next year when her academic program was expected to become international.

One of the benefits of Linda's program, as with most of the video education programs, was the corporate underwriting that kept the tuition low. This had come as another spinoff of sports. Once corporations became involved in sponsoring college football bowl games, colleges and universities eliminated the middle-level people and teamed up with appropriate companies to sponsor their athletic teams. In exchange for substantial corporate donations to the institutions, the schools allowed the companies to run ads in school bulletins, on the school networks, during the games, and so forth. Some colleges were even considering changing their mascots to reflect the corporate tie.

After Linda had completed her class registration, a video syllabus was transmitted to her and recorded on a videodisc as an integrated-interactive assignment, reading, and exam support system. Linda's instructor now was asking all students to call up a practice investment simulation from the syllabus. After running the simulation on one of the side monitors, Linda transmitted her solution. Wrong answer. Because she had missed on the simulation, Linda's name was logged into the instructor's master data file to indicate that she was required to work on the simulation as a homework assignment.

Companies with large educational and training functions had turned out to be particularly good partners for education. Because of similar educational missions, comparable resource units from education and business had come together to create strong business-education partnerships. One of the student benefits was the use of a portion of the corporate donation to make up the shortfall in state funding, keeping tuition low for postsecondary education. The corporations were also interested in the alumni that the affiliated institutions produced through their universal-access video educational programs as potential well-educated new employees.

Professional sports had followed a path similar to that of the colleges and universities with each pro sport owning and operating specialized pay-for-view networks. The price per event turned out to be very reasonable because so many people bought into the concept. The federal government then stepped in and mandated a ceiling on player salaries and a special tax on corporate revenues. Those federal revenues went into a sports welfare fund that made systems like HT2S available to needy families at a modest subsidized price. Families receiving this equipment were required to commit to enrolling all adults and school-aged children in educational programs designed by a family educational adviser. Full participation and successful completion were monitored through the video system. This federal program had made *universal access to education* possible through a convenient and affordable program for all citizens.

Responsiveness and Flexibility

The history of postsecondary education and training in America started over three hundred years ago with colonial liberal arts colleges that adapted European forms of higher education. Institutions for the elite few were, in effect, professional schools of theology. The late 1800s saw the evolution of universities, driven by the utilitarian need to incorporate new fields of study, such as science and modern languages, in order to address the requirements of an expanding society. This movement toward more practical or applied knowledge led to the 1862 Morrill Act, which granted federal lands to states for the endowment of universities. This practical side of higher learning was further enhanced in 1887 by the Hatch Act, which provided federal funds for the establishment of agricultural experiment stations in connection with land-grant colleges.

The new idea of *public service* in higher education, joining *teaching* and *research* as the threefold mission for higher education, was perhaps best exemplified at the turn of the century by Charles McCarthy, whose *Wisconsin Idea* made the boundaries of the university the boundaries of the state. In 1906, this concept helped to revitalize the University of Wisconsin Extension Division. McCarthy also sponsored legislation in 1911 that was the nucleus for the creation of an extensive statewide vocational and adult education system (Brubacher and Rudy, 1958).

The ever-expanding student population in American higher education was again deliberately broadened by policies such as the 1944 G.I. Bill of Rights, which revolutionized accessibility to postsecondary education. James Bryce "observed that by making higher education accessible to all classes, American universities had achieved what had never been done before." They had "'led all classes of the people to believe in the value of university education and wish to attain it'" (Brubacher and Rudy, 1958, p. 173). The rise of community colleges in the 1960s and 1970s is another example of this phenomenon. Clearly, higher education in the United States has had a history of extending access to more and more people.

Martin Trow proposed a model of postsecondary education that assimilates various educational structures and describes the problems experienced by institutions in transition. He argues that change in higher education has led to the creation of three types of postsecondary organizations. The first, or the *elite higher education institution,* exists to shape the mind and character of the ruling class and to prepare students for broad elite roles in government and the learned professions. *Mass higher education institutions* prepare a broader range of elites that includes the leading strata of all the technical and economic organizations of society. Third are the emerging *universal-access institutions,* whose role is to prepare the public for life in an advanced information society and to maximize the adaptability of that public to a culture with rapid social and technological change (Trow, 1973).

Trow defines *elite higher education* as highly structured and reflecting academic notions of degree coursework. Instruction primarily consists of tutorials or seminars, with a strong personal relationship between student and teacher. Students move directly from secondary or preparatory school into residence on a full-time basis until a degree is completed. The institution is homogeneous, with high, broadly shared standards. Elite institutions tend to be relatively small, with two to three thousand students and sharp, clear semi-impermeable boundaries.

Mass higher education institutions offer a curriculum that is modular and semistructured, with a sequence of courses that earns credits. There can be movement between major fields of study as well as between institutions. Instruction is conducted through large lectures and seminars. Students typically come directly from high schools but many delay their start and often take longer to complete degrees, spending some time in other pursuits. There is a mix of residential and commuter students, and institutional diversity is significant and desired. These institutions tend to be large—up to forty thousand students in some cases—and comprehensive, with a variety of standards that can vary from one part of the institution to another. Mass higher education institutions have boundaries, but students flow easily in and out of them, which results in a lessening of the idea of membership.

Educational organizations making extensive use of telecommunications-based education, as described in this book, closely match the characteristics of emerging or *universal-access institutions,* as described by Trow. They may be either new institutions or in transition from mass higher education. These institutions focus on a curriculum that is still modular but with relatively unstructured instruction. Course boundaries and requirements are not strictly or consistently defined. The traditional academic structure and standards may be rejected as learning and life flow together. There is a major reliance on numerous forms of electronic technology to deliver instruction. The institutional boundary is nonexistent, and the location of the student is the only parameter for defining institutional shape. Students tend to postpone the start of their postsecondary education at these institutions, often leave for a time, and usually bring occupational experience to the learning environment. Universal-access institutions are very diverse and are unlimited in size. Most of the students never see the central campus and do not seek community with the institution and fellow students. Academic standards focus on the value added as a result of the educational experience.

It is likely that existing organizations and institutions that are broadly committed to telecommunications-based education and training are appropriately designed to provide universal-access education. They are in effect mass education institutions in transition to universal education. Could the influx of electronic technology be a barometer of educational responsiveness, flexibility, and transition? Quite possibly, but we must consider specific technical applications. An elite institution that decides to broadly apply technology in order to empower its academic community and student population by providing new technical tools may only perceive itself to be staying current. The multicampus, mass education organization or institution that simply connects its sites to improve communication among its existing staff and students is not in transition. However, the mass education institution that uses telecommunications-based education to reach new students, expand its service area, and provide a variety of educational programs (noncredit or personal growth programs, for example) is in transition to universal education. The evidence of this is demonstrated through its responsiveness and flexibility, resulting in change and conflict.

Trow nicely summarizes these transitional relationships in three categories: (1) "the functional relationships among the various components or aspects of given systems" (for example, the debate over the relative quality of face-to-face and telecommunications-based education), (2) "the problems arising during the transition from one phase to the next when existing, more or less functional, relationships are progressively disrupted by uneven and differently timed changes in the patterns and characteristics of the system" (for example, when seasoned professors are required to change their entire method of doing their jobs), and (3) "the problems arising in the relations between institutions of higher education and society and its economic and political institutions, as higher education moves from one phase to the other" (public accountability, for example) (Trow, 1973).

Transformative Forces

As a product of our times, universal-access institutions reflect major current changes in American culture. Indeed, the universal-access institution seems to be the educational prescription for a society moving along the parameters suggested by John Naisbitt in the so-called field guide of the future, *Megatrends,* which described the following "ten new directions transforming our lives" (Naisbitt, 1982):

1. Industrial society $\longrightarrow$ Information society
2. Forced technology $\longrightarrow$ High-tech/high-touch
3. National economy $\longrightarrow$ World economy
4. Short term $\longrightarrow$ Long term

5. Centralization ——➤ Decentralization
6. Institutional help ——➤ Self-help
7. Representative democracy ——➤ Participatory democracy
8. Hierarchies ——➤ Networking
9. North ——➤ South
10. Either/or ——➤ Multiple option

Postsecondary education has already moved toward a decentralized structure and is more committed to a curriculum that allows multiple options for the learner. The adult part-time learner is now the majority in many postsecondary educational settings. Two patterns the older learner's presence has established as part of the educational scene are lifelong or long-term learning in order to remain up-to-date and the self-help mode of learning fostered by independent, self-motivated, and self-designed value-added learning objectives. These independent learners survive in part in spite of institutional barriers, because of their ability to network with other learners. It is noteworthy that most educational institutions still have much to change to accommodate their students' needs.

Universal-access institutions flourish because of the networks they create with their publics and the for-profit organizations that need their educational services, and as a result of the political bodies that see a need for their services. Undoubtedly community colleges currently best exemplify the universal-access institutional characteristics as set forth by Trow. They also seem to be best positioned to meet the social needs and changes suggested by Naisbitt. However, numerous public universities are also in transition. This suggests that the transition from mass higher education to universal-access education is at work across postsecondary institutions. In addition, many independent postsecondary institutions and corporate training centers have been created that will refine and define the universal-access model. One current example is a hybrid organization universities have formed consisting of national consortia that develop and offer undergraduate and graduate programs nationwide by means of cable television. Mind Extension University has generated much interest and support and will be accessible to millions of people through one of the nation's major mass media. "It appears to be the wave of the future," says Bob Aaron, director of the Office of Communication, National Association of State Universities and Land-Grant Colleges (Thomas, 1991, p. 32). Even the source of this reference, *Better Homes and Gardens,* confirms the boundless appeal of access to universal education.

Nevertheless, Derek Bok argues that postsecondary education has done relatively little through the curriculum "in conveying to undergraduates enough knowledge of other languages and other cultures to give them the international background they will need for their careers" (Bok, 1990, p. 36). This observation suggests that we are still a long way from providing academic programs capable of producing the informed citizenship skills necessary to support a vibrant, culturally diverse, and participatory democracy.

Today, the use of electronic technology for research, organizational communication, and universal access to postsecondary education is embedded in our educational system. Managers of new or growing educational telecommunications systems, therefore, need to develop new perspectives on their organization. Will educational telecommunications be a tool to improve the existing organization? Will the organization in transition to some form of universal-access institution need to rely on telecommunications-based education to meet its mission and long-range plan? Is the manager in fact part of a universal-access institution? Telecommunications managers must provide answers to these questions, built on a vision of the future, in order to participate in the strategic plan of the organization, since their position places them in a unique position to see the organization as no one else.

While *Megatrends 2000* may not be a prescription for the future, managers may find clues embedded in the following trends that are relevant to their own setting and that can help in visioning the next steps (Naisbitt and Aburdene, 1990):

1. The booming global economy of the 1990s
2. A renaissance in the arts

3. The emergence of free-market socialism
4. Global life-styles and cultural nationalism
5. The privatization of the welfare state
6. The rise of the Pacific Rim
7. The decade of women in leadership
8. The age of biology
9. The religious revival of the new millennium
10. The triumph of the individual

Perhaps an eleventh megatrend should be added:

11. Access to universal education

Quality and Service for Adult Learners

The bipolar instructional environment that exists between the mass education structure, which is a teacher-centered model, and universal access, a learner-centered paradigm, presents new opportunities for both educators and managers of educational telecommunications systems to participate in a paradigm shift. Telecommunications-based programs designed for traditional students typically follow the well-known "stepwise, sequenced, institutional model of program development" associated with the mass education organization (Brookfield, 1986, p. 207).

Studies of adult learning styles, however, demonstrate that adult learning patterns are distinctly different from those of younger students and that individual differences abound. Given this different pattern and the fact that the part-time adult public is the most significant growth segment in higher education, it is important for managers to understand and facilitate adult learning by designing their programs in a fashion that will individualize the learning experience — for example, through the use of instructional-design techniques. This will be a critical factor for successful programs provided by universal-access educational organizations. It will also be important for mass education institutions that are serving a segment of the public in the manner of universal access.

The shift to a more learner-centered educational environment suggests that the educational telecommunications manager will need to become well acquainted with adult learning theory. As discussed throughout this book, the proposition of providing programs for learners with different learning styles presents unique opportunities to refocus attention on how people learn.

While Brookfield (1986, pp. 25–39) argues that a general theory of adult learning is not known, it is possible to identify a number of characteristics that program developers, and therefore managers of telecommunications-based programs, should consider when creating learning opportunities. Brookfield (p. 38) reports the finding of W. B. James, who suggests nine principles of adult learning that should be taken into consideration when designing programs:

1. Adults maintain the ability to learn.
2. Adults are a highly diversified group of individuals with widely differing preferences, needs, backgrounds, and skills.
3. Adults experience a gradual decline in physical/sensory capabilities.
4. Experience of the learner is a major resource in learning situations.
5. Self-concept moves from dependency to independency as individuals grow in responsibilities, experience, and confidence.
6. Adults tend to be life-centered in their orientation to learning.
7. Adults are motivated to learn by a variety of factors.
8. Active learner participation in the learning process contributes to learning.
9. A comfortable, supportive environment is a key to successful learning.

These principles raise a number of important questions that the manager may wish to consider in the future development of telecommunications-based education. Can telecommunications effectively serve a diverse group of individuals simultaneously? How will programs account for and take advantage of the experience of individual learners? Will they allow the independent and self-centered learner to grow to the greatest extent possible? Will they motivate learners? What kind of learning environment is the distance learner using to participate in distance education, and is that environment conducive to successful learning? It may be that the strong desire of the adult learner to participate in the learning process, as suggested by the eighth principle and recommended by Moore (1983a, 1989), will provide the guiding principle around which managers can design their programs to best meet the needs of the publics primarily served by universal-access programs.

Brookfield (1986, pp. 38–39) further reports that James found, in a questionnaire administered to adult educators, a difference in the way adult educators of distinct adult populations perceived their implementation of these principles: "Hospital patient educators, university extension instructors, community college instructors, and agricultural extension instructors all perceived themselves as implementing all the principles identified 'frequently,' while business and industry personnel perceived themselves as implementing principles one, two, and eight 'sometimes' but the others 'frequently.' An interesting difference was also revealed regarding the principle ranked highest by these practitioners. In hospitals, universities, community colleges, and agricultural extension, principle nine—'a comfortable, supportive environment is a key to successful learning'—was ranked as the most important. In business and industry, however, principle three—'adults experience a gradual decline in physical/sensory capabilities'—was ranked highest." Surprisingly the principle referring to active learner participation in the learning process was ranked rather low by all five groups!

These findings suggest that in practice adult educators continue to use rather traditional modes of instructional design. It appears that the traditional mass education models of education (the stepwise, sequenced, institutional model of program design) still predominate as the most common ways to organize programs. Clearly there is still a good deal of academic program development and design work facing current and future managers of telecommunications-based programming if they are to make their programs more effective for learners.

Brookfield (1986, pp. 258–259) suggests four features for effective program development of adult learning. Managers must consider including these themes in current and future program-development processes and must encourage system design capabilities that allow for their implementation:

1. "Programs that are based on learners' characteristics and engage learners in a dialogue about content, aims, and methods are likely to provide settings for meaningful learning."
2. "[Educational telecommunications] programmers should recognize that contextual distortion of neatly planned programs is likely to be a recurring feature of their professional practice."
3. "Linked to this second point is a third concerning the necessity of recognizing and encouraging the legitimacy of adaptive, improvisational practice."
4. "[Managers of educational telecommunications systems] should recognize the multiplicity of methods and techniques that might appropriately be used in program development."

At an applied level, Aslanian and Brickell have studied adult learning patterns and their data describe a number of program parameters that confirm adult learning theory and that can be applied productively to educational telecommunications systems (Aslanian and Brickell, 1988). Their national survey of adults showed that at any time, approximately 12 percent of adults are engaged in a formal learning program (an organized activity with prescribed objectives) and 37 percent participate in informal learning (less structured and often self-designed learning such as reading a book to learn a new skill), while 51 percent of adults are nonlearners (not involved in a learning activity at that time).

Adults also move freely and frequently between the three categories. A year's time between surveys would show that many individuals had crossed from one group to another (learners moving to the nonlearning mode and vice versa). These transitions are triggered by demands placed on the individual's life-centered needs. The triggers vary from career demands to family or health changes or avocational interests.

When Aslanian and Brickell asked adults to provide reasons for choosing a program, the top four responses were:

1. Nearby location
2. Type of program
3. Low cost
4. Academic quality

The services in highest demand were:

1. Evening registration hours
2. Registration by mail
3. Parking space
4. Registration by phone
5. Financial aid
6. Student loans
7. Discounts for more than one course
8. Laboratories for practical application of course material
9. Job placement assistance

One assertion that emerges from these two lists is the strong desire by adults for program access—convenient program sites, minimal barriers to enrollment, and so on, all of which can be provided by educational telecommunications. These needs would seem to support the observations of the respondents in the James study that a comfortable environment (implying the absence of disturbing, painful, or distressing features) was the most important feature for successful learning. This observation not only reaffirms the need for educational telecommunications systems but places access as the primary motive for selecting a program.

A second observation is the relatively minor emphasis that adults tend to put on determining academic quality when they select an educational program. The learner's employer's emphasis on educational credentials or the salary rewards that a degree, certificate, or training program can bring are two strong motivations that have led people to find the easiest but not necessarily the best path to completing the next step on the educational ladder (Stewart and Spille, 1988, pp. 9–22).

Regrettably, distance-learning programs for nontraditional students have been a fertile arena for "diploma mills," characterized by Stewart and Spille as organizations that grant fraudulent or academically deficient degrees or credentials to the unsuspecting and unscrupulous alike. As the move continues toward the less structured universal-access form of education, it is likely that this condition will persist.

Quality needs to be the foundation for program development and design. But quality and access must be blended as American higher education evolves to meet society's needs. In summarizing the major developmental phases of our postsecondary educational system, Ernest L. Boyer describes the work of Harry S. Truman's President's Commission on Higher Education (Boyer, 1990, p. 11). "In its landmark report, this panel of prominent citizens concluded that America's colleges and universities should no longer be 'merely the instrument for producing an intellectual elite.' Rather, the report stated, higher education must become 'the means by which every citizen, youth, and adult, is enabled and encouraged to carry his education, formal and informal, as far as his native capacities permit.'"

Summary

The American educational system has for centuries moved systematically from an elite to a universal form of education. Telecommunications-based education is simply the latest catalyst to influence reactions to the demographic, economic, and social changes that will alter teaching and learning relationships forever. Some of the trends that characterize the last decades of the twentieth century include changes from an industrial to an information society, a national to a world economy, short-term to long-term planning, and multiple options and institutional help to self-help. In the 1990s and beyond, institutions will become increasingly interconnected and decentralized. These trends will increase the motivation of both learners and nonlearners to participate in secondary and postsecondary education as they recognize that our rapidly changing society demands continual education.

Part-time learners (working adults, military personnel, members of minority groups, and older adults, for example) are the fastest-growing population in higher education. Nationally, almost 40 percent of prebaccalaureate students attend part-time and more than 65 percent of master's degree candidates are part-time learners. To continue to be vital and growing institutions, all segments of the educational enterprise (the public schools, privately and state-supported higher education, and for-profit training organizations) must embrace and adapt to the needs of the new educational majority — part-time, diverse, adult students. In order of priority, the adult part-time learner prefers the following characteristics in an educational program: convenient location, tailored program, low cost, and, finally, quality. All four characteristics should guide programming decisions.

This book has presented a number of persuasive perspectives on the changing paradigm of off- and on-site education and training, and its impact on the mission of educational organizations. This dynamic situation is further influenced by the emerging multimode student who is neither traditional nor nontraditional, who must integrate education into a variety of lifestyles and priorities, and who will be presented with formal learning experiences through a myriad of electronic technologies. This student clientele now represents a learner group of all ages that wishes to access education and training resources at all levels for many purposes. Managers of educational telecommunications systems must come to terms with the complexities of this new environment and be prepared to manage and provide leadership as teaching and learning systems evolve.

New distance-learning strategies will profoundly affect the conduct of education and training. This chapter has argued that these effects will require different frames of reference and behavior from educators and trainers who view such programming as their province. We have offered evidence that telecommunications-based programming is already moving from the periphery to the mainstream of academic and training endeavors.

Matters of teaching and training as related to learning outcomes and the quality of the learning experience have also been considered. Distance learning in an independent format within distributive technical delivery systems provides ample opportunities for lax or unethical program design and certification of academically deficient learning experiences. Quality control will be included in the distance-learning equation in ways that are new to educational institutions. We have suggested that the intense focus on teaching and training skills required by telecommunications-based education will revitalize teaching and training in traditional environments.

While telecommunications-based education will not by itself change the nature of educational delivery systems, it will be a catalyst for incremental change to move education along — "a necessary revolution," as described by Tom Peters (1988, p. xi). According to Peters, "predictability is a thing of the past" (p. 9). It will be difficult to know from day to day the value of commodities or services. He says, "We don't know whether merging or de-merging makes sense, and we have no idea who will be partners with whom tomorrow or next week, let alone next month. We don't know who our competitors will be, or where they will come from" (p. 9). In this volatile environment, Peters argues that electronic technology is a wild card affecting every aspect of doing business. Extrapolating from his business context to an educational setting, technology is changing how we *design* the curriculum and how we teach (Peters uses the word *manufacture*). A case in point is computer applications to education. Most relevant to the theme of this book is the way educators and trainers will perceive (or *define and distribute*) their educational programs (or *products*) and the role that managers of telecommunications-based education will play in this new context (Peters, 1988, pp. 3–11). It seems clear that the revolution Peters speaks of will express itself in education through the development of educational organizations that use electronic technologies to provide universal access to formal learning.

Our publics are also changing. Increased awareness of quality, the rapid rise in the number of women returning to education, changes in the kinds of jobs available, the needs of a multicultural work force, and demand that is shifting to "customized alternatives with special features tailored for ever narrower market segments" requires that educators and trainers become more familiar with the needs of these diverse publics. "The fact is that no firm can take anything in its market for granted" (Peters, 1988, pp. 10–11).

Recall our discussion on Deming and Total Quality Management in Chapter Nine. By integrating TQM with Peters's "passion for excellence," the catchwords for the future in education, as catalyzed by telecommunications-based education, must be:

1. Enhanced responsiveness and flexibility
2. Transformation
3. Quality and service
4. Continuous innovation and improvement

●●●●●●●●●●●●●

Glossary of Telecommunications Terms

Other sources for selected definitions used here include National University Continuing Education Association (1988) and Wagner (1991).

Audio bridge: a synonym for "bridge," an electronic device that interconnects three or more locations, usually over telephone lines.

Audioconferencing: interactive audio communications between individuals or groups at three or more locations.

Audiographics: use of audio lines, such as regular telephone lines, to transmit data that are converted to graphics at the receiving end.

Audio telecommunications: a synonym for audioconferencing.

Bandwidth: the spread between the highest and lowest frequencies a communications channel is capable of carrying. The broader the bandwidth, the greater the amount of information that can be carried.

Bibliographic searches: the process of reviewing and compiling by reference editions, dates, authorship, and so forth, books and other writings; in this context, using electronic technology to review the literature.

Bridge: an electronic device that interconnects three or more locations, usually for audio communication using telephone lines.

Bridging: the act of electronically interconnecting with multiple locations for audio communication, usually over telephone lines.

Broadcast signal: transmission of information in one direction that is available to an undifferentiated audience.

Cable TV: a broadband transmission system that has the capacity to deliver multiple channels of programming to residential and institutional subscribers over a coaxial cable.

Capital equipment budget: a budget that plans the expenditure of funds for capital items, such as electronic hardware, often over several budget cycles.

CODEC (to code and decode): an electrical device that converts a signal into digital form to be sent through some type of transmission medium to another CODEC, where it is decoded back to its original form.

Compressed-video system: a digital transmission technique used to reduce a normal broadband video signal into a narrowband form before transmission.

Computer-assisted design: design projects that are assisted by a computer.

Computer-assisted instruction: a system in which the student receives individualized instruction by interacting with a computer.

Computer-based instructional management: computer applications that address management and instructional activities equally rather than focusing exclusively on one or the other.

Computer-based telecommunications system: a telecommunications system that makes use of a computer as the platform for processing and transmitting information.

Dedicated system: an educational telecommunications system designed to operate twenty-four hours a day.

Direct-broadcast satellite: a communication satellite designed specifically to transmit video signals directly to small rooftop receiver systems owned or leased by members of the general public who subscribe to such services.

Distance education: an educational activity in which the teacher and learner are physically separated and one or more techniques are used to exchange information between them.

Downlink (dish): the ground equipment, including a dish and other electronic components, used to receive signals from a satellite.

Educational telecommunications system: an organizational unit composed of hardware, software that provides direction for the operation of the hardware, a transport system to move information from point to point, and staff who lead, manage, and use the system.

Electronic mail (E-mail): the use of computers and terminals as message centers for users.

Fiber-optic system: a telecommunications system that transports signals by means of a pulsating beam of light over a network of glass fibers.

FM-broadcast station multiplexing: radio signals that are frequency modulated, which allows for the simultaneous transmission of multiple signals.

General funds: funds that are controlled and allocated by the parent organization.

Instructional Television Fixed Service (ITFS): narrowcast television channels, assigned by the Federal Communications Commission for nonprofit use, which require a special antenna for signal reception.

Interactive educational telecommunications system: a system that allows for some form of two-way communication between users, most often as real-time communications.

Interactive videodisc system: computer-assisted instruction using videodiscs, which allows instantaneous changes in the lesson delivery based on student input to the system.

Land-based lines and facilities: a telecommunications transmission system that uses land-based facilities.

Live-via-satellite system: a telecommunications system based on the live transmission of signals using satellite transport.

Low-power TV: a technology that uses transmitters to amplify and rebroadcast television signals over distances of ten to twenty miles.

Master budget: an all-inclusive budget for a unit that assembles all budgets from its centers or subunits.

Media services center: an organizational support unit that assists with audio, video, and occasionally computer technologies and applications.

Microwave transmission: the transmission of information over distances by means of signals of microwave length.

Modeling: the use of computers to create representations of situations or objects.

Montage funding: a funding approach that makes use of a variety of revenue sources to support an activity.

Multimodel design: the application or blending of more than one technique or technology to address a project or situation such as distance education.

Narrowcast signal: electronic transmission of information to a specific audience rather than the general public.

On-demand system: an educational telecommunications system designed to operate only at times when there is a demand for its use.

Operating lifetime: a period of time that experience has shown to be the average useful time over which a device will function properly and reliably.

Origination site: the point of origin of an activity or program.

Program budget: a line-item budget of expenditures and revenues for a single activity.

Program center budget: a composite of related line-item program budgets under one manager for a specific time period.

Radio talkback: a microwave technology that uses frequencies at the high end of the ITFS band to transmit voice communication from remote sites to the origination point of a network.

Rate card: a document that defines and states the fees a unit charges for the various services it offers.

Receive equipment: equipment used at a receive site to receive, process, and present a program.

Receive site: the point of reception of an activity or program.

Redundancy: the systematic inclusion of duplicative equipment in an educational telecommunications system as protection in case of primary equipment failure.

Satellite: an electronic retransmission device serving as a repeater, which is normally placed in orbit above the Earth in a geosynchronous orbit (having a constant position above one spot on Earth) for the purpose of receiving and retransmitting electromagnetic signals.

Satellite downlink: see *Downlink.*

Satellite uplink: see *Uplink.*

SCA (subsidiary carrier authorization) radio: special FM radio frequencies approved for certain uses, such as radio reading services for the blind, by the Federal Communications Commission.

Self-supporting system: a system that is required to generate all revenue necessary for operation.

Sending equipment: equipment used at an origination site to process and send a program signal to receive sites.

Service center budget: an expenditure-only budget for a unit that is not required to generate revenue.

Simulation and gaming: a variety of applications in which it is possible through use of computers or detailed scenarios to simulate real-world strategies and decision-making situations.

Slow-scan TV: a telephone-based technology that captures still-frame pictures and displays them on television monitors.

Strategic plan: a long-range planning process that depends on assessments of organizational strengths and weaknesses, external factors, annual evaluations, and planning updates.

Subsidized system: a system that is underwritten by outside or donated funds.

Subsidy budget: a budget that expends an allocation from a reserve or development fund.

T-1 transport (DS1): a digital carrier capable of transmitting 1.54 megabits per second of electronic information, equivalent to twenty-four telephone lines.

Transmission equipment: a variety of types of equipment used to transmit signals to receiver equipment at other locations.

Transponder: a channel of a satellite used for receiving and retransmitting signals.

Transport: methods for sending and receiving information between different locations.

Uplink: the ground equipment, including a dish and other electronic components, used to transmit signals to a satellite.

Useful lifetime: see *Operating lifetime.*

User fee: a charge made to users of a service unit.

Video graphics: still video images that are electronically processed for projection or transmission to remote sites.

Video telecommunications system, one-way: a telecommunications system with the capacity to transmit video signals only from an origination site to receive sites.

Video telecommunications system, two-way: a telecommunications system with the capacity to transmit video signals between all sites.

Videoconferencing: interactive video communications between individuals or groups at three or more locations.

Videotext-teletext: the process of delivering computer-generated data in text or graphic form into homes using a TV set as the receiving equipment.

Voice: the content of a telecommunications system with capability to transmit two-way audio communication solely or in addition to transmitting other content such as data and one-way or two-way video.

References

Apps, J. W. *Higher Education in a Learning Society: Meeting New Demands for Education and Training.* San Francisco: Jossey-Bass, 1988.

Apps, J. W. "Beliefs, Values and Vision Making for Continuing Higher Education." *Continuing Higher Education Review,* 1990, *54*(3), 124–136.

Aslanian, C. B., and Brickell, H. M. *How Americans in Transition Study for College Credit.* New York: College Entrance Examination Board, 1988.

Beckhard, R. "The Executive Management of Transformational Change." In R. H. Kilmann, T. J. Covin, and Associates, *Corporate Transformation: Revitalizing Organizations for a Competitive World.* San Francisco: Jossey-Bass, 1987.

Beer, M. "The Critical Path for Change: Keys to Success and Failure in Six Companies." In R. H. Kilmann, T. J. Covin, and Associates, *Corporate Transformation: Revitalizing Organizations for a Competitive World.* San Francisco: Jossey-Bass, 1988.

Bennis, W. "The Four Competencies of Leadership." *Training and Development Journal*, 1984a, *38*(3), 14–19.

Bennis, W. *On Becoming a Leader.* Reading, Mass.: Addison-Wesley, 1984b.

Bok, D. *Higher Learning.* Cambridge, Mass.: Harvard University Press, 1986.

Bok, D. *Universities and the Future of America.* Durham, NC: Duke University Press, 1990.

Bolman, L. G., and Deal, T. E. *Reframing Organizations: Artistry, Choice, and Leadership.* San Francisco: Jossey-Bass, 1991.

Boyer, E. L. *Scholarship Reconsidered: Priorities of the Professoriate.* Princeton, N.J.: Princeton University Press, 1990.

Briggs, L. J., and Wager, W. W. *Handbook of Procedures for the Design of Instruction.* Englewood Cliffs, N.J.: Educational Technology Publications, 1981.

Brockett, R. G. (ed.). *Ethical Issues in Adult Education.* New York: Columbia University Press, 1988.

Brookfield, S. D. *Understanding and Facilitating Adult Learning: A Comprehensive Analysis of Principles and Effective Practices.* San Francisco: Jossey-Bass, 1986.

Brown, L. D. "Planned Change in Underorganized Systems." In T. Cummings (ed.), *Systems Theory for Organizational Development.* New York: Wiley, 1980.

Brubacher, J., and Rudy, W. *Higher Education in Transition.* New York: HarperCollins, 1958.

Brumbaugh, K., and Crossland, B. "What Should a Center for Educational Technology Provide?" *Technological Horizons in Education Journal*, 1991, *18*(9), 78–80.

Brush, J. M., and Brush, D. P. *Private Television Communications: The New Directions.* Cold Spring, N.Y.: H I Press, 1986.

Cameron, K. S., Sutton, R. I., and Whetten, D. A. (eds.). *Readings in Organizational Decline: Frameworks, Research, and Prescriptions.* Cambridge, Mass.: Ballinger, 1988.

Cameron, K. S., and Whetten, D. A. "Models of an Organizational Life Cycle: Applications to Higher Education." In K. S. Cameron, R. I. Sutton, and D. A. Whetten (eds.), *Readings in Organizational Decline: Frameworks, Research, and Prescriptions.* New York: Ballinger, 1988.

Carkhuff, R. R., and others. *ISD, Instructional Design Systems.* Amherst, Mass.: Human Resource Development Press, 1984.

Carnevale, A. P. "The Learning Enterprise." *Training and Development Journal,* 1989, *43*(2), 26–33.

Carroll, A. B. "In Search of the Moral Manager." *Business Horizons,* 1987, *30*(2), 7–15.

Cervero, R. M., Azzaretto, J. F., and Associates. *Visions for the Future of Continuing Professional Education.* Athens: University of Georgia, 1990.

Clark, R. "Reconsidering Research on Learning from Media." *Review of Educational Research,* 1983, *53,* 450.

Clark, T. A., and Verduin, J. R., Jr. "Distance Education: Its Effectiveness and Potential Use in Lifelong Learning." *Lifelong Learning,* 1989, *12*(4), 24–27.

Cohen, M. D., and March, J. G. *Leadership and Ambiguity: The American College President.* New York: McGraw-Hill, 1974.

Cowan, R. *Teleconferencing: Maximizing Human Potential.* Reston, Va.: Reston Publications, 1984.

Cross, K. P. "The Changing Role of Higher Education in the Learning Society." *Continuum: The Journal of Continuing Education,* 1985, *49*(2), 101–110.

Curtis, J. A., and Biedenbach, J. M. *Educational Telecommunications Delivery Systems.* Washington, D.C.: American Society for Engineering Education, 1979.

Davie, L. E., and Wells, R. "Empowering the Learner Through Computer-Mediated Communication." *American Journal of Distance Education,* 1991, *5*(1), 15–23.

Davis, J. L. "The Demands of the Decade." In C. A. Wedemeyer (ed.), *The Brandenburg Memorial Essays on Correspondence Instruction,* Vol. I. Madison: University of Wisconsin, University Extension, 1963.

Deming, W. E. *Out of Crisis.* Cambridge, Mass.: Massachusetts Institute of Technology Center for Advanced Engineering Study, 1986.

Dillon, C., Blanchard, D., and Price, M. *The Emerging Role of Telecommunications in Higher Education — Improving Teaching at a Distance: A Guide to Resources.* Norman: University of Oklahoma, 1990.

Dillon, C. L., and Gunawardena, C. *Learner Support as the Critical Link in Distance Education: A Study of the Oklahoma Televised Instruction System.* Norman: University of Oklahoma, 1990.

Dively, D. D. "Principles and Guidelines for a Coordinated Telecommunications Plan." In M. A. McGill and R. W. Jonsen (eds.), *State Higher Education Policies in the Information Age.* Boulder, Colo.: Western Interstate Commission for Higher Education, 1987.

Enarson, H., Widmayer, P., and Trendler, C. *Challenges and Opportunities for Nebraska Higher Education — A Call to Action.* Widmayer and Associates, 1990.

Gagne, R. M., Briggs, L. J., and Wager, W. W. *Principles of Instructional Design.* Troy, Mo.: Holt, Rinehart & Winston, 1988.

Garrison, D. R., and Baynton, M. "Beyond Independence in Distance Education: The Concept of Control." *American Journal of Distance Education,* 1987, *1*(3), 3–15.

Gooler, D. D. "Criteria for Evaluating the Success of Nontraditional Postsecondary Education Programs." *Journal of Higher Education,* 1977, *68,* 78–95.

Gooler, D. D. "Using Integrated Information Technologies for Out-of-Classroom Learning." In J. A. Niemi and D. D. Gooler (eds.), *Technologies for Learning Outside the Classroom.* San Francisco: Jossey-Bass, 1987.

Gray, W. H., and Sullins, W. R. "Comparative Analysis of the Barriers to Rural Postsecondary Education in Two Regions of the United States." *Continuing Higher Education Review,* 1988, *52*(1), 29–39.

Greiner, L. E. "Evolution and Revolution as Organizations Grow." *Harvard Business Review,* 1972, *50*(4), 37–46.

Grieder, T. "Remarks." In *Proceedings of the Invitational Symposium on Emerging Critical Issues in Distance Higher Education,* pp. 39–44. Albany, N.Y.: Regents College, 1990.

Gunawardena, C. N. "New Communications Technologies and Distance Education: A Paradigm for the Integration of Video-Based Instruction." Unpublished doctoral dissertation, University of Kansas, Lawrence, 1988.

Gunawardena, C. N., and Saito, M. "Instructional Design Considerations in the Development of Computer-Assisted Interactive Video." Paper presented at fifth annual Conference on Teaching at a Distance, Madison, Wis., August 1989.

Hanna, D. E. "Planning Programs to Enhance Institutional Image." In R. G. Simerly and Associates, *Handbook of Marketing for Continuing Education.* San Francisco: Jossey-Bass, 1989, pp. 89–102.

Hannum, W. H., and Hansen, C. *Instructional Systems Development in Large Organizations.* Englewood Cliffs, N.J.: Educational Technology Publications, 1989.

Hayes, E. "Adult Education: Context and Challenge for Distance Educators." *American Journal of Distance Education,* 1990, *4*(1), 25–38.

Hesser, J. E., Spears, J. D., and Maes, S. C. "Action Priorities for Rural Adult Education." *Continuing Higher Education Review,* 1988, *52*(1), 11–20.

Hezel Associates. *Statewide Planning for Telecommunications in Education.* Washington, D.C.: The Annenberg/Corporation for Public Broadcasting Project, 1990.

Holden, C. D. "How Every Staff Person Can Be a Salesperson." In R. G. Simerly and Associates, *Handbook of Marketing for Continuing Education.* San Francisco: Jossey-Bass, 1989, pp. 309–319.

Hosmer, L. T. "Managerial Ethics and Normative Philosophy." In L. T. Hosmer (ed.), *The Ethics of Management.* Homewood, Ill.: Irwin Press, 1987.

Jacobson, T. "Editorial." *The On-Line Journal of Distance Education and Communication,* May 1991.

Johansen, R. *Groupware: Computer Support for Business Teams.* New York: Macmillan, 1988.

Johnson, K. A., and Foa, L. J. *Instructional Design: New Alternatives for Effective Education and Training.* New York: American Council on Education and Macmillan, 1989.

Johnson, W. O. "Sports in the Year 2001." *Sports Illustrated,* 1991, *75*(4), 40.

Keller, G. *Academic Strategy: The Management Revolution in American Higher Education.* Baltimore, Md.: Johns Hopkins University Press, 1983.

Kilmann, R. H., Covin, T. J., and Associates. *Corporate Transformation: Revitalizing Organizations for a Competitive World.* San Francisco: Jossey-Bass, 1987.

Kimberly, J. R. "The Life Cycle Analogy and the Study of Organizations: An Introduction." In J. R. Kimberly, R. H. Miles, and Associates, *The Organizational Life Cycle: Issues in the Creation, Transformation, and Decline of Organizations.* San Francisco: Jossey-Bass, 1980, pp. 1–17.

Kitchen, K., Wagner, E., and Ward, A. A. *Planning for Telecommunications: A School Leader's Primer.* Portland, Oreg.: US West Communications and National School Board Association, 1989.

Knox, A. B. "Emerging Imperatives for the Continuing Professional Educator." In R. M. Cervero, J. F. Azzaretto, and Associates, *Visions for the Future of Continuing Professional Education.* Athens: University of Georgia Press, 1990.

Kotler, P. *Marketing for Nonprofit Organizations.* Englewood Cliffs, N.J.: Prentice Hall, 1984.

Kouzes, J. M., and Posner, B. Z. *The Leadership Challenge: How to Get Extraordinary Things Done in Organizations.* San Francisco: Jossey-Bass, 1987.

Langdon, D. G. *Interactive Instructional Designs for Individualized Learning.* Englewood Cliffs, N.J.: Educational Technology Publications, 1973.

Lenth, C. S. *State Priorities in Higher Education.* Denver, Colo.: State Higher Education Executive Officers and Education Commission of the States, 1990.

Lenz, E. *Creating and Marketing Programs in Continuing Education.* New York: McGraw-Hill, 1980.

Lodahl, T. M., and Mitchell, S. M. "Drift in the Development of Innovative Organizations." In J. R. Kimberly, R. H. Miles, and Associates, *The Organizational Life Cycle: Issues in the Creation, Transformation, and Decline of Organizations.* San Francisco: Jossey-Bass, 1980.

London, M. *Change Agents: New Roles and Innovation Strategies for Human Resource Professionals.* San Francisco: Jossey-Bass, 1988.

Long, H. B. *Adults and Continuing Education.* New York: Columbia University Teachers College Press, 1983.

Lorsch, J. W. "Managing Culture: The Invisible Barrier to Change." *California Management Review,* 1986, *28*(2), 95–109.

Lynton, E. A., and Elman, S. E. *New Priorities for the University: Meeting Society's Needs for Applied Knowledge and Competent Individuals.* San Francisco: Jossey-Bass, 1987.

McCannon, R. S., and Crom, R. L. "Whose Role Is It to Serve Rural Learners? Can/Should Continuing Higher Education Assume the Leadership?" *Continuing Higher Education Review,* 1988, *52*(1), 3–10.

McNeil, D. R. *Wiring the Ivory Tower: A Round Table on Technology in Higher Education.* Washington, D.C.: Academy for Educational Development, 1990.

Martin, L. G., and Ross-Gordon, J. M. "Cultural Diversity in the Workplace: Managing a Multicultural Work Force." In J. M. Ross-Gordon, L. G. Martin, and D. B. Briscoe (eds.), *Serving Culturally Diverse Populations.* New Directions for Adult and Continuing Education, no. 48. San Francisco: Jossey-Bass, 1990, pp. 45–54.

Matkin, G. W. *Effective Budgeting in Continuing Education: A Comprehensive Guide to Improving Program Planning and Organizational Performance.* San Francisco: Jossey-Bass, 1985.

Merriam, S. B., and Caffarella, R. S. *Learning in Adulthood: A Comprehensive Guide.* San Francisco: Jossey-Bass, 1991.

Miles, R. H. "Findings and Implications of Organizational Life Cycle Research: A Commencement." In J. R. Kimberly, R. H. Miles, and Associates, *The Organizational Life Cycle: Issues in the Creation, Transformation, and Decline of Organizations.* San Francisco: Jossey-Bass, 1980, pp. 430–450.

Miles, R. H., and Randolph, W. A. "Influence of Organizational Learning Styles on Early Development." In J. R. Kimberly, R. H. Miles, and Associates, *The Organizational Life Cycle: Issues in the Creation, Transformation, and Decline of Organizations.* San Francisco: Jossey-Bass, 1980, pp. 44–82.

Miller, D., and Friesen, P. H. "A Longitudinal Study of the Corporate Life Cycle." *Management Science,* 1984, *30*(10), 1161–1183.

Mitchell, A. *The Nine American Lifestyles: Who We Are and Where We Are Going.* New York: Warner Books, 1983.

Mitroff, I. I. *Stakeholders of the Organizational Mind: Toward a New View of Organizational Policy Making.* San Francisco: Jossey-Bass, 1983.

Moe, J. F. "The Dream Deferred: Minority Adult Participation in Higher Education in the United States." *Continuing Higher Education Review,* 1989, *53*(1), pp. 35–49.

Moe, J. F. "Education, Democracy, and Cultural Pluralism: Continuing Higher Education in an Age of Diversity." In J. M. Ross-Gordon, L. G. Martin, and D. B. Briscoe (eds.), *Serving Culturally Diverse Populations.* New Directions for Adult and Continuing Education, no. 48. San Francisco: Jossey-Bass, 1990, pp. 31–44.

Moore, M. G. "On a Theory of Independent Study." In D. Stewart, D. Keegan, and B. Holmberg (eds.), *Distance Education: International Perspectives.* London: Croom Helm, 1983a.

Moore, M. G. "Self-Directed Learning and Distance Education." ZIFF Papiere 48. Hagen: FernUniversität, 1983b.

Moore, M. G. "Three Types of Interaction." In M. G. Moore and G. C. Clark (eds.), *Readings in Principles of Distance Education.* University Park: American Center for the Study of Distance Education, Pennsylvania State University, 1989.

Moore, M. G., Thompson, M. M., Quigley, B. A., Clark, G. C., and Goff, G. G. *The Effects of Distance Learning: A Summary of Literature.* University Park: American Center for the Study of Distance Education, Pennsylvania State University, 1990.

Morgan, G. *Images of Organization.* Newbury Park, Calif.: Sage, 1986.

Morgan, G. *Riding the Waves of Change: Developing Managerial Competencies for a Turbulent World.* San Francisco: Jossey-Bass, 1988.

Nadler, D. A. "Organizational Framebending: Types of Change in Complex Organizations." In R. H. Kilmann, T. J. Covin, and Associates, *Corporate Transformation: Revitalizing Organizations for a Competitive World.* San Francisco: Jossey-Bass, 1988.

Naisbitt, J. *Megatrends.* New York: Warner Books, 1982.

Naisbitt, J., and Aburdene, P. *Megatrends 2000.* New York: Morrow, 1990.

National University Continuing Education Association (ed.). *Distance Education Through Telecommunications.* Washington, D.C.: National University Continuing Education Association, 1988.

Niemi, J. A., and Gooler, D. D. (eds.). *Technologies for Learning Outside the Classroom*. New Directions for Adult and Continuing Education, no. 34. San Francisco: Jossey-Bass, 1987.

O'Brien, E. M. "Continuing Ed Programs Not Reaching Minority Populations, Officials Admit." *Black Issues in Higher Education*, Mar. 1, 1990, pp. 6–8.

Offerman, M. J. "Matching Programmatic Emphases to the Parent Organization's Values." In R. G. Simerly and Associates, *Strategic Planning and Leadership in Continuing Education: Enhancing Organizational Vitality, Responsiveness, and Identity*. San Francisco: Jossey-Bass, 1987, pp. 71–86.

Olcott, D., Jr. "Bridging the Gap: Distance Learning and Academic Policy." *Continuing Higher Education Review*, 1991, *55*(1, 2), 49–60.

Peters, T. *Thriving on Chaos*. New York: Knopf, 1988.

Pew Higher Education Research Program. "Keeping the Promise." *Policy Perspectives*, 1992, *4*(2), 1A–8A.

Quinn, R. E., and Anderson, D. F. "Formalization as Crisis: Transition Planning for a Young Organization." In J. R. Kimberly and R. E. Quinn (eds.), *New Futures: The Challenge of Managing Corporate Transitions*. Homewood, Ill.: Dow Jones–Irwin, 1984.

Quinn, R. E., and Cameron, K. S. "Organizational Life Cycles and Shifting Criteria of Effectiveness: Some Preliminary Evidence." *Management Science*, 1983, *29*, 33–51.

Quinn, R. E., and Cameron, K. S. "Organizational Paradox and Transformation." In R. E. Quinn and K. S. Cameron (eds.), *Paradox and Transformation: Toward a Theory of Change in Organization and Management*. New York: Ballinger, 1988, pp. 1–18.

Rapp, S., and Collins, T. L. *MaxiMarketing: The New Direction in Advertising, Promotion, and Marketing Strategy*. New York: McGraw-Hill, 1987.

Reilly, K., "Remarks." *Proceedings of the Invitational Symposium on Emerging Critical Issues in Distance Higher Education*, pp. 31–33. Albany, N.Y.: Regents College, 1990.

Richey, R. *The Theoretical and Conceptual Basis of Instructional Design*. London: Kogan Page, 1986.

Riggs, J. K. "Determining an Effective Marketing Mix." In R.

G. Simerly and Associates, *Handbook of Marketing for Continuing Education.* San Francisco: Jossey-Bass, 1989, pp. 125–137.

Rink, P. "Planning and Responsiveness in Continuing Higher Education: Setting Goals and Seizing Opportunities." *Continuing Higher Education Review,* 1987, *51*(3), 39–45.

Romiszowski, A. J. *Designing Instructional Systems: Decision Making in Course Planning and Curriculum Design.* London: Kogan Page, 1981.

Ross-Gordon, J. M., Martin,L. G., and Briscoe, D. B. *Serving Culturally Diverse Populations.* New Directions for Adult and Continuing Education, no. 48. San Francisco: Jossey-Bass, 1990.

Rumble, G. *The Planning and Management of Distance Education.* London: Croom Helm, 1986.

Ryan, J. H. "The Continuing Educator: Change Agent or Prisoner?" *Continuum: The Journal of Continuing Education,* 1985, *49*(2), 129–134.

Saettler, P. *The Evolution of American Educational Technology.* Englewood, Colo.: Libraries Unlimited, 1990.

Sarason, S. B. *The Creation of Settings and Future Societies.* San Francisco: Jossey-Bass, 1972.

Schon, D. A. *Beyond the Stable State.* New York: Random House, 1971.

Schwartz, J. "Close Up: Talking Heads." *Communications Week,* 1991, *335,* 35–38.

Simerly, R. G., and Associates. *Strategic Planning and Leadership in Continuing Education: Enhancing Organizational Vitality, Responsiveness, and Identity.* San Francisco: Jossey-Bass, 1987.

Simerly, R. G., and Associates. *Handbook of Marketing for Continuing Education.* San Francisco: Jossey-Bass, 1989.

Smith, K. G., Mitchell, T. R., and Summer, C. E. "Top Level Management Priorities in Different Stages of the Organizational Life Cycle." *Academy of Management Journal,* 1985, *28*(4), 799–820.

Sobol, T. "Opening Remarks." *Proceedings of the Invitational Symposium on Emerging Critical Issues in Distance Higher Education,* pp. 7–8. Albany, N.Y.: Regents College, 1990.

Stewart, D. W., and Spille, H. A. *Diploma Mills.* New York: Macmillan, 1988.

Tarr, D. L. "Learning More About Your Market: Sources and Uses of Data." In R. G. Simerly and Associates, *Handbook of Marketing for Continuing Education*. San Francisco: Jossey-Bass, 1989, pp. 30–48.

Thomas, J. B. "Earn Your Degree by Cable TV." *Better Homes and Gardens*, 1991, *69*(8), 32.

Threlkeld, R. M., Behm, R. J., and Shiflett, M. "Live and Interactive: Is It Really Important?" Unpublished paper, California State Polytechnic University, Pomona, 1991.

Tichy, N. *Managing Strategic Change: Technical, Political and Cultural Dynamics*. San Francisco: Jossey-Bass, 1983.

Tichy, N. M. "Problem Cycles in Organizations and the Management of Change." In J. R. Kimberly, R. H. Miles, and Associates, *The Organizational Life Cycle: Issues in the Creation, Transformation, and Decline of Organizations*. San Francisco: Jossey-Bass, 1980, pp. 164–183.

Tichy, N. M., and Devanna, M. A. *The Transformational Leader*. New York: Wiley, 1986.

Total Quality Management: A Guide for the North Dakota University System. Bismarck, N.D.: State Board of Higher Education, (undated).

Trow, M. *Problems in the Transition from Elite to Mass Higher Education*. Berkeley, Calif.: Carnegie Commission on Higher Education, 1973.

Tushman, M., Newman, W., and Romanelli, E. "Convergence and Upheaval: Managing the Unsteady Pace of Organizational Evolution." *California Management Review*, 1986, *29*(1), 29–44.

U.S. Congress, Office of Technology Assessment. *Linking for Learning: A New Course for Education*. OTA-SET-30. Washington, D.C.: U.S. Government Printing Office, 1989.

Vaill, P. B. *Managing as a Performing Art: New Ideas for a World of Chaotic Change*. San Francisco: Jossey-Bass, 1989.

Van de Ven, A. H. "Early Planning, Implementation, and Performance of New Organizations." In J. R. Kimberly, R. H. Miles, and Associates, *The Organizational Life Cycle: Issues in the Creation, Transformation, and Decline of Organizations*. San Francisco: Jossey-Bass, 1980.

Van de Ven, A., and Poole, M. S. "Paradoxical Requirements

for a Theory of Organizational Change." In R. E. Quinn and K. S. Cameron (eds.), *Paradox and Transformation: Toward a Theory of Change in Organization and Management.* New York: Ballinger, 1988, pp. 19–63.

Van Kekerix, M. J. "The SUN Experience: A Historical Analysis of the State University of Nebraska Program Utilizing the Organizational Life Cycle Perspective." Unpublished doctoral dissertation, University of Nebraska, Lincoln, 1986.

Verduin, J. R., Jr., and Clark, T. A. *Distance Education: The Foundations of Effective Practice.* San Francisco: Jossey-Bass, 1991.

Votruba, J. C. "From Marginality to Mainstream: Strategies for Increasing Internal Support for Continuing Education." In R. G. Simerly and Associates, *Strategic Planning and Leadership in Continuing Education: Enhancing Organizational Vitality, Responsiveness, and Identity.* San Francisco: Jossey-Bass, 1987.

Wagner, E. D. *Teaching on Tele-Systems: A Faculty Development Handbook.* Greeley: University of Northern Colorado, 1991.

Walsh, J. P., and Dewar, R. D. "Formalization and the Organizational Life Cycle." *Journal of Management Studies,* 1987, *24*(3), 215–231.

Walshok, M. L. "Developing a Strategic Marketing Plan." In R. G. Simerly and Associates, *Strategic Planning and Leadership in Continuing Education: Enhancing Organizational Vitality, Responsiveness, and Identity.* San Francisco: Jossey-Bass, 1987, pp. 149–167.

Walter, D., and Carey, L. *The Systematic Design of Instruction.* Glenview, Ill.: Scott, Foresman, 1985.

Weick, K. E. *The Social Psychology of Organizing.* Reading, Mass.: Addison-Wesley, 1979.

Weidemann, C. D. "Making Customers and Quality Service a Priority." In R. G. Simerly and Associates, *Handbook of Marketing for Continuing Education.* San Francisco: Jossey-Bass, 1989, pp. 114–124.

Weinstein, A. *Market Segmentation: Using Demographics, Psychographics and Other Segmentation Techniques to Uncover and Exploit New Markets.* Chicago: Probus, 1987.

Whetten, D. A. "Sources, Responses, and Effects of Organizational Decline." In J. R. Kimberly, R. H. Miles, and Associates, *The Organizational Life Cycle: Issues in the Creation, Transformation, and Decline of Organizations.* San Francisco: Jossey-Bass, 1980.

Whetten, D. A. "Organizational Growth and Decline Processes." In K. S. Cameron, R. I. Sutton, and D. A. Whetten (eds.), *Readings in Organizational Decline: Frameworks, Research, and Prescriptions.* New York: Ballinger, 1988, pp. 27–44.

Whittington, N. "Is Instructional Television Educationally Effective? A Research Review." *American Journal of Distance Education,* 1987, *1*(1), 47–57.

Willis, S., and Bridwell, S. E. (eds.). *Directory of Distance Education Through Telecommunications.* Washington, D.C.: National University Continuing Education Association, 1988.

Index

Index